reviewing
leadership

Julie Godwin

Tyndale Seminary

Engaging Culture

WILLIAM A. DYRNESS
AND ROBERT K. JOHNSTON,
SERIES EDITORS

The Engaging Culture series is designed to help Christians respond with theological discernment to our contemporary culture. Each volume explores particular cultural expressions, seeking to discover God's presence in the world and to involve readers in sympathetic dialogue and active discipleship. These books encourage neither an uninformed rejection nor an uncritical embrace of culture, but active engagement informed by theological reflection.

reviewing
leadership

a christian evaluation of current approaches

second edition

bernice m. ledbetter, robert j. banks,
and david c. greenhalgh
foreword by max de pree

Baker Academic

a division of Baker Publishing Group
Grand Rapids, Michigan

© 2004, 2016 by Bernice M. Ledbetter, Robert J. Banks, and David C. Greenhalgh

Published by Baker Academic
a division of Baker Publishing Group
P.O. Box 6287, Grand Rapids, MI 49516-6287
www.bakeracademic.com

Printed in the United States of America

Library of Congress Cataloging-in-Publication Data
Names: Ledbetter, Bernice M., author. | Banks, Robert, 1939– Reviewing leadership.
Title: Reviewing leadership : a Christian evaluation of current approaches / Bernice M. Ledbetter,
    Robert J. Banks, and David C. Greenhalgh ; foreword by Max De Pree.
Description: Second Edition. | Grand Rapids : Baker Academic, 2016. | Series: Engaging culture |
    Rev. ed. of: Reviewing leadership : a Christian evaluation of current approaches / Robert Banks
    and Bernice M. Ledbetter ; foreword by Max De Pree. c2004. | Includes bibliographical references
    and index.
Identifiers: LCCN 2016010851 | ISBN 9780801036293 (pbk.)
Subjects: LCSH: Leadership—Religious aspects—Christianity.
Classification: LCC BV4597.53.L43 B36 2016 | DDC 253—dc23
LC record available at http://lccn.loc.gov/2016010851

17   18   19   20   21   22   23   8   7   6   5   4   3   2

To
our friend and mentor, Max De Pree,
who taught us a great deal about leadership
through his writings, example, and influence.
—Bernice M. Ledbetter and Robert J. Banks

To
the colleagues and students of Eastern University's PhD program who
have inspired and challenged me over the years.
—David C. Greenhalgh

contents

foreword

I don't read many books on leadership, but the practice of good and ethical leadership is something I have thought a lot about. During my years at Herman Miller Inc., especially as CEO, I tried to integrate my work and my faith—that's always been important to me and still is.

This book surveys the evolution of understanding about leadership and asks important questions about faith and leading that are necessary to consider if leadership is to have a future. I have come to believe that asking the right questions may be more important than getting to the answer. Questions help us to bring to the surface what is most important, and this book does just that.

Reviewing Leadership helps us to gain an understanding of the influences on leadership, things such as culture, timing, events in one's personal history, and one's faith. Leadership is a complex enterprise, and we do well to pay attention to influencing factors.

Peter Drucker once said that leadership and faith share a common core. They are both acts of intention, and this leads to integrity. Integrity in leadership is at an all-time low, and people need a reason to trust in leadership once again. Leadership is barren and hollow when it does not have integrity at its core. The examples of faithful leaders offered in *Reviewing Leadership* give us good reason to hope that the core of leadership remains intact for those leaders who fight the good fight of faith and remain strong.

The authors of this book are right to discuss the spiritual importance of leadership, which cannot be overstated. Leadership has always had a spiritual dimension, and now is the time to underscore the importance of this vital leadership component. Good, effective, moral leaders have a compass, something that guides them from the inside out, and faith is a good candidate for providing a clear set of moral principles to guide one's leading and following. The authors touch on the vital importance of the character of a leader by discussing the ripple effect of leadership on people, projects, and processes in organizations. In fact, the character of a leader may be one of the most important factors in determining the success of an organization because it really does spread throughout an entire organization, helping it to be beautifully whole or sadly fractured and broken.

Reviewing Leadership is a book about leading from one's spiritual center, which is the right thing to do and is not as easy as it sounds. It is really a journey of discovery about oneself and God and how one intends to lead based on who one intends to be.

The authors, whom I consider my friends, have offered some ways to think about this challenge that I encourage you to consider.

Max De Pree

preface to the second edition

Since the first edition of this book the field of leadership has only grown deeper and wider. There continue to be many, many books on leadership published each year. Yet as time has marched forward little attention has been given to the theological dimension and evaluation of current views on leadership. As the cultural importance of leadership has expanded, the topic has gained greater relevance for this series on engaging culture.

This book intentionally seeks to develop a substantially theological—rather than purely practical or even biblical—assessment of current leadership literature. It does this from a biblical base and with the conviction that what is best theologically ultimately leads to what is best practically. As the old but little appreciated adage goes, there is nothing more hands-on than a good theory. While we deal with leadership theory in this volume, we also attempt to critique and evaluate these ideas through the lens of theology. Thus, this book has a particular and unique shape. It is a summary of academic approaches and concrete experiences as much as it is a fruit of biblical investigation and reflection on our own leadership learning and experience.

Moreover, we believe this book is an exercise in cultural analysis and theological exploration. It is derived from historical and current writings on leadership and personal observations of past and present role models. Behind this diverse range of influences lie the convictions that, however normative biblical revelation may be, truth comes from God in a variety of ways, and all truth is God's truth.

The introduction provides the historical backdrop for this book: the origins that led to the writing of the first edition. We thought it would be helpful to provide the context behind the initial impetus for this work. The introduction concludes with areas for future investigation, which we address in this second edition.

The opening chapter begins by acknowledging the ongoing interest in leadership as a topic of investigation. A review of the history of the study of leadership provides insights and reveals limitations in our understanding of the theory and practice of leadership. Definitions and the distinction between leadership and management along with the ideas associated with followership are considered. Chapter one foreshadows several themes that are addressed within the book, including ways culture influences an understanding of leadership and, of course, the intersections between leadership, Christianity, and spirituality.

The second chapter offers a brief historical perspective on leadership, beginning with Jewish views on leadership and followed by Paul's innovative understanding and practice of leading. It then surveys historical models of leadership in the church, each containing a theological dimension. Application for leadership today is drawn from this historical and theological discussion.

The third chapter explores the religious, spiritual, and ethical dimensions of leadership by examining implicit and explicit expressions of spiritual and ethical leadership with implications for organizations. Through popular writing and significant examples, the implicit themes of spirituality and religiosity in leadership are presented. After addressing explicit approaches to spirituality and leadership, the text discusses specifically Christian approaches.

The fourth chapter begins by surveying a number of popular writings on leadership that include an overtly religious dimension. From this it moves on to discuss the strengths and weaknesses of a number of leading theological perspectives on leadership revolving around Jesus, biblical life stories, and the Trinity, the latter of which informs an understanding of women in leadership and the use of power.

The fifth chapter discusses translating ideas about leadership into practice. It examines the roles of imagination, emotion, and wisdom with the goal of a more holistic understanding of leadership and then turns to three key aspects of character: faithfulness, integrity, and a servant-like attitude.

The sixth chapter explores leadership development and spiritual development and addresses this question: How does one learn to lead ethically from a solid moral grounding? The themes of moral stress and resilience are discussed. Finally, a biblical understanding of leadership legacy is presented.

The seventh chapter considers the topic of leadership at the senior level by examining governance and the perils of success. The practice of faith-based leadership is considered through the lens of major religious views on what it means to lead.

The last chapter considers some exemplary role models of Christian leadership. These include examples from within the realms of national leadership, leadership in a parachurch context, leadership in the city, leadership in the marketplace and the wider community, and leadership in a congregation. The case studies demonstrate the potential Christians have in various walks of life to articulate and embody a distinctive and integrated Christian approach. The book concludes with some reflections on how to nurture leadership of this kind for the future.

In writing this book, Rob and Bernice are grateful for our previous work expressed through leadership at Fuller Theological Seminary and founding the Max De Pree Center for Leadership, where we had the great privilege of working with Max De Pree. This work partnership gave rise to our collaboration on the first edition. David entered our fold through our affiliation with the International Leadership Association, and we are grateful for his partnership and insightful critique of the first edition and substantive contribution to this second edition. For all three of us our teaching opportunities have spanned the globe: from the Centre for the History of Christian Thought & Experience, Macquarie University (Sydney, Australia); to the Graziadio School of Business and Management at Pepperdine University (Malibu, California); to Eastern University (St. Davids, Pennsylvania). Our teaching has certainly shaped our thinking and practice of leadership; we are grateful to our many students who have helped us refine our thinking about the ideas in this book and made us better teachers and scholars. We also want to acknowledge and express our appreciation to the series editors, Bill Dyrness and Robert K. Johnston of Fuller Theological Seminary, as well as our executive editor at Baker Publishing Group, Robert N. Hosack, for their enthusiastic support for extending our work into the second edition of this book.

introduction

We begin with background concerning the trends that led to the writing of the first edition of *Reviewing Leadership: A Christian Evaluation of Current Approaches* to set the context for the second edition.

Historical Background: The Faith at Work (FAW) Movement

It is important to mention the work of David Miller, project director for the Faith & Work Initiative at Princeton University and author of the book *God at Work: The History and Promise of the Faith at Work Movement*.[1] The FAW movement is a lay-led, non-church-based movement that began as a means for people of faith, mainly Christians, to address a central question: What does it mean to be a person of faith in the marketplace? Feeling that the institutional church did not do much to address this concern, laypeople began meeting together for support and to share ideas. This movement began in the late 1800s and continues to the present. However, from the beginning of this movement this notion of faith and work faced a particular and serious challenge: how to connect religion with economics, in which economic gain is seen as contrary to encouragement to live a simple life, not focused on material gain. Coauthor Robert J. Banks was a very significant leader in this movement in Australia and later in the United States.

Fast-forward to the 1980s, when the FAW movement included a movement within a movement that came to be known as the Ministry of the Laity. This movement sought to connect Sunday with Monday. The central question for this phase of the movement was: How does faith inform work? How can we see the laity as involved in a kind of ministry Monday through Friday? This period was fraught with tension, as the church saw Ministry of the Laity more in terms of how laypeople used their gifts to serve within the church, whereas the laity sought insight as to how one's faith gives meaning to one's work.

Banks was integral to the Ministry of the Laity movement, and much of his work and research focused on empowering laity even in the context of training people for ordained ministry.[2] Banks wanted ordained clergy to understand the importance of emergent leadership in the laity.

In the next turn in the movement, going into the 1990s and the early part of the twenty-first century, we see the central question relating to the capacity to integrate faith with work. In this stage of FAW there is a greater opening to speak about faith in the marketplace. This newfound openness is in part thanks to baby boomers who hold top positions in organizations; this generation seeks—though not always successfully—integration, including faith and spirituality into their work, particularly in applying faith in practical ways to daily life.

This recent turn toward greater openness to spirituality and faith in the workplace is further confirmed by Andre Delbecq, noted scholar of management and spirituality. He identified a clear shift in the late 1980s and early 1990s in the discussion of faith integration with work through his teaching at Santa Clara University and his consulting with tech leaders in Silicon Valley, who expressed a longing for increased spiritual integration in life and work.[3]

Theoretical Struggle: Gaining Legitimacy

In many ways, practice precedes theory. As we will see, oftentimes practitioners bring new insight and pressing questions to the foreground, thus providing the impetus for advancing theory in the academic context. Because practitioners began asking questions about ethics, leadership, and spirituality, acceptance and then research in these areas eventually flourished. It is quite interesting to note that ethics, leadership, and spirituality each fought an uphill battle to be recognized in the academy. There was a time when ethics was considered the purview of the philosophy department, and not in any substantial way was it related to business, management, or leadership.

Ethics began to enter the business school curriculum, and thus joined the conversation concerning the workplace and management, in the 1980s and 1990s. *People Magazine* in 1978 featured a story about the dean at Stanford University, who was lauded for introducing ethics into the MBA curriculum, which was unheard of at the time. The article cites increased enrollment as a result of this decision![4] And a page from popular media in 1990 highlights the importance of asking moral questions about business conduct.[5] The same vexing challenges continue to appear on the front pages of our e-newspapers today, and we continue to wonder: Can ethics be taught? Can moral behavior be learned? The point is, ethics moved beyond the philosophy department to practitioners in the workplace vis-à-vis the business school, and this was a very important shift.

Similarly, leadership studies in many ways found its beginning with the seminal work *Leadership* by James MacGregor Burns in 1978.[6] However, Frederick Fiedler's work in the 1960s, from an organizational psychology perspective on a theory of leadership effectiveness, was certainly important as well.[7] During the 1990s Joseph Rost made a major contribution to the field of leadership studies.[8] In that same decade (1992) the Jepson School of Leadership Studies, the premier undergraduate leadership program in the nation, opened, and Peter Northouse published his first edition of *Leadership: Theory and Practice* (1997).[9] The 1980s and 1990s were crucial for the study of leadership to gain a foothold in academia. Most now consider leadership a discipline, and output from programs like that at Eastern University continue to add substantive research to the field.

One of the chief concerns levied against leadership studies is the lack of a central theory. This comes from the scientific approach that claims all substantive knowledge contained within a discipline must be based on a central theory and, further, that standard measures are needed to substantiate claims; results must be replicable and generalizable. Fair enough, if the focus of study is splitting the atom or measuring the speed of light. In 2005 James MacGregor Burns and a team of top scholars collaborated to develop a general theory of leadership; their book, *The Quest for a General Theory of Leadership*, appeared in 2006.[10] However, the team was unable to develop a general theory of leadership because of the multiple contingencies that surround the phenomenon of leadership. Still, leadership studies has found its place within the academy, building a multidisciplinary base from the fields of psychology, sociology, philosophy, communications, and political science.

It should be noted as well that not all that long ago leadership was considered values-free—that values were not part of leadership and that those two concepts should be kept separate.[11] This debate continues up to the present. The thought of even discussing faith, spirituality, or religion in the secular classroom was unheard of in the 1980s, with the exception of, say, in the religious studies department, but even there no attempt was made to connect faith with daily life, much less leadership. Around the year 2000 scholarship in the area of faith, spirituality, and religion in management and work began to take off.

Clearly the 1980s and 1990s, leading into the turn of the century, brought a broadening of thoughtful research-based discussion of these three important areas—ethics, leadership, and spirituality/faith/religion. As we welcomed the new millennium, ethics became common in business schools; leadership studies emerged as one of the fastest-growing disciplines in the academy, and spirituality became part of the public discourse and even part of curricula in many academic departments, including medicine, nursing, and business.

It was against this backdrop that we set out to write the first edition of *Reviewing Leadership: A Christian Evaluation of Current Approaches*.[12] Clearly a door was opening, and because the intellectual discourse was emerging we stepped into this interdisciplinary discussion. In so doing we set out to think about leadership faith/spirituality from a decidedly biblical and theological perspective to advance an understanding of leadership, ethics, and faith. We sought to create a substantive intersection between the business literature on leadership and biblical theology, and to do so at a deeper level, moving beyond personal motivation and inspiration, which were common in popular-media offerings at that time. To do this required collaboration across disciplines and academic departments that is unusual and rare, combining solid biblical theology with substantive leadership theory. We felt quite good that we accomplished what we set out to do.

Now that these heretofore radical fields of inquiry have matured considerably, what occupies the discourse at this disciplinary intersection? We would argue that the purpose of leadership continues to be a central concern. In a certain way this gets at the question of definitions of leadership. Many will be familiar with a common definition of leadership: influence toward goals, which implies that leadership ought to have a direct impact on organizational performance or some sort of outcome. However, research has been highly inconclusive on this critical point: Can we demonstrate that certain forms of leadership lead to certain organizational performance outcomes? The question remains open, which raises a further problematic question: If leadership does not affect organizational outcomes, is leadership needed? In our quest to put forward a determinative position for leadership we have perhaps shot ourselves in the proverbial foot insofar as much of our research on leadership has set out to prove scientifically that leaders have a direct impact on organizational performance, and while this is not altogether inappropriate, it certainly may be insufficient.

A group of Harvard researchers points out that early scholars in the field "were not concerned with leadership because of its ability to explain economic performance. Instead, leadership was deemed important because of its capacity to infuse purpose and meaning into the lives of individuals."[13] While economic performance was not irrelevant in the early stages of theory development of leadership, it simply was not the central focus. If we are to take a cue from our scholarly ancestors, then we must judge the importance of leadership's ability to infuse purpose and meaning into the organizational experience.

To answer the question of what the purpose of leadership is while considering leadership's role in advancing purpose and meaning, Max Weber wrote in 1946, "Modernization implied an ever increasing rationalization of all aspects of life, as the dry logic of bureaucratic institutions steadily replaced the meaning systems derived from the wonder and enchantment of religion, respect for tradition, or awe of charisma."[14] Weber is suggesting that efficiency in organizations had come to be seen as a cultural norm for measuring value—efficiency was, we might argue, a sort of taken-for-granted social good. As organizations became more bureaucratized, efficiency became the norm and therefore served as the definition of the value attributed to organizations. To offset this tendency to put efficiency before meaning, Weber pointed to extraordinary individuals or leaders who were capable of creating alignment between the actions individuals undertook in the organization and the meaning that they sought. Weber called this charismatic leadership, which for him came to be seen as a counter to the inevitable decline in meaning. Charismatic leaders possess a sort of magical, even mystical, presence that compels people to follow them. That gift is needed and should be used to reinfuse organizations with meaning, according to Weber.

To understand and add clarity to this idea of meaning in organizations, it is necessary to look to G. W. F. Hegel and Jean-Jacques Rousseau. Let us begin by looking to social theory, in particular Hegel's idea that meaning derives from actions guided by the absolute value of ethics, aesthetics, or religion entirely for its own sake, apart from any measure of external success.[15] In addition, Rousseau's idea of social interconnectedness informs an understanding of meaning at work. His idea that the quest for meaning is obtained through social communion and solidarity through relationships with others fits well with an understanding of organizations as communities.[16] Finally, Émile Durkheim, writing just after World War II, added his perspective that organizational life was replacing the traditional meaning-making role of religion because the collective was now found at work and in industry, which was playing a central role in the 1940s and 1950s.[17] Building on these ideas and placing them into the current context of our present-day organizations, we conceive of meaning-making action as supportive of some ultimate end that the individual personally values, and affirming individuals' connection to the community of which they are a part. In sum, what we all long for in our work is activity that is of intrinsic, personal value and a community of connection.

However, leadership scholarship moved away from seeing meaning making as central to leadership in favor of a more functional approach, connecting leadership to economic or other measurable forms of performance. But this longing related to our work that we all have as humans has never gone away, nor has the pressing question of what is the *purpose* of leadership. It seems that at such a time as this, when the world is open and inviting critical thinking concerning faith and leadership, there is great opportunity to move the discourse on the purpose of leadership back to its original consideration. Could it be that the contemporary integration of leadership and spirituality is actually a return to the origins of leadership, where the leader was thought to infuse purpose and meaning into the organizational experience? Indeed, transformational leadership is certainly one way in which the aspect of meaning is reintroduced into the leadership equation, insofar as this form of leadership activates beliefs and values, and raises the level of moral maturity for both leader and led.

In this book we try to get at this modern-day challenge of leadership purpose by looking to the apostle Paul's idea of community as a form of "organization" that creates and leverages a strong center of community as well as the centrality of faith-based values as critical to understanding individual valuation of particular actions. If we agree that one problem that confounds leadership scholarship is coupling leadership with economic performance, what then is the answer to this dilemma? Do we decouple this pairing? Obviously a leader, and for that matter followers, cannot infuse meaning over time unless the organization can survive, and since survival depends on a level of performance, we cannot expect to create organizations with the capacity to create meaning if we fully exclude performance from the discussion of leadership.

In an effort to hold together what we might consider the a priori of leadership—meaning making—with the functional reality of performance, we would do well to exercise restraint when attempting to establish a causal relationship between meaning making and performance. Though some research has supported this connection, still more is called for. To exercise restraint we need to develop compelling ways to assess meaning before we can draw definitive conclusions about the impact of meaning and economic performance. And it is important to note the causal relationship can flow in the other direction as well: individuals might perform at higher levels when they derive meaning from their work. In this regard, performance might be seen as an indicator of the ability to infuse meaning into an organization. And, likewise, we could hypothesize that individuals will derive little meaning from organizations that underperform. These are critical questions facing leadership researchers right now.

Areas for Further Investigation

Future areas of investigation regarding the intersection of leadership and faith /spirituality/religion that may help us return to the centrality of meaning and purpose associated with leadership are described below. We take up several of these themes in this second edition.

1. *Ethics.* The influence spirituality has on ethical decision making and ethical leadership is significant.[18] For many this is the most direct way in which faith/spirituality/religion influences leadership—by establishing a high threshold for ethical conduct and basing standards on biblical principles. This area, of the integration of faith as it informs ethical decision making, is ripe with possibility and in need of further investigation.

2. *Ethical leadership.* Similar to yet different from the first area, here we take up what the responsibility of ethical leaders is. Articles by J. B. Cullen and B. Victor,[19] as well as Cullen, P. K. Praveen, and Victor,[20] discuss ethical work climates—which the authors describe as egoistic, benevolent, or principled—and address the role of the kinds of organizational cultures ethical leaders create. As might seem obvious, the benevolent culture holds great promise for investigating the intersection of leadership and spirituality. Such a climate might, for instance, increase the possibility for the spiritual development of members. Benevolent norms might encourage individuals to have a sincere interest in the well-being of everyone, regardless of stakeholder status or position, in an environment where community and finding meaning in work are common.

3. *The theory of spiritual leadership.* This theory has been developed within an intrinsic model that incorporates vision, hope/faith, and altruistic love, based on theories of workplace spirituality and spiritual survival. The purpose of spiritual leadership is to tap into the fundamental needs of both leader and follower for spiritual survival through calling and membership. A good instrument has been developed by L. W. Fry and others that links spiritual leadership with organizational commitment, and—guess what—it results in productivity and continuous improvement.[21] More work is called for in this critical area of spiritual leadership. Fry's model is the prevailing construct; building on this foundation is needed.[22]

4. *Absence of hubris.* Here some good work by Andre Delbecq has investigated how the absence of spiritual maturity and virtue leads to the fall of leaders.[23] The offset for hubris comes straight from the spiritual traditions, especially humility and love.[24] Could it be that egoistic ethical climates (as mentioned earlier) possibly do not foster the development of spirituality among members, by putting self first and seeking outcomes that support self-interest? The role faith and spirituality play in offsetting hubris is an intriguing area for further research.

5. *Spiritual values.* Robert Giacalone has explored the area of expansive values, as contrasted with materialistic values, that focus on achievement of money, power, and status. He argues those holding expansive values are more concerned

with creating a higher quality of life through achieving more humanistic goals for themselves, their communities, and future generations. They are concerned about issues of personal transcendence and spirituality. Giacalone believes the number of those holding expansive values is increasing around the globe. If Giacalone's predictions materialize, this will affect the way organizations operate if they hope to attract workers holding expansive values. Attracting such workers will require leaders skilled in and capable of leading with spiritual values.[25]

Also, the area of spiritual values is rich for exploring multireligious dimensions and commonalities, holding promise for the advance of interfaith dialogue and community.[26]

6. *Holistic approaches (whole-person awareness, or WPA).* Such values as described above increase longing for and awareness of more holistic ways of being and doing. Also on the increase are researchers, particularly in the neurosciences, who are exploring whole-person awareness, which includes spiritual along with physical, emotional, intuitive, and intellectual awareness. This is very mainstream research.

Ian Mitroff and Elizabeth Denton point out that spirituality can be useful in helping people to bring their whole selves to work—to "deploy more of their full creativity, emotions, and intelligence."[27] In other words, a whole-person approach at work may even be a source of soul nourishment. WPA approaches and models provide a fruitful area for further investigation concerning the intersection of leadership and spirituality, exploring how the interaction between whole-person components enhances leadership and perhaps even supports the expression of spirituality in leaders.

7. *Resilience (perseverance, suffering).* Margaret Wheatley argues that leaders need to look to the spiritual traditions for guidance for coping with turbulent times. She sees a clear movement of questions emanating from the domain of spirituality to leadership—for example, What is the purpose of life? Why is there suffering? and the like. "As our world grows more chaotic and unpredictable, we are forced to ask questions that have historically been answered by spiritual traditions."[28] Wheatley argues we should expect to see practices of enrichment, like spiritual practices that lead to growth, occurring more in organizations. This is a fascinating area of investigation.

8. *Organizational level of analysis.* There is still a good deal more work to be done looking at the organizational level of analysis of spirituality. Most work has been done at the individual level, whether focused on leader or follower. Margaret Benefiel[29] and Judith Neal[30] have done good work in this area; still, uncovering factors that lead to spiritual organizations in the marketplace and creating measurements to assess spiritual organizations are critical for greater understanding in this area. Benefiel makes clear that such research will require

new, holistic methods that consider the intangible, unmeasureable factors of faith. This is a burgeoning area of exploration.

One challenge in this area of research is dealing with the reality of most organizations—that is, by their very nature organizations are control oriented and instrumental. The field of Critical Workplace Spirituality examines the ways in which organizations can use spirituality to control and manipulate, this is done by asking what the outcome is of other-made meaning in organizations.[31] When the leader is the one making meaning, how is that different from the individual uncovering of meaning? Likewise, Critical Workplace Spirituality looks at the management of meaning versus meaningful work. There is no model that includes positive and negative effects of workplace spirituality at the organizational level of analysis.

The first and last question each of us will wrestle with concerning leadership is: *Leadership for what?* We have defined and validated many theories, approaches, and styles of leadership. We stand on the shoulders of those who did the first heavy lifting in this field, and we now have a growing great cloud of witnesses as the first generation yields the baton to the succeeding generations. It is our conviction that we owe a great debt to our world to use our scholarship to advance peace and justice. Leadership for what? May it be peace.

If you seek to take up the challenge of studying and investigating leadership, faith, and spirituality, it will turn back on you and examine you by asking gently: How is it that you are integrating your spirituality, your faith, into your leadership as a scholar and practitioner? This work is convicting, and it will not let you stand at a distance and examine it in purely analytical terms. Rather, it will invite you to the deeper place of the inner self, where spirit resides. For this work and this calling, we wish you strength and peace for the journey.

leadership: an emerging academic discipline

Leadership is a big, intriguing idea, and it has been for a long time. It's easy to recognize, yet difficult to define or prescribe. It touches each of our lives every day. With good leadership, we flourish; without it, we flounder; with the wrong kind, we suffer. Leadership is on the same level as other big concepts like organization or community or justice. It's an applied wisdom. Understanding and appropriating the nature of good leadership is challenging and worthy of our best thinking and efforts. Yet unpacking its complexities could assist many of our endeavors.

Talk about leadership continues to abound today. Voices on many sides deplore its absence or mediocrity, betrayal or corruption. The young are suspicious of it, the middle-aged tend to resent it, and the elderly long for it. Articles in newspapers and magazines, material in surveys and reports, and titles of popular and serious books highlight leadership as an important issue. A growing band of consultants offers advice on developing it, new centers focusing on various aspects of leadership continue to appear, and every year a regular round of seminars, workshops, and conferences feature well-known experts in the field. It would seem, then, that leadership has become a leitmotif of our culture, one of its pivotal concerns.[1] The topic has become an integral part of intellectual and everyday discourse.

And yet leadership has not been recognized as a unique discipline within the academy. At best it's been a subset of business management, organizational studies, or industrial psychology. This may be changing. Leadership studies could be either a passing fad or an emerging discipline that will find its legitimate place. Sociology had a similar story when it was first introduced. It's too early to tell for leadership, but we do know that a whole industry has grown up in the past twenty-five years that has fueled the study of leadership as a unique and a stand-alone subject. Hundreds of academic programs around the world testify to this. However, "stand-alone subject" is a slightly misleading descriptor, since leadership is a multidisciplinary subject that draws from classical literature, psychology, and sociology, and applies to business, nonprofit, education, and public sectors. Its interdisciplinary nature makes it difficult to place in the traditional classification schemes of the academy. Nevertheless, the fervent press for insights, the richness of the research efforts, and the continual demands of the public have created a burgeoning niche that is finding its way.

To one degree or another, every age has exhibited some interest in leaders. It had to, for sometimes it lived or died, or at other times was better or worse off, at the hands of such people. Even when people had little power over who led them—in the village, city, or country—it paid to know who was in charge and what they might do. But the current fascination with the subject goes far beyond this. It involves not just leaders as such but wider concerns about leadership itself. While this is not the first time reflection on the nature, scope, and methods of leadership has arisen, there is arguably a broader and more systematic interest in the topic today than in any time past.

One example of the systematizing of this rising interest is the establishment of academic programs devoted to the study of leadership and the commensurate associations and their academic journals. The first leadership studies program was founded by John Adair at Exeter University in the United Kingdom. The first American programs were founded at Catholic institutions; the first PhD in leadership was founded at the University of San Diego in 1979, and at Gonzaga University at about the same time. Since the founding of those programs, over fifteen hundred post-secondary institutions in the world now offer academic programs. This is a new phenomenon. New courses, certificates, diplomas, undergraduate majors and minors, master's degrees, and doctorates have all been introduced in the past two decades. Two associations in particular support this new expansion: the International Leadership Association, based in the United States and founded in 1999, and the International Studying Leadership Conference, based in the United Kingdom and founded in 2002. The International Association of Leadership was formed after scholars and practitioners recognized the need for an umbrella organization to facilitate the growing interest in leadership. Since then, the International Association of Leadership has become the largest international and interdisciplinary membership organization devoted solely to the study and development of leadership. It is one of the few organizations to actively embrace academics, practitioners, consultants, the private industry, public leaders, not-for-profit organizations, and students. Commensurate with these academic programs and associations has been the rise in supporting peer-reviewed academic journals, including *Leadership Quarterly* (1990), *Journal of Leadership and Organizational Studies* (1993), *Leadership* (2002), *Journal of Leadership Studies* (2007), and *Leadership and the Humanities* (2013). For decades popular media and trade journals have generated a plethora of books and articles, but for the first time competitive peer-reviewed journals are now available to the serious student.

Christian institutions parallel the same trends. The colleges and universities that belong to the Council of Christian Colleges and Universities have begun new academic programs, including new doctoral programs at Azusa Pacific University, Eastern University, Indiana Wesleyan University, and Regent University in Virginia. Seminaries report new courses and a sharp increase in the number of these that address leadership. A simple Google search for the terms "Christian," "leadership," and "development" will generate over one thousand hits, identifying consulting agencies, institutes, conferences, resource centers, newsletters, and blogs.

All this growth raises more questions: Why this burst of interest? What have we learned so far? Has it made a difference? Have we reached a saturation point, and will the interest soon fade? These are important questions but somewhat speculative. If you are eager to delve into this topic, the more relevant questions are: Where do I begin? What are the major schools of thought? How do I approach the study of leadership? What resources are available to me? What are the current issues? And, if you are a committed Christian: How does my faith inform my study?

Building a Conceptual Framework? Categories, Definitions, and Historical Roots

It has been said that there is a new leadership book published every five minutes, which seems the case if one frequents airport bookstores. Databases of journal articles, blogs, e-newsletters, discussion groups, and apps provide daily advice on how to be a more effective leader. SmartBrief on Leadership is a good example.[2] Many books and online sources have excellent insights and advice, but the volume is overwhelming. How does one sort all this out? Which literature is worth reading, and which is poorly grounded? The serious student needs to form some working categories, a frame of reference, to organize this material and at times sift out the chaff.

First, the student will benefit from recognizing and drawing from literature that stems from both the humanities and from social science. The humanities—theology, philosophy, history, literature, and language—provide a rich source of leadership material stemming from ancient times. This includes the biblical narratives around Moses, Joshua, Samuel, Saul, David, the prophets, Nehemiah, Daniel, Jesus, and Paul, as well as the classical literature from East and West, including Plato, Aristotle, Sun Tzu, Xenophon, Marcus Aurelius, Machiavelli, Shakespeare, Carlyle, and Gandhi. As philosopher Joanne Ciulla states, "Perhaps the most important benefit of the humanities approach to leadership studies is that it does not allow us to study leader effectiveness without looking at the ethics of what leaders do and how and why they do it."[3] This perspective has been recently affirmed with the founding of the European journal *Leadership and the Humanities*. In contrast, social science literature is only about one hundred years old, with a proliferation of research and publications in the past thirty-five years. Social science literature is driven by empirical research and always asks the question: Where is the data? As this kind of research matures, it leads to theory development and generalizations. Both domains, humanities and social science, provide helpful insights, though they approach the subject with different methods.

A second useful categorization is leader versus process. Literature focused on the leader emphasizes traits, personality, character, skills, and behaviors necessary to be effective. This dimension has dominated the leadership literature for decades and continues to interest researchers and the public. The basic question is: What are the essential qualities of a leader? The process literature asks: How does leadership manifest itself? What is the interaction between follower and leader? What is the leadership dynamic and impact within the organization? How does the situation affect leadership? These are largely descriptive questions where the social sciences make a significant contribution.

Third, the student can organize the literature as either normative or contextual. Normative literature has to do with answering the question: What is good or moral leadership? This domain cuts across time and place and is considered universally applicable. This literature has more to do with the ethical dimensions of leadership and draws heavily from the humanities. In contrast, a large body of leadership literature is focused on the context of leadership, taking into account such things as culture, cross-cultural issues, gender, age, and changing circumstances. One of the challenges of leadership research is to appropriately account for the obvious reality that every situation is unique. Readers will need to develop a critical sophistication that can extrapolate general insights from normative and contextual studies and at the same time make appropriate application to their particular situations.

There are more categories to be introduced, but for now just understanding these three sets—humanities versus social science, leader versus process, and normative versus context—will help the reader build a frame of reference for approaching the study of leadership. This brings us to the need for a working definition of leadership.

Joseph Rost, a leadership scholar focused on the post-industrial twenty-first century, defined leadership as "an influence relationship among leaders and followers who intend real changes that reflect their mutual purposes."[4] Note the four essential elements: (1) that the influence relationship is multidirectional, (2) the influence is non-coercive, (3) it involves meaningful change toward a purpose, and (4) followers are active participants. Even though scholars do not agree on a universally accepted definition, there would be wide agreement with these elements. It should be recognized by now that even though we have an intuitive understanding of its meaning, leadership studies, like other disciplines, has many layers of complexity, and while a working definition may be useful, it's only a starting point to explore its many dimensions. Ciulla wisely cautions that "scholars in history, biology and other disciplines don't necessarily agree on a definition *of their discipline* and even if they did, it would not help them to understand it better."[5] The same is true for leadership.

Besides the limitations of any definition, it is enlightening to realize that definitions of leadership have dramatically changed over time. Consider this definition, published in 1927: "Leadership is the ability to impress the will of the leader on those led and induce obedience, respect, loyalty and cooperation."[6] Compare that with this definition, written in the 1990s: "Leadership assists in mobilizing a group to make a hard decision."[7] The change in these definitions reflects the changing times, from a time of focus on the leader and power to a less authority-bound definition where leadership emerges from wherever someone mobilizes others to address significant challenges. "Mobilizing" is a much softer term and infers the critical role of followers with an emphasis on mutuality and empowerment. This underscores the changing understanding of leadership based on shifts in the larger culture. Definitions reflect the conditions of life at a particular time in a particular society and the values that are important to either the public or the leaders. Definitions of leadership are social constructions.

Students are helped when authors expand a succinct definition and include key components or essential aspects of leadership. One example is the work of Keith Grint in his book *Leadership: A Very Short Introduction*. He uses a four-fold typology that encompasses many of the aspects of leadership. It includes *positional* aspects, that is, what do those in authority do; aspects focused on the *person*, what are the traits of leaders; an emphasis on *process*, that is how leaders get things done; and finally *results*, what leaders achieve. These four dimensions are an example of one helpful conceptual tool that strengthens a definition of leadership to clarify what particular aspect of the leadership spectrum is being addressed. There are many such examples.

Streams of Focus

It would be too strong to suggest that formal schools of thought have developed over the years. Rather, leadership studies have clustered around key elements as indicated in the definition above, such as the qualities of the leader, the dynamics of the process between leader and followers, and the expression of leadership in unique contexts or cultures. These three streams of focus frame the following section.

Focus on the Leader

Typically this focus is mentioned first, since it has the longest tradition. It is rooted in Thomas Carlyle's nineteenth-century theory of great men, which argues that history is the history of great men. But before Carlyle did so, Lao-Tzu, Homer, Plato, Aristotle, and Machiavelli also identified the qualities of effective leaders. It seems intuitive that we should recognize great leadership in history and then parse out the particular qualities or traits of that leader. Once those traits are understood, one could simply identify them in others or promote them for others to emulate. Scientifically, this line of inquiry was active for the first fifty years of the twentieth century, and after a thirty-year hiatus has had a resurgence of interest. The emphasis here is on traits or certain stable dispositional characteristics that are consistently manifest across a variety of situations. They have more to do with one's genetic make-up. Traits like intelligence, self-confidence, perseverance, sociability, and integrity are commonly recognized and have been extensively tested.

This stream of study was abruptly stalled by Ralph Stodgill, a researcher from Ohio State, who said in 1948 that "a person does not become a leader by virtue of the possession of some combination of traits."[8] After reviewing numerous studies, Stodgill recognized that the wide variation of lists of traits generated by one study after another was inconclusive in terms of any definitive list, and, equally importantly, traits were only one dimension of the leadership dynamic. Other dimensions needed to be studied.

In spite of the limitations of this stream of study, people easily recognize leadership traits in a person. Gifts of certain personality features are evident to the common observer, and there is widespread agreement that unless those gifts are cultivated they will wither. So even though trait study stalled for thirty years, about 1950 through 1980, and situational approaches prevailed, the notion of inborn traits remained. By 1980 new life was infused into trait studies, after it became evident that the same leaders who emerged in one group situation were also effective across different situations, even though they required different leadership responses.

A more recent extension of trait theory has been a focus on the cognition and information processing of leaders and followers. This line of inquiry was largely prompted by the challenge that leadership is legitimized not so much on the actual traits of leaders but rather based on what followers implicitly believe leadership should be. Sorting out this issue further opened up this stream of inquiry to address cognition and the behaviors of leaders and followers.

The second dimension of focused study is the behavior of the leader. Another way to express this is that leader-centric research can be divided into two spheres, specifically leader identity, or who the leader is, and leader behavior, or what the leader does.[9] This focus on the leader's behavior infers an optimistic assumption—namely, if I know the effective behaviors of a leader, then with practice and experience these behaviors can be learned.

Studies from 1930 to 1960, primarily at Ohio State University and the University of Michigan, synthesized numerous behaviors under two large categories, initiating structure and consideration. Through use of questionnaires, leaders could find out whether they were typically task oriented or relationship oriented in their preferred style of leadership. Individuals could get some general insight about themselves, but as is so frequently the case in answering a questionnaire, the participant wants to shout out, "It depends on the situation! When I need to be focused on the task, I am; other times I need to focus on relationships." Thus the results of decades of research indicated that there was no consistent evidence of a universally preferred leadership style across tasks or situations.[10] This seems rather intuitive, even simplistic, for anyone who has experienced organizational life. On the one hand, there is a goal or a vision, and the required tasks to get there, and on the other hand, the successful achievement of that goal requires the cooperative effort of the people of that organization—goals and tasks versus people and process. It's a both-and equation, and frequently the two are in tension with each other. Logically, leadership research moved from a leader's behavior to now understanding the nature of the situation. However, before we leave the leader-centric focus, there are two other related developments to consider.

In 1978 James MacGregor Burns published his seminal work, simply titled *Leadership*.[11] The focus was on the behavior of the leader, but a large demarcation was drawn between what he called transactional behavior and transforming behavior. Burns argues that transactional behaviors are management oriented and have to do with the day-to-day tasks that most of us are familiar with in our respective organizations. The label "transaction" is used because employers and employees fulfill the tasks of their mutual obligations, typically wages for fulfillment of a job description. As important as this is, Burns argues that this is not leadership. Rather, he argues, leadership happens when a person engages with others and creates a connection that raises the level of motivation and morality in both the leader and the followers, transcending one's own self-interest for the sake of the organization. This was lofty thinking, but it lifted scholarship from the sterility of behavioral analysis and launched a new direction for leadership studies. Burns's work was picked up by Bernard Bass and others, who led a rich investigation into the elements and dynamics of what became known as transformational leadership. That investigation spawned numerous other studies, which in turn led to the largest body of research on any particular leadership theory and was eventually relabeled the full range model of leadership.

As the research developed, the distinction between transactional and transformational leadership became more of a continuum rather than distinct categories. At the top of the continuum were four very specific features that have become known as the "Four I's." They include *idealized influence*, the power of example when leaders are respected and trusted role models whom others want to emulate; *inspirational motivation*, the behaviors that enthusiastically provide meaning and challenge to others; *intellectual stimulation*, inviting innovation, reframing problems, and encouraging creativity; and *individualized consideration* by paying attention to each individual's need for achievement and growth by acting as coach or mentor. There is an intuitive appeal to transformational leadership and from it grew other hybrids, including the work of Warren Bennis,[12] and James Kouzes and Barry Posner.[13]

A second development was an outgrowth of the first. Burns's distinction between transactional and transforming leadership led to a more generalized sharpening of the difference between management and leadership. In general, the purpose of management is to provide order and consistency to organizations, while the primary function of leadership is to produce change and movement. Management is about seeking order and stability, whereas leadership is about seeking adaptive and constructive change.[14]

Leadership produces change by communicating the vision for an organization and the values that support the vision. Leaders also translate that vision and the values into understandable and attainable acts and behaviors. They then help to create coalitions of people who can bring their gifting into alignment in carrying out the vision. Leaders set a direction by collecting information and data both within and outside the organization, looking for patterns, relationships, and links. Leaders watch the big picture and monitor factors such as market changes, key trends, competitors, and market share. Leaders watch internal indicators such as performance, the growth or decline of a product or service, costs, innovation, and the morale of people in the organization.

Managerial planning compliments the leadership role of strategic direction setting. The two work hand in hand to support the goals of the organization. Planning helps to ground the direction setting in reality by asking: Can this plan be implemented? Is it feasible and reasonable? Do we have the tools and the resources to turn this direction into a reality? Managers achieve their goals by organizing and staffing. This includes various functions such as creating an organizational structure, staffing jobs with qualified individuals, and devising systems to monitor implementation. Management is concerned with creating human systems that can implement plans with precision and efficiency. They are the blueprints of how work will transpire in an organization.

Despite their differences, managers and leaders are on a spectrum rather than on either side of a line. Most leadership positions require a degree of managerial ability, and managerial positions contain possibilities for the exercise of leadership. Neither role should be minimized in terms of its complexity and demanding nature.[15] Both leadership and management are needed for organizations and, most important, for the people in those organizations to do their work in effective, productive, and life-giving ways.

A final thought before we leave the leader-centric focus is to recognize the limitations of a leader-centric approach. First, we need to recognize that the person in charge of a unit, a division, or an entire organization may have the greatest responsibility for exercising leadership, but the position does not equate to the totality of the leadership dynamic. Beyond describing the qualities and behaviors of the leader-in-charge, the one with the broadest title in the hierarchy, we easily recognize that there is more to it. Most obvious is the context, the situation in which the leader-in-charge is working. The situation may dictate a different set of skills best illustrated when things are chaotic or in crisis, for example, in a hospital emergency unit. This will be explored further in our next section, but for now the point is that a leader-centric approach to understanding leadership is only one dimension of a much broader and deeper dynamic. Understanding the leader doesn't tell the whole story.

If the first limitation is about the scope of the leadership dynamic, then the second limitation is the problem of ascribing appropriate expectations of the leader. Organizations live with the tension that things will not get done unless there is some measure of hierarchy and decision-making authority versus the knowledge that power and authority is easily abused. We frequently err on either side of the tension. On the one hand, we elevate the leader-in-charge with unreasonable expectations; some would refer to this as the heroic mentality. On the other hand, over time we've become so disillusioned with leaders and their gross failings that we want to stringently contain their power even at the risk of diminishing their abilities to effect positive change. Americans tend to err on the side of the heroic, Europeans on the side of marginalization. We all have an image of what we think effective leadership should be, which scholars refer to as an implicit theory of leadership. We ascribe that image to our leaders and expect them to fulfill the commensurate expectations. Different cultures ascribe different values and expectations, but all want effective leadership that will benevolently allow all to flourish.[16]

A third and dramatic limitation of a leader-centric focus is the continual disheartening moral failure of so many leaders. Many have suffered under toxic leaders either because of their abuse of power, narcissistic behavior, lack of self-awareness, emotional indifference, irrational ideology, vacuous spiritual foundation, or corrupt moral compass. The damage they cause is immense. Awareness of the moral failure of leaders was heightened in the nineties with the news of several high-profile business leaders who were found guilty of criminal behavior and imprisoned. A body of literature from leadership scholars arose focused on the *authentic* leader, with a fresh look at ethics and accountability. In contrast, several important works on toxic leadership were published. The work of authenticity and toxicity revealed the limitations of a leader-centric focus and opened the avenue to a less heroic perspective and a greater emphasis on the leader-follower dynamic.

Fueling the diminishing of a heroic mind-set is the ongoing cultural shift brought on by technology. In a word, the world has become flat. Organizational charts show more decentralized teams, and collaborative efforts bring individuals together that cross traditional departmental boundaries. Teams and collaborative efforts frequently need very little formal authority structure. Of course, this is facilitated by the ever-expanding applications of the internet and social media. Leadership is shared and happens within the dynamic of the work, and it emerges as needed. It's a new age, and leadership studies is only in the early stages of addressing this phenomenon of shared leadership.[17]

We will visit these themes again, but for now, in this discussion of a leader-centric focus, we can summarize that not only is a leader-centered focus limited in achieving a full understanding of the leadership dynamic, but also it's a focus that has dramatically declined in the past fifty years, particularly in the era of globalization and social media.

Focus on the Followers

The cliché says, "The best test of leadership is whether or not anyone is following." This seems to be an obvious axiom, and it immediately moves us beyond the focus on the leader and opens up the whole dimension of followership. Questions include: What does it mean to be a follower? Since not all followers have the same motivation or competency, how do leaders address this? How do followers impact leadership? What's the effect of the relationship between leader and follower? Important theories and research have developed around each of these questions.

Before we explore that research, the term "follower" needs clarification. Within our respective organizations, most of us would describe ourselves as an employee, a team member, a committee member, or some other term that more closely describes our role, but rarely would we use the term follower. We would typically reserve that term for a cause, or for someone who is symbolic of a movement, a vision, or a set of values. In this case we would voluntarily identify ourselves with that cause and its leadership. The key word is "voluntary." Most roles in organizational life are not voluntary; they are contractual. We receive a paycheck for fulfilling the roles for which we were hired. Even though we may have great admiration for a leader in the organization, few of us would describe ourselves as followers. A more apt term seems to be "worker" rather than "follower," but "worker" also has its problems, with its inference of either mindless compliance or being limited to transactional behavior. Such are the inadequacies of our language. The leadership literature has used the term "follower" in numerous books and articles.[18]

The role of the follower and its relevance to understanding leadership logically grew out of the limitations of focusing exclusively on the leader, particularly the realization that no exhaustive list of leader characteristics existed.[19] As a response, four prominent theories emerged: contingency theory, developed by Frederick Fiedler in 1964;[20] situation leadership, developed by Paul Hersey and Kenneth Blanchard in 1969;[21] path-goal leadership, developed by Robert House in 1971;[22] and leader-member exchange theory, developed by F. Dansereau, G. G. Graen, and W. Haga in 1975.[23] Each of these theories underwent several revisions and was tested and applied to the workplace. Each provides some important insights into the leader-follower dynamic.

Consistent with our ongoing effort to develop a working conceptual framework, different authors have provided some help. Brad Jackson and Ken Parry, in their helpful book, *A Very Short, Fairly Interesting and Reasonably Cheap Book about Studying Leadership*, which introduces the study of leadership, use the work of Boas Shamir to frame follower-centered perspectives. They include descriptions of followers as:

1. *Recipients of leadership*. This is the traditional view that followers are passive receptacles and do not play an active role in the leadership process.
2. *Moderators of leadership*. Due to the characteristics of the follower, leaders will have to adapt their leadership style. However, followers are still not active participants in the leadership process.
3. *Substitutes for leadership*. This is a category in which followers need very little leadership because their high level of competence and motivation are in sync with the goals and mission of the organization, or the tasks are so routinized and structured that again no leadership is needed.
4. *Constructors of leadership*. The focus here is on how followers make or construct leadership in their thought process. Succinctly, if followers don't recognize it as leadership, then it's not leadership.
5. *Leaders (shared leadership)*. This is a recognition that the smart thing to do in our global economy is to move away from a command-and-control hierarchy to an increasingly flattened, laterally integrated networked workplace in which leadership throughout the organization is recognized and empowered.
6. *Coproducers of leadership*. The focus here is on the dynamic between leaders and followers. It puts the "ship" in leadership at the center of interest and affirms the recognition that the relationship between leaders and followers as a mutual exchange produces the leadership needed for a flourishing organization.[24]

Reversing the lens of leadership from leader to follower opened up a whole body of fresh and lively research. The four theories mentioned above illustrate the progression of an increasingly follower-centric focus.

Fred Fiedler is credited for pioneering contingency theory that essentially says a leader's effectiveness depends on a match of his or her style with the situation. Fiedler's focus was on an understanding of the situation, specifically the clarity of the work, the relative authority of the leader, and the quality of relationship between leader and followers. Fiedler was not convinced that leaders were able to adapt to new situations.[25]

Hersey and Blanchard advanced contingency thinking and popularized what became known as situational leadership. The focus was on leaders adapting to the needs of followers. Those needs are on a continuum from followers needing clear explicit instructions because they lack confidence and knowledge of the task, to followers being empowered to do the task because they are both knowledgeable and have relationally gained the trust of leadership.[26]

Robert House also advanced contingency thinking with his path-goal theory. His focus was on the psychological and material motivation of the followers.

Leaders ask: What motivates followers, and how do I capture that motivation to keep followers on the path or attending to the tasks related to the goals of the organization? The leader's primary role is to clarify the tasks, remove or reduce the obstacles on that path, and enhance personal satisfaction along the way.[27]

Dansereau, Graen, and Haga proposed the leader-member exchange theory in 1975. They shifted the focus of contingency thinking from asking: How do leaders adapt based on their understanding of the needs of followers? to How do leaders adapt based on the mutual understanding of their relationship and exchange with individual followers? Intuitively, this strikes a cord. We seem to be getting at the heart of the leadership dynamic—namely, what's going on between leader and follower. Leader-member exchange theory opened up a whole category of research that continues today.[28]

Since servant leadership includes a significant orientation toward followers, it fits well in the discussion here. However, it would not be accurate to include it as part of the contingency paradigm or even consider it follower-centric. Servant leadership was introduced by Robert Greenleaf after years of reflecting on corporate management practices.[29] Though eschewed by many in business, servant leadership has made remarkable inroads in the mind-set of our institutions in the realms of business, education, and nonprofits. His work generated research at Gonzaga University, supported by the Lilly Foundation. Greenleaf's "best test" reveals his orientation toward followers. He asks, "Do those served grow as persons? Do they, while being served, become healthier, wiser, freer, more autonomous, more likely themselves to become servants? And what is the effect on the least privileged in society? Will they benefit or at least not be further deprived?"[30] For Greenleaf, both leaders and institutions should serve the realization of the greater good.

The language of servant leadership resonates with Christians in part because it explicitly connects with the language of the New Testament. For example, Jesus Christ describes his mission in Mark 10:45 as follows: "For even the Son of Man did not come to be served, but to serve, and to give his life as a ransom for many." In relationship to his followers, a servant mind-set was dramatically modeled when Christ washed their feet. Paul links this to a deeper theological understanding when he wrote,

> Do nothing out of selfish ambition or vain conceit. Rather, in humility value others above yourselves, not looking to your own interests but each of you to the interests of the others. In your relationships with one another, have the same mindset as Christ Jesus: Who, being in very nature God, did not consider equality with God something to be used to his own advantage; rather, he made himself nothing by taking the very nature of a servant, being made in human likeness.

And being found in appearance as a man, he humbled himself by becoming obedient to death—even death on a cross! (Phil. 2:3–8)

For Christian leaders and followers these are powerful passages that challenge us to perceive humble service as the fundamental character required for leadership.

Focus on the Culture

The third focus of leadership literature is a focus on culture, which has two major dimensions to consider: the internal culture of the organization and the external culture that hosts that organization. The values and customs of both dimensions need to be understood by leaders. The first dimension asks: How do I assess the culture of the organization? How do leaders influence the culture of an organization? How does the culture of an organization enable or restrain leadership? The second dimension asks: How do leaders engage the culture of the society in which they work? What influence does the external culture have on the work of the organization? How do leaders adapt to or manage that influence? The reader can readily recognize the importance of these questions. When the internal culture of an organization is positive and motivating it has a powerful effect on the performance of the enterprise as a whole, and vice-versa. When the external culture is chaotic, corrupt, or unduly bureaucratic, the leadership challenges are compounded.

Another way of speaking about the internal culture is to recognize that leadership does not work in a vacuum; rather, it operates within a specific context. The "where" and "when" questions become an important part of the analysis. To state it more emphatically, if you isolate leadership from context your understanding of leadership is limited and some would say misconstrued. Throughout the 1980s the linkage between leadership and culture received considerable attention. Edgar Schein became the foremost thinker on the topic of organizational culture and leadership.[31] According to Schein, managing and shaping the internal culture is a critical responsibility. His analysis of primary mechanisms (e.g., who gets hired, who gets rewarded, who are the role models, what gets measured) and secondary mechanisms (e.g., organizational design, stories, rituals, layout of physical space, mission statements) fostered the creation of a legion of consultancies that popularized cultural audits, revitalization programs, and executive coaching, all to help leaders shape the culture of an organization.

At the same time, it should be recognized how difficult it is to understand and define culture. Its complexities have been debated by anthropologists for millennia, so a degree of humility and caution is required for the serious student who tries to link leadership and culture. One could say that leadership is essentially a cultural activity burgeoning with issues of values, beliefs, and customs. From that perspective, there is something intriguing about understanding the relationship of leadership and culture, something very intellectually challenging in the consideration of the multitude of variables and something that we intuitively know is powerful for the flourishing of any organization.

Interest in leadership and the external culture, the focus of the second dimension, has accelerated in recent decades—due in part to globalization. There are a multitude of questions: What are the protocols of engaging the host culture? How are people respected? What are the implications for the work place? Are there gender differences? Are there different ethical standards? How are disputes handled? How do we effectively cope with language differences? Globalization, led by multinational companies, has made such questions increasingly relevant. Working cross-culturally has been a challenge since the establishment of ancient trade routes, but today we experience the impact of global affairs every day. Our interdependence across national borders is evident as we experience the effects of a recession, the threat of extremism, disequilibrium of wealth and poverty, the blessing and curse of technological innovation, the migration of peoples, increasing urbanization, the joy of freedom and prosperity, and so on. Is a different kind of organizational leadership required for each of these external contexts? What is different and what is similar for leaders working cross-culturally, whether in business, nonprofits, education, churches, military, or government? What can leaders learn from anthropology?

Out of this milieu has come the concept of cultural intelligence. Its three components include knowledge of the host culture, mindfulness (paying attention in a reflexive way), and competence (acquired cross-cultural skills applied appropriately). Leaders need to become culturally intelligent in order to bring individuals together from diverse national and cultural contexts, transcending their own childhood acculturation. The work of several important scholars has shown how rich and complex it is to acquire such cultural intelligence.

Hofstede's study of one hundred thousand IBM employees in 49 countries was completed between 1967 and 1973.[32] Hofstede proposed four dimensions that are critical for leaders to understand in order to work effectively within a particular culture: individualism/collectivism; hierarchy/status/power distance; uncertainty avoidance; and masculinity/femininity. His four dimensions became a starting point for many other studies, including what has become the most prominent ongoing study, the so-called Globe Project. Initiated by Robert House in 1991, the study has grown to include 200 investigators from over 70 countries with data gathered from 17,000 managers in over 900 organizations.[33] The study continues to invite investigation and analysis of the data collected.

The fact that the study is still ongoing on a large scale, using a wide variety of methodologies and generating numerous publications as well as helpful insights, seems unprecedented in social science research. Any serious student interested in such questions as How do the people of a culture perceive the nature of leadership? or What is effective leadership in a particular culture? or What are some methodologies to study cross-cultural leadership? needs to investigate this work. Of course, the complexities of culture keep this study from being exhaustive in its understanding, and there are critics who provide important cautions.[34]

In summary, the focus on culture and leadership, divided into the two dimensions—the internal culture of an organization and the external culture in which the organization must operate—has generated a large body of scholarship in the last forty years. Due to the complexities of culture, this research, though maturing, remains open for fresh scholarship to understand the value and dignity of the local while recognizing the ever increasing presence of the global and the negotiation between the two.

Critical Theory and Method

Critical theory ushers in a new way of thinking about leadership. The term "critical theory" has roots in sociology and literary criticism and essentially means a perspective based on critique. One stream of critical theory is rooted in a Marxist critique and has a focus on the nature of power. As applied to leadership, critical scholars have become increasingly wary of leadership theory developed exclusively by research methods rooted in positivism. This is the view that the only authentic knowledge is scientific knowledge gleaned through the application of strict scientific method. The rigor of the scientific method has repeatedly proven its value, and there is an appropriate application in all disciplines, particularly the natural sciences but also the humanities and social sciences. However, there are limitations. A troublesome example would be the use of a scientifically validated questionnaire used to determine whether an individual is, for example, task or relationship oriented, transactional or transformational, authentic or untrustworthy. Such questionnaires are usually self-reports, administered at one point in time and, most important, not linked to a particular context. Critical theorists rightly question the adequacy of this methodology and the theories that are rooted in such an epistemology. Other ways of knowing are needed.

One way to get at these other ways of knowing, which are crucial for understanding context and therefore a richer understanding of leadership within particular contexts, is through the research method of phenomenology. Without an understanding of context, our understanding of leadership is bound to be limited, if not superficial. Phenomenology can help. "Like positivism, phenomenology is a philosophy of knowledge that emphasizes direct observation of phenomena. Unlike positivists, however, phenomenologists seek to *sense* reality and to describe it in words, rather than numbers—words that reflect consciousness and perception."[35] There are tools here that can help the scholar focus on the actual behavior and activities that impact the leadership process. Phenomenology takes into account the subjective world of the participant and researcher, including the physical setting, their psychological disposition, their previous experience, their motivations, and their process of meaning-making. The phenomenologist places the subjective as central to understanding leadership dynamics. This reflects an important shift from a focus on either the leader or the follower or the culture to the leadership dynamic—that is, the interaction between all of these elements and their context in which leadership emerges.

The reader should recognize a parallel shift here. It is a shift from the idea that there is a universally applicable set of elements needed to be successful in leadership to a practice-process model that is based on the idea that each situation, each context, and even each relationship is unique and subject to change and requires a praxis designed and redesigned specifically for that context and its evolution. This challenges the competency frameworks and their instruments that have been the dominant paradigm for many decades in management and organizational life and assume that their models are not only useful for analysis and prescription for one's immediate context but are also normative for other contexts. We know this is not always true as we come to understand the uniqueness of each context and the very subjective nature of the perceptions by the participants of their relationships with each other. Phenomenology has provided the philosophical foundation to support this challenge and has opened up leadership studies to the possibility that the study of each context and the subjectivities involved in determining leadership praxis within that context may be a richer more useful analytical approach. In fact, a movement of study in this direction, leadership as practice, has gained considerable momentum as exemplified by this shift.[36]

Thinking Christianly about Leadership

As with any important study, Christians begin with a particular epistemology. No matter the method, whether critical analysis of ancient text, experimental design, or the interpretation of qualitative data, Christians consider the Bible authoritative for life. The Bible affirms a God of history who revealed himself to humanity and established a foundation for being, purpose, morality, and community. So we come to know by faith, by reason, and by experience—all guided by the biblical narrative. This foundation informs our efforts to understand leadership and acts as a filter for any research findings. Typically, Christians think in categories that inform their lives and worldviews. These categories typically include creation, fall, and redemption. Below are a few salient theological perspectives that have direct connection to notions of leadership. These perspectives reflect a broad catholic and evangelical tradition as developed by Augustine, Thomas Aquinas, Martin Luther, John Calvin, and Karl Barth.

Creation

1. God is the author and sustainer of creation. All life is sacred, and the whole of it stands under the blessing, judgment, and redeeming purposes of God. The creation is infinitely interesting and open to exploration. This ranges from the investigation of the stars to the dynamics of human relationships. The complexities of leadership are part of the wonder of creation, worthy of study and greater understanding.
2. Uniquely, men and women are created in the image of God. There is something sacred about every human being, and thus each person is worthy of respect, dignity, and care. Leadership is a process that engages fellow humans, and the sacredness of each person must be honored.
3. Like the amazing diversity of the biosphere, human development of community and culture is richly diverse. As social beings, we creatively come together to solve problems and support one another. Effective leadership recognizes the value of diversity and facilitates creativity and healthy community.

Fall

1. Christians believe that all humans have a fallen nature that negatively affects their understanding of self, relationships with others, and their engagement with the world. Leadership, as a process that engages other humans, is fraught with danger and pitfalls. Accurate self-understanding and appropriate engagement with others requires mentoring, feedback, accountability, and maturation. The most egregious sins of leadership stem from pride, selfish ambition, and a misuse of power.
2. Part of our fallen nature is a distorted understanding of purpose. For Christians, humankind is made for God and for fulfilling God's will as

individuals and communities. All other purposes are secondary to this and should be shaped by this larger purpose.

3. Evil is what's wrong with the world, and it includes trouble in nature as well as in human nature. It includes disease as well as theft, birth defects as well as character defects. Christians define evil as any spoiling of *shalom*, any deviation from the way God wants things to be. Good leadership is not naive about evil and will recognize its interplay with creation. Light and shadow are always present within the dynamics of our endeavors.

Redemption

1. Central in the biblical narrative is the notion of redemption—that is, a restoration of relationships with God and humankind. Evil and resulting brokenness need not inevitably result in despair. Rather, Christians believe meaning, healing, peace, and justice are possible and thus remain hopeful and committed to positive change. Hope is not a fantasy but a reality grounded in historical example and a faith in a meaningful future. The incarnation, atonement, and resurrection of Jesus Christ are central to redemption and the ultimate platform for every Christian enterprise.

2. The Bible is most explicit about the redeeming of individual character. Laws of the Hebrew Bible, commandments of Christ, and exhortations from his disciples Peter, Paul, James, and John emphasize the virtues of kindness, gentleness, self-control, love, compassion, humility, patience, and a host of others. Such transformation is the expectation of Christian maturity.

3. From a Christian point of view, noble purposes aligned with personal integrity and the respect of persons undergird our understanding of leadership.[37] It is only when the direction and the method are in line with God's purposes, character, and ways of operating that godly leadership takes place.

A Note about Spirituality and Christianity

The modern use of the term "spirituality" embraces the deepest values and meanings by which people live. Not all spirituality is religious, but all religions espouse a distinctive spirituality. For example, Christians have delineated several spiritual disciplines, Muslims practice the five pillars, Buddhists have the Noble Eightfold Path, and Hindus have a wide range of practices called Sadhana.

Similarly, secularists, in an attempt to be guided by their deepest values, may practice a form of reflection and meditation. Purpose and meaning are widely recognized as essential to human flourishing, and so spirituality has become increasingly acceptable as a dimension of the workplace and an element of the curriculum in the academy. This broader notion of spirituality has created a space for religious faith, as a subset of spirituality, to be more transparent in the work of the academy. Perhaps this is most evident in the *Journal of Management, Spirituality and Religion*, a publication started in 2004 by one of the interest groups of the Academy of Management and the scholarship of Louis Fry on spiritual leadership. Leaders, including Christian leaders, have a unique opportunity to winsomely integrate "the human spirit, fully engaged" as part of their ventures.[38]

2

biblical, historical, and denominational perspectives on leadership

Although the first chapter touched on the contemporary study of leadership, before going further we need to go back in time. This chapter identifies the earliest Jewish and Christian approaches to leadership as well as those developed by influential denominations and religious orders throughout the centuries. These include the Benedictine, Lutheran, Presbyterian, Quaker, Methodist, and Pentecostal traditions. While these are often examined for what they have to say about the nature and the pattern of ministry, only in passing has this examination focused on its leadership dimension.

The earliest Jewish and Christian writings offer a range of challenging insights into the nature and practice of leadership. This topic is not central to their main plot—the developing story of God's dealings with humankind. Nor is it one of their main themes—creation, providence, faith, justice, redemption, love, community, and hope. However, the issue of leadership does surface regularly within them. Alongside occasional prescriptive statements, there are many stories about and evaluations of leaders. Rather than always telling us what to conclude about the leadership portrayed, more often these writings draw us in to working out what to make of what they describe.

Early Jewish Approaches to Leadership

Although there is no exact equivalent to the word "leader" in the Hebrew Bible, the idea is certainly present. In the first instance, it is associated with God, chiefly through references to his actively "guiding," "going before," and "preparing the way for" his people or a particular individual. Where "leader" is used of human figures, the following features regularly stand out.

1. There are different types of leadership, which complement and correct one another. Politically, this is embodied in the king, but there is a strong insistence that he is subject to, not above, the law. At crucial moments, prophets act as his divine guide and conscience, sometimes clarifying but more often challenging his actions. There is also a class of wise advisers who are guardians of the learned experience that can inform and help him to communicate his judgments. Finally, various levels of priests provide instruction and should be role models in religious and ethical matters. Stellar examples of these four types of leadership are Solomon, Moses, Daniel, and Ezra. These groups are always in creative, and frequently dissonant, tension with one another and are an early form of the "separation of powers" found in modern democracies.[1]

2. Within the framework provided by these main forms of leadership, other kinds subsist. There are, for example, army generals (such as Joab), prophetic assistants (such as Baruch), city or town elders (such as Boaz), and part-time as well as full-time priests. While these mostly undertake the wishes of the most significant leaders, at times they also clash with them when they overstep the limits of their respective authority. More generally, leadership is also expressed at the familial level in the forms of heads of households and local landlords (both of whom were generally, but not always, male).

3. At the heart of leadership lies the radical notion of "servanthood." Iconic leaders like Moses are regarded as such because they exemplify this quality in the highest degree. This does not mean that servanthood is primarily defined as other-centered or as simply providing what people want. It is first and foremost God-centered and involves articulating, embodying, and enacting God's vision, heart, and will for his people. A second leading metaphor to describe leadership is that of "shepherding." While this is another relatively lowly occupation, the qualities needed to be a good shepherd are similar to those required in a good leader. As the well-known Psalm 23 shows, God himself provides the highest expression of what this involves.

4. Leadership does not always come from the more privileged sectors of society but also from those in lower or marginal positions whom God discerns as possessing what leadership requires. There are many examples of this. Joseph is an immigrant from an oppressed people who becomes the chief administrator in Egypt. Deborah is a woman who becomes a judge and prophetess among her people at a critical time. David is a young shepherd from a rural district who becomes Israel's second and most illustrious king. Samuel, the child of a devout mother, is marked out to become the leading prophet in the land. Amos is a simple herdsman unexpectedly called to challenge both Israel's elite and surrounding foreign rulers. Underlying the rise of such individuals is God's preeminent interest in what is in their hearts rather than in their outward status and position.

5. Leadership is not always a solo affair and often takes place through the partnership of one or more figures whose contributions complement each other. The link between these partnerships varies—for example, family ties, bonds of friendship, persons with complementary responsibilities, links forged by training for service—and can cross both gender and status lines. Examples include the joint contributions of three siblings (Moses, Aaron, and Miriam), an uncle and niece (Mordecai and Esther), two friends (David and Jonathan), a political and a religious leader (Nehemiah and Ezra), and four colleagues in exile (Daniel and his associates).

6. There are different and various ways of communicating to people what characterizes leadership. The earliest Jewish writings contain stories, and occasionally autobiographies, of how people became and operated as leaders. There are parables of how leadership should or should not be undertaken. There are direct instructions about what it involves and about the consequences of doing it well or badly. There are wise maxims or proverbs, riddles or questions, to guide or warn those in positions of responsibility. All of these have their place, mostly complementing, sometimes standing in creative tension with, one another.

7. Even the greatest leaders make bad mistakes and experience failure. Moses and David are prime examples of this. Leaders are not idealized or eulogized but portrayed with all their weaknesses as well as strengths.[2] They are not spared the repercussions of their self-serving, misguided, or evil decisions, nor are those close to them or under them. If they become aware of their wrongdoing, some learn from it, while others do not. When they do, forgiveness is available and new opportunities await them, even if these may be affected by the consequences of their previous actions. Leaders' fallibilities demonstrate how much they need to be envisioned, directed, and empowered by God as well as open to the advice of those God has placed around them.

8. The legacy of these leaders is frequently documented. Interestingly, this is often unpredictable, for it depends less on what kind of leader they are than on how God blesses or judges their contributions. Good leaders sometimes fail to shape the future as much as expected and experience a kind of "divine inutility." This may be due to the intransigence of others around them, the effects of unexpected circumstances, or the apathy of those for whom they are responsible. Correlatively, sometimes God is able to turn the decisions of bad leaders to better effect. In other words, a leader's legacy is not simply a case of cause and effect but is caught up in a wider divine providence and purpose.[3] Increasingly in these writings, however, there is talk of a future reckoning that will fully evaluate, judge, or vindicate each leader's contribution.

9. Although these writings' depictions of leadership are secondary to their main purposes and themes, they often intersect with these and are shaped by them. As a result, several key features of divinely approved leadership regularly come to the fore. These include keeping promises, encouraging creativity and design, maintaining covenants or contracts, developing trust through behaving trustworthily, describing reality rather than embroidering it, practicing good stewardship of resources and sharing prosperity, giving voice to and acting affirmatively toward the marginal and disadvantaged, building relationships and community, expressing a vision, and generating hope for the future. These characteristics are not presented as mere principles or generalities but as specific projects, discrete behaviors, and concrete actions.

At the practical level, these early Hebrew writings contain numerous stories that, with a little contemporary updating and cultural adjustment, can be profitably used as case studies today. Good examples of this are how to develop a relationship with the head of another corporate body with whom there have been tensions and even enmity (David's approach to the king of Tyre); how to oversee a restorative project in a postconflict situation with limited resources and aggressive opponents (Nehemiah's reconstruction of Jerusalem after the return of his exiled countrymen); and how to lobby from a position of relative disadvantage in the presence of a rival who has greater power (Esther's approach to countering Haman's attack on the Jews).

The Major Early Christian Exponent

Among the early Christians, Paul most clearly and fully articulates an understanding of leadership. As his work and writings are the key source for Western

Christianity and a seminal influence on other Western social and political structures, it is strange that until recently he has been overlooked in leadership studies. It is only in the past decade that Paul has begun to gain attention. As Mark Strom says: "He was a thoroughly urban man. He readily employed his audience's vocabulary, literary techniques, intellectual models, social conventions and even clichés. He seems to have improvised from whatever was at hand in order to engage the needs and world views of his audiences. Today we take such adaptability for granted, but there was little precedent for Paul."[4]

The first discussion of Paul as an important figure for leadership studies appeared in the original edition of this volume. It was then taken up by biblical scholar Richard Anscough and business consultant Stephen Cotton in their more extensive treatment of Paul as a passionate visionary leader.[5] Mark Strom is the latest to recognize Paul's past significance and present relevance in this area by making him the final and major case study in his book on transformative wisdom leaders.[6] As we shall see, however, this adaptability was rooted in a set of deeply held convictions arising from his profound encounter of the living God as revealed through Jesus Christ. In the course of establishing a far-flung network of local groups in various cultural settings through an itinerant mission team, Paul developed a clear understanding and practice of leadership that was quite contrary to conventional approaches to leadership at the time. Though he does not provide a systematic account of the nature and practice of leadership, his approach to it was radical for its day and is still suggestive for ours. The following discussion considers two interrelated kinds of governance that arose in his churches: the ongoing task of grassroots leaders and the sporadic role of Paul himself and his team.[7]

Leadership in the Local Churches

For modern people, questions of governance are often of primary interest. Leadership is a central concern in any democratic and bureaucratic society. This is also the case in church life, which is more democratized and bureaucratic than in previous times. In social and religious arrangements, people prize order; it is not only a preoccupation but also a virtue, not only a means but also an end. As already noted, the issue of leadership influences attempts to understand chains of command and lines of authority. As a result, there is a danger of reading the priority we accord these matters into Paul's ideas about the church. He was certainly concerned about the church conducting itself in an orderly manner and about members being properly cared for and guided. But other than when a church's actions were inadequate, he says very little about such matters. For him, they appear to be secondary rather than primary issues.

The Language of Leadership

If we begin by looking simply at the basic words Paul uses in speaking about these issues, what strikes us first is the infrequency of terms related to those at the top, to formal power, and to organization. Of more than three dozen terms used of people in leadership positions in his day, the only high-ranking one Paul uses is in reference to Christ (Col. 1:18). Reference to order, or the need to be orderly, occurs infrequently in Paul's writings (1 Cor. 14:40; Col. 2:5), and only once is it clearly associated with the church, coming at the close of his instructions to the Corinthians about what should happen in their meetings (1 Cor. 14:13–40). Its opposite is *unruliness*, which is associated with disharmony (1 Cor. 14:33; cf. 2 Cor. 12:20). Paul never suggests that it is the role of one or a few people in the assembly to regulate its gatherings. This is everyone's responsibility as the people discern and share what the Spirit is saying (1 Cor. 12:7–11; 14:28, 30, 32). Organization stems from a highly participatory and charismatic process and is not determined in advance by a few. Likewise, the word "authority" rarely appears in Paul's writings. Only in two places does he use the word in regard to his own position—never in regard to those in leadership in local churches—and only then when his apostolic link with a church is being challenged (2 Cor. 10:8; 13:10). At Corinth, he certainly wishes to reestablish his unique relationship with the church as its founder (2 Cor. 10:13), but he disassociates himself from the authoritarian way the "false apostles" conduct themselves. He does not seek to influence the members by improper means (2 Cor. 10:3), boast of his preeminence (2 Cor. 10:12–15), dazzle the church with rhetoric (2 Cor. 11:5–6), or manipulate and control his converts (2 Cor. 11:16–19; cf. 2 Cor. 1:24). His "authority" is exercised only for constructive purposes, and he prefers that the church take appropriate corrective action before he arrives so that he does not have to engage in it.

Basic Metaphors for Understanding Leadership

In talking about organization and authority, Paul draws on several metaphors to provide an overall frame of reference or paradigm for his view. Basic to this are metaphors and analogies drawn from family life. This is not surprising, for the language of family is the primary way of talking about the relationship between God and his people. Just as God is viewed as "Father" and believers as "children," so Paul describes himself as a "father" to his "offspring" in the faith (1 Cor. 4:14–15; 2 Cor. 12:14; 1 Thess. 2:11). This conveys an affectionate but responsible parental rather than patriarchal bond. Paul also speaks of himself as a "mother" who suffers labor pains (Gal. 4:19) and as a nurse who cares for her charges (1 Thess. 2:7; cf. 1 Cor. 3:2). This cluster of metaphors emphasizes both the affectionate relationship between Paul and his converts and his sense of responsibility for them. But it would be wrong to conclude that Paul encouraged a childlike dependency on him, for he treated believers as adult children and urged them to "grow up" in Christ and to become mature adults in the faith (e.g., 1 Cor. 14:20; Eph. 4:14). Other metaphors in Paul's writings, such as farmer (1 Cor. 3:6–9) and builder (1 Cor. 3:10–15), are drawn from the world of work and stress his fundamental role in starting and designing the Corinthian church. The metaphor of the body (1 Cor. 12:12–27; Eph. 4:1–16), especially the reference to the unifying and structuring role of the ligaments, reveals something about the central role of key people in the church whose primary responsibility is to help maintain unity and engender growth.

Participation in Leading the Gatherings

For Paul, what happens at church gatherings originates in the Spirit and flows through the entire membership for the benefit of all. Everyone is caught up in this divine operation (1 Cor. 12:7). The process itself is described through the use of action verbs that stress its dynamic character: Contributions to the meetings are energized, manifested, and distributed by the Spirit (1 Cor. 12:6–7, 11). Paul uses a variety of nouns to capture the diversity of what takes place. It is an exercise of "gifts," a variety of "services," different kinds of "working" (1 Cor. 12:4–6). The activities that result from these gifts highlight the diversity of the Spirit's working (Rom. 12:4–8; 1 Cor. 12:8–11; Eph. 4:11–13). Since, for Paul, everyone in the church is under an obligation to discern the validity of contributions to the meeting, this task is not in the hands of one person, a leadership team, or a worship committee, even if certain people play a more prominent role in shaping what takes place (1 Cor. 12:10; 14:30). While Paul provides some general guidelines for what should happen during a meeting (1 Cor. 13:1–3; 14:9–32; Eph. 4:12–15), if everyone respects these guidelines, there is no need for a planned order of service or for one person to lead it.

No Status Distinctions

Reference to certain people in the community playing a greater role than others leads to a consideration of key people within the churches. The language of priesthood appears only metaphorically in Paul's writings, never of a literal person or group, in regard to a wide range of devotional, compassionate, financial, and evangelistic activities (cf. Rom. 15:16, 27; 2 Cor. 9:12; Phil. 2:17 in the original language). Paul's point is that the kinds of ceremonial activities God required of only some people in the Old Testament are now required of all Christians. This desacralizes and democratizes the role of those who have a significant part to play. The central corporate action in the churches was the Lord's Supper, which was held weekly and was a full, not a token, meal. Nowhere in Paul's letters, disputed or undisputed, is anyone identified as the official presider. This role probably fell to the host, in whose home the meal was held. If Paul's practice is at all typical, baptism also took place through other than leading figures in the movement (1 Cor. 1:14–17). As far as the usual terms for secular offices are concerned, only one of the more than thirty that existed in the first century appears in Paul's writings, but it is used exclusively of the governing role played by Christ in the church (Col. 1:18). Instead, the language of servanthood dominates. In the first century, however, this language did not necessarily conjure up ideas of lowly people undertaking inferior tasks. Servants of important social and political figures had considerable status and carried on high-level managerial and bureaucratic work. A servant's master determined that servant's status, and many servants had a higher social standing than free men or women who belonged to socially inferior families. In addition, because Christ is the Lord of Christians, their servant work has dignity and should be respected, and because he is the ultimate model of servanthood, he provides the profoundest example of how this should be undertaken.

Effective Functioning Rather Than Appointed Positions

On the whole, verbs rather than nouns are used more often in regard to those making a fundamental contribution to the church. What is crucial, therefore, are the functions people perform rather than the positions they occupy. For example, Paul refers to those who "work hard," "admonish," and are "instructor[s]" (Gal. 6:6; 1 Thess. 5:12) and to the way certain people proved themselves through conflict in the church (1 Cor. 11:19). When nouns are used, as of those who are "helpers" or administrators (1 Cor. 12:28), they tend to be used in regard to fairly ordinary rather than dramatic contributions. Apart from the Pastoral Letters (e.g., 1 Tim. 5:17), the term "elders," referring to older, respected Christians who probably had a corporate responsibility for a cluster of churches in a city, does not occur in Paul's writings (but cf. Acts 14:23). The word "overseer" occurs just once and in the plural (Phil. 1:1), serving as a description rather than a title and as an ancillary to "God's holy people" in general. Ordination, as we know it, does not appear in the Pauline letters. The laying on of hands is mentioned, but this was used for such diverse procedures as giving the Spirit (Acts 8:17), healing from illness (Acts 9:17), and commissioning a person for itinerant service (Acts 13:2–3). While, according to Acts, Paul and Barnabas "appointed elders" in every church (Acts 14:23), this seems to have involved ratifying a community's choice, as was the case with the laying on of hands on the seven (Acts 6:3–6). When Paul identifies certain people in the church in Corinth as having made a fundamental contribution to its life, he merely asks the congregation to "order themselves" under such people and instructs them to extend this attitude "to everyone who joins in the work and labors at it" (1 Cor. 16:16). This suggests a nonformal, community recognition of a group, not an individual, that is based on the quality of the ministry people are already engaged in rather than on external qualifications.

The Necessity of Practical Qualifications

As the Pastoral Letters indicate, people should be appointed overseers and helpers in the community only if they have first proven themselves in their households. But houses were workplaces as well as domestic spaces and involved the tasks of supervising slaves in addition to raising families. Proven experience and a good reputation in managing workers were therefore also qualifications for leadership in the church. It is not inappropriate to assume that this is the background for people singled out by Paul such as Titius Justus (Acts 18:7), Aquila and Priscilla (Rom. 16:3), Gaius (Rom. 16:23), Nympha (Col. 4:15), and Philemon and Apphia (Philem. 1–2). The social status of such people provided the basis for their having preeminence in the group, but only if, as Stephanas and his household did, they "devoted themselves to the service of the Lord's people" (1 Cor. 16:15). This is not to say that in this case traditional authority replaced charismatic authority, for these people needed more than social status to qualify for this responsibility. What we find is an approach to authority that recognizes the charismatic gifts or social prominence of certain people but requires that other qualities such as commitment and servanthood also be present. Paul names women among this group, indicating that they often played a significant role in congregational life as well as among the itinerant group of apostles (Rom. 16:6–7) and prophets (1 Cor. 11:5). Women may also have operated as evangelists (Phil. 4:3), and among Paul's associates was a wife-and-husband team involved in at least occasional high-level instruction (Acts 18:26). Paul rises above the gender as well as the status distinctions of his time.

Motivating by Persuasion Rather Than Command

Paul plays a visible role in the birth and ongoing life of the churches he founded. With other churches, he cannot and does not assume a preeminent position (cf. Rom. 1:11–13). Yet the day-to-day ordering and governing of affairs in the churches Paul founded lay in the hands of the congregations themselves.

In churches where things are going relatively well, such as the church at Philippi, Paul addresses problems without reminding believers of his foundational role in their lives or of his apostolic authority. In churches in which things are not going so well and his role is being challenged, such as the church at Corinth, Paul reminds his converts of his seminal role in the church's life (1 Cor. 4:15) and, from a distance at least, plays a more directive part in their affairs. But nowhere does he exhibit an authoritarian stance. He is more concerned that his converts "imitate" him rather than "obey" him (1 Cor. 11:1; Gal. 4:12; Phil. 3:17), and he instructs others by means of appeals (1 Cor. 4:16) based on love (Philem. 1:8–9) far more than by means of "commands" (cf. 1 Cor. 14:37). His few calls for obedience have to do with responding appropriately to his loving urgings (2 Cor. 2:9), remaining faithful to the gospel (cf. Phil. 2:12), and yielding to the prompting of the Spirit (1 Thess. 4:8).

The Contribution of Paul and His Team

Paul's Role in the Local Churches

Paul's noncoercive and nonauthoritarian stance toward his communities accords with certain characteristic features of his method of operation. Since they have the gospel (1 Cor. 15:3), basic instruction (1 Thess. 4:1), Paul's own example (Acts 20:34–35), the Old Testament (1 Cor. 14:34), a few sayings of Christ (1 Cor. 7:10), and some general rules (1 Cor. 11:16), Paul is confident that his communities have the resources to mature. He is available if they need advice on certain matters (e.g., 1 Cor. 7:1; 1 Thess. 4:13) and occasionally visits them to see how they are doing (Acts 15:36). In a situation requiring discipline, he can still lay down the law, but not, however, as an external, hierarchical authority as much as a significant fellow member whose spirit is present in their deliberations even when he is absent (1 Cor. 5:3–5; Col. 2:5). Even those with little status have the wisdom to deal with some disputes in the community (1 Cor. 6:4–5), though on other occasions the entire church should do so (1 Cor. 5:1–5). Paul's aim is to build up a community's ability to look after such matters, to "work with" the members rather than "lord it over" them (2 Cor. 1:24). If he is forced to confront them, the rod that he brings is the rod of the Word (2 Cor. 10:3–6), and his preference is to come "in love and with a gentle spirit" (1 Cor. 4:21). His basic authority stems from the gospel he has been commissioned to preach, not by right from his apostolic commission. Only as long as his words reflect that gospel (Gal. 1:9) or are in accord with the Spirit (1 Cor. 7:40) should the churches give him a hearing. His authority is instrumental, not inherent, and, though powerful because of God's call, subject to his converts' Christian discernment.

The Roles of Paul's Team in the Churches

Associates such as Timothy and Titus have only functional or derived authority based on the reputation of the work they have undertaken or on the task of transmitting Paul's message to the churches. They do not have an automatic right of entry. Often Paul has to argue their case, pointing out their involvement with him and knowledge of his affairs as well as their fidelity to the apostolic task, sometimes at risk to their own lives (1 Cor. 16:10–11; Phil. 2:19–23; Col. 4:7–8). When visiting churches, these colleagues have a role to play as itinerants (cf. 2 Cor. 7:15), not as residents. The Pastoral Letters are revealing here. Paul's associates do not have a settled and official role in the congregations but an ambassadorial and exemplary one. They do not reside among the congregations but only visit them for a defined period of time and exert spiritual rather than formal authority through the quality of their love and faithfulness to Paul's teaching (1 Tim. 2:12–15; 6:1–12; 2 Tim. 1:8; 2:22–24; 3:10; Titus 2:7). They are to relate to people in the churches in a familial way, reflecting their limited age and experience, rather than from a position of command (1 Tim. 5:1–2). They are to provide instruction for ordering certain aspects of worship and for governing the church rather than to control and regulate the specifics of how church worship and government are conducted (1 Tim. 3:2; 2 Tim. 2:2–7; Titus 2:1–9). The key roles in the churches are for proven individuals and couples within their own ranks (1 Tim. 3:1–13; Titus 1:5–9). Paul's associates can help identify these people only through knowledge provided by the churches themselves.[8]

Paul as a Collegial Leader

Paul's mission team was commissioned by a particular church, the church at Antioch, and at intervals reported back to it (Acts 13:1–3; 14:26–28). Yet it had a largely independent existence throughout the Mediterranean world. It always contained a number of core members who traveled much of the time with it but broke off now and again to fulfill a particular undertaking. It also contained a number of short-term members who came from various churches as the need or opportunity arose. Paul's team involved women and men, couples and singles, young and old, Greeks and Jews. It has been estimated that at times it contained up to forty members. Its prime tasks were to preach the gospel, plant churches among those who responded to it, and help network those churches and encourage them through occasional visits and letters. It was essentially a nonprofit organization engaged in mission activities.

The members of the group were drawn into the orbit of one person's ministry: Paul's. Paul is the one who is generally spoken of as "choosing," "sending," or "leaving" people and who generally decides, though with the agreement of his coworkers, what the next step in the work will entail (Acts 15:40; 16:1–3, 9; 18:1, 18–21; 19:21; 20:13, 16–17). Despite this, or rather because of Paul's understanding of his ministry as rooted in the gospel and embodied in Christ, Paul operates in a highly consultative and collegial way. He describes his staff as "coworkers" (Phil. 2:25) and as "brothers and sisters" (Acts 18:18) and regards them as having a ministry in their own right. They are not merely extensions of him and his work. This is clear from the way he names several of them separately at the beginning of many of his letters (as in 1 Cor. 1:1). His attitude reflects his hope that his fellow workers are welcomed and encouraged by the communities they visit (1 Cor. 16:10–11; 2 Cor. 8:22, 24; Phil. 2:20–22, 25–28; Col. 4:7, 12–13). Though there is a subordination to Paul, it is voluntary and personal rather than coercive and formal (1 Cor. 4:17; 2 Cor. 8:17).

Qualities That Mark Paul's Leadership

According to the first commentator to emphasize the apostle's importance for leadership studies, "Paul created a self-perpetuating model of leadership . . . that intentionally created other leaders, who in turn created other leaders." For him, leaders were "worthy of imitation," and followers became "imitators" of leaders and "examples for others to follow."[9] Each left a legacy for others to continue. The key characteristics of his leadership include displaying boldness amid opposition; influencing motives rather than asserting authority; being affectionate and emotional, vulnerable and transparent, authentic and sincere; exemplifying a follower-centered, not self-centered, approach. In this way his motives and methods corresponded to one another and were anchored in a standard outside of himself—that is, in Jesus. This enabled Paul to influence people in a spiritual and moral rather than formal and authoritarian way. The real measure of his effectiveness was changed lives and new leaders.[10]

While J. Lee Whittington writes from a leadership studies perspective, over the past fifteen years a number of biblical scholars have contrasted Paul's approach to leadership with that dominant in the Greco-Roman culture of his day, and this has also been a focus of contributions in several issues of the *Journal of Biblical Perspectives in Leadership*. Biblical scholar Richard Ascough and leadership consultant Sandy Cotton summarize Paul's underlying principles of leadership as follows:

- Paradigm busting
- Sharing vision ✶
- Creating shared space ✵

- Prioritizing relationships
- Encouraging followers
- Maintaining transparency
- Networking continuously
- Priming joint leadership
- Building community
- Clarifying boundaries
- Celebrating diversity
- Confronting opposition
- Advocating for others
- Giving up control
- Embodying compassion[11]

In this section we have focused on general early Jewish and a specific early Christian understanding of leadership. In a later section we shall assess popular treatments in the management literature of the two main figures in the Old and New Testament writings: Moses and Jesus. Here we turn next to the differing developments of these biblical approaches in religious organizations in the subsequent centuries.

Historical Models of Leadership in the Church

Long and rich traditions of leadership exist in subsequent Jewish and Christian history.[12] In what follows we focus on the latter, especially on denominational church networks and on religious orders with a particular mission alongside these. From such approaches, we can gain relevant applications to leadership today.

The Benedictine Order

In the Benedictine Order, monks are viewed as preservers of tradition. Historically they served as scribes who carefully copied manuscripts, thereby saving many treasures of classical antiquity during the so-called Dark Ages. Benedictine monasticism has flourished for more than fifteen hundred years in a variety of settings and in various cultures. Its fundamentals are contained in the Rule of St. Benedict, a formative document that has been influential in much communal development in the West to this day. It sought to provide a model of leadership that avoided overemphasizing the arbitrary or dysfunctional whims of either a single leader or the majority of the community. As the leader of a monastery, the abbot is expected to hold together the creative tension between organizing and pastoring, between attending to the common good of all and the particular good of individuals. The abbot is viewed as a kind of spiritual parent. In fulfilling this role, the abbot is expected to pass on wisdom (the sacred doctrine and tradition) as well as provide prudent guidance in a disciple's search for God. In addition, he is expected to understand the spiritual connection between administrative and pastoral duties.[13]

The temporal arrangements of a monastery are ordered as such to serve the spiritual good of the monks. Consequently, the abbot's spiritual leadership necessarily involves a concern for the practicalities of life. In this way he is a steward of both the spiritual and the material resources of the monastery (Rule of St. Benedict 64). His stewardship expresses itself in delegating key tasks to others to direct the elements of the daily life of the community. The abbot is also directed by the Order of St. Benedict to see himself as a physician (Rule 28). He must know how to "diagnose" the spiritual maladies of individual monks and the entire community, and he must know how to apply the right remedy. The Benedictine abbot is also seen as a teacher (Rule 2:11–15). Beyond his responsibility to teach monastic doctrine is his duty to teach a way of life. While he is to teach by word, he is also required to teach by the example of his life and actions. Though he is a guardian of tradition, the abbot must possess "a treasury of knowledge from which he can bring out what is old and new" (Rule 64:9).[14]

In considering a monk for the office of abbot, a community must look for a person who demonstrates "wisdom in teaching" and "goodness of life" (Rule 64:2). The notion of wisdom carries with it the element of discretion. We might also call this prudence or discernment. The abbot must be able to size up the monks, taking note of their individual needs and gifts. He must know how to challenge the strong to greater advance in their spiritual journeys and also how to encourage the weak (Rule 64:17–18). The Rule goes on to encourage the abbot to include the community in key decisions, taking into account the thoughts of even the youngest members. In this way, discretion is used to make good participatory decisions. Interestingly, the Rule is one of the few leadership documents from the past that contains guidance for the selection and job description of the "second-in-command" in an organization (in this case, the prior).

The complex character of Benedictine leadership is best exhibited in the multiple roles the abbot undertakes simultaneously and seamlessly. Because he understands the long-term impact of his leadership on both his organization and his followers, like a parent or a guide, he exercises a combination of wisdom and care. Like a physician, the abbot serves as one who can identify and attend to the needs of his followers. Like a teacher, the abbot fulfills an instructional role through encouraging the personal and professional growth of his followers. He, like a manager, leads by exercising good and discreet stewardship of human and other resources. The abbot is comfortable delegating tasks while at the same time leading by example. These roles aptly capture the complexity of leadership required in today's world. Leaders must serve as guides, stewards, physicians, teachers, and empowerers, leading by example, displaying wisdom, and living lives of goodness.

The Lutheran Understanding

Lutheran theology has always stressed God's complex work in the world, including God's ability to affirm the goodness of created things and offices, and the appropriateness of worldly vocations. Reason plays a central role, as does the application of common sense, in living life in the world.

The historical circumstances that gave birth to the Lutheran tradition provide a view of leadership as an act of reformation in the context of resistant systems. When Martin Luther is used as an exemplar of this approach to leadership, it expresses itself in three distinct tasks: (1) critique of the status quo or "defining reality," (2) constructive experimentation or risk taking, and (3) consolidation that has as its chief end continuity within the new order. This is a reformation model of change that requires courage, collaboration, and commitment and takes place within the context of Luther's conviction of the priesthood of all believers. This conviction enabled him to see every Christian as having full access to God, being able to express to others the full forgiveness of God, and exercising the divine right of sharing God's Word and reflecting God's Spirit.

What qualifies one for leadership from a Lutheran perspective? To begin with, one must understand the means of grace as it comes through the preached Word, baptism, the Lord's Supper, and the conversation and consolation of the community. Indeed, understanding one's baptism as a primary reminder of one's position as a child of God in the context of the commitment and fellowship of the faith community is highly relevant to understanding leadership. Doing so enables the believing person to live a life of security in the faith. As a leader, Luther constantly took himself back to the fundamental principles of the faith, to his security in baptism, and to his place in the community of faith. A leader is one who, like Luther, always keeps before him these key understandings.

This reformational understanding of leadership provides a model that is inward looking with respect to the person of the leader and outwardly focused on the tasks of leadership. A leader is one who with humility embraces his or her security in the faith, represented by baptism and confirmation of the benefits of living life within the faith community—namely, consolation, conversation, and communion. This inward confirmation of one's place in the world enables a leader to lead freely, intently, and openly. The Lutheran understanding of the priesthood of all believers helps leaders to view themselves less as overlords of their communities and more as representatives of them, exercising a role that belongs to every member even as it requires expression particularly in one.[15]

The Presbyterian Model

For Presbyterians, leadership is best portrayed by the classic Reformed understanding of the threefold office of Christ: prophet, priest, and king. In ancient Israel, these leadership functions were expressed separately by three people, and each was legitimate and necessary for carrying out God's will for the people. Prophets brought the message from God to the people, priests represented the needs of the people before God, and kings governed society according to God's will. In Presbyterian polity, these roles are expressed by ministers of the Word, who proclaim God's will to the church; deacons, who serve the felt needs of the people; and elders, who administer God's rule in the congregation.

In Christ, these three roles merge into one to create a complementary whole. As redeemer, Christ was at once prophet, priest, and king: he proclaimed the Word of God, exhibited mercy, and through his power healed the sick, forgave sins, and subdued the storm.[16] Since Christ encompasses all, it follows that, in the Christian community, those who profess Jesus as Lord should also seek to serve as prophet, priest, and king in a unified rather than a separate fashion. We can never again isolate the three offices; we must see them as a whole. This is not to say that a person must exhibit all three roles. Rather, all three must be represented in leadership.

The Presbyterian model offers significant insights for contemporary leadership. The priestly function reveals the need for empathy, a critical skill that has gained wide appeal in recent years. Empathy, often seen as a "soft" skill, has proven to be necessary for building relationships and understanding the perspectives of others. Effective communication is another key function of leadership and certainly ties in with the prophetic function. Leaders skilled at communicating a vision or a plan with clear, compelling, inspiring, and honest communication pave the way for enthusiastic implementation of their ideas. The ruling or kingly function is akin to the direction-setting ability of a leader. This is the ability to see the big picture.[17]

The Quaker Alternative

At the heart of the Quaker (or Friends) tradition is a rich belief in shared leadership. A designated or assigned individual leader is an alien concept. The Friends method of governance relies not on hierarchical structure to make decisions but rather on a "sense of the meeting" by the entire group. In this model of decision making, the emphasis is on the presence of Christ in the gathered community, and the practice of silence is used by all to discern the leading of the Spirit. Silence is not a vacuum or the absence of noise but a fullness, a space in which to hear the still, small voice of God. The gathered submit themselves to waiting on the Holy Spirit and to listening to one another in expectation that God's direction for the group will be revealed. Participants are expected to contribute their insights by speaking simply, without repetition, rhetoric, or argumentativeness. Decisions are made through consensus rather than majority vote.[18]

The Quaker process of shared decision making is built on the fundamental belief that "all of us in this world are interdependent and must be responsible for each other."[19] No one is above anyone else, and the Spirit can speak through anyone in a Friends' meeting. Everyone has the responsibility to participate, whether orally or not, and each has the potential to offer insight. If one cannot improve on the silence, one does not speak. The spiritual power of group silence is recognized, and shared silence is a medium for group discovery and a way of sharing oneself with others and with God. Friends view silence as a highly accessible treasure. It is with silence that meetings begin and end, signaling dependence on the source of wisdom and giving time to open one's self to the workings of the Spirit.

This model invites organizational leaders to use their positional power to promote dialogue. The assigned leader is also a participant in seeking new solutions to pressing organizational issues. In the vulnerability of this approach, there is freedom for the assigned leader to contribute, listen, learn, and share his or her power. Quakerism opens up a way to better understand a style of shared leading and responsibility.[20]

The Methodist Approach

Methodism's view of leadership has been strongly influenced by its founder, John Wesley.[21] At its heart lies a passionate commitment to know the living God, proclaim the reality of Christ, and seek justice for those denied it. This expresses itself in several basic principles.

For Wesley, leadership sprang not from his personal style, gifts, or ministry but from a concern for people. This encompassed their material and social as well as spiritual needs. His approach explains why he attracted so many ordinary people who were unmoved by the appeals of other religious leaders of the time. Wesley then took the further step of going to the people wherever they were rather than expecting them to come to him. In the early days Methodism was more a movement than an institution. Its organizational structure, including churches, sprang up as a consequence of, rather than strategy for, reaching out to people. This is why Methodism outpaced other denominations as the American frontier expanded westward. As a consequence, significant leaders of social, worker, and prison reform, as well as those devoted to the abolition of slavery and elevation of women, were raised up among the early Methodists.

These principles were expressed in several distinct leadership practices. First among these was the recognition that leadership could be exercised by a variety of people. "There was no one route to leadership. . . . Leaders were male and female, ordained and lay, of noble birth and modest origin and—particularly in America—'black and white.'"[22] The development of lay preachers was a new phenomenon. Female oversight of small "class" meetings and larger "societies" was unusually common. Unlike Anglicanism, leadership extended beyond the upper class to include middle- and working-class people. Second, one could lead not only from the center but also from the margins, as Wesley did, starting from a position of social status but becoming a critic of the religious establishment. Working from the margins taught him the role of struggle, tension, and ambiguity in leadership. Third, there was openness to a range of opinions and sometimes "third alternatives" between conventional and radical options. Finally, there was an emphasis on a horizontal network of local organizations that were in conference with one another rather than the hierarchical, centralized structure of older denominations.

In varying degrees, Holiness or socially conscious denominations developing out of Methodism, such as the Church of the Nazarenes and Salvation Army, exhibited some of its particular characteristics. As Methodism itself became more respectable, it increasingly lost its character as a movement and became more institutional, bureaucratic, and centralized.

The Pentecostal Perspective

In the perspective of Pentecostalism, which has a much shorter but still influential history, an understanding of self emerges from an understanding of God as the giver of gifts and power. In this context, leadership is not viewed as a purely human characteristic. It is not a set of skills or knowledge that can be obtained or learned; rather, leadership begins with understanding that one is a follower of Jesus and a vessel for the power of his Spirit. God is the chief leader who chooses human leaders. In this way, leadership is something that is derived from the sovereign operation of the God of the Bible. The greatness of human leadership is measured by how well the leader is a follower of God.

On the basis of Acts 2, Pentecostals believe that God pours out the gifts of the Spirit equally on all who earnestly seek the Spirit. They therefore view Christian leadership as transportable, adaptable, and personal. Within the Pentecostal movement, then, every member is a potential leader. All genuine leadership is based on spiritual power coming from the Spirit of God, and it emerges in the context of a loving community. Young people are encouraged to learn and publicly recite Scripture and to express their gifts of the Spirit. Guidance and nurture are offered along with correction. In this environment, one emerges as a leader from within a context of mentoring and support.

According to the Pentecostal perspective, leadership can also be described as a spiritual calling, one that begins with being a good and faithful follower. A leader sees him- or herself as a vessel through which the power of God takes action to fulfill God's will on earth. Responding to the call is to take part in the present and future kingdom of God and enable the purposes of God to be accomplished in the here and now. Since any and all can be called, leadership is not for just a chosen few. It is open to all. From the Pentecostal perspective, therefore, leaders emerge from the community of faith in the context of support and encouragement, enabling the emergent leaders to grow and develop over time.[23]

Implications for Leadership in Daily Life

The approaches to leadership outlined above are not the only ones evident in Western societies. We could also explore the more military form of governance present in the Jesuit movement and the more representative character of congregational church structure. These approaches and those outlined above have had an influence on the wider understanding of leadership in the West. In areas dominated by Catholicism and Anglicanism, this influence came through the close connection between church and state. On other occasions, as in some Protestant circles, it came through the gradual extension of church-based forms of leadership into civic and political structures as Christians began to realize that if they could govern their own religious affairs, they had the capacity to take on broader societal responsibilities. This happened in England, for example, in Presbyterian and independent churches between the sixteenth and eighteenth centuries.[24] Here and there even more radical Christian structures provided models of leadership that indirectly influenced the way leadership was understood and practiced. As yet, apart from documenting the influence of dissenting churches on the development of democratic forms of government between the Reformation and the Enlightenment, little research has been undertaken to demonstrate the specific connections between these traditions and wider social life.

These ecclesiastical traditions—in particular, the Benedictine, Lutheran, Presbyterian, Quaker, Methodist, and Pentecostal—offer rich and useful models of leadership applicable to today's organizations and groups.

While an abbot serves as the leader of a group of monks who share a common vision and values, he still needs to form the community and to uphold and pass on the received tradition of the faith—its history, ethos, and fundamental values. His task is to form and re-form the community's basic identity and vision. The Benedictine abbot, then, must attend to the needs of the present, always with an eye to the future. The abbot is not only the preserver of the past but also the innovator of the future. Holding these two fundamental roles in tension is what makes the Benedictine abbot a unique leader.

Some important implications for leadership can be seen in the Lutheran understanding. First, effective leadership carries with it a sense of calling, that is, one is led to lead. Second, leadership occurs within a shared community of followers and leaders; it is not an isolated activity. Third, foundational to good leading is knowing oneself, especially knowing oneself in God. This includes knowing one's strengths and weaknesses, embracing both success and failure, and keeping one's ego in check by remaining humble and grateful. An important extension of the Lutheran model occurs in the life and activities of theologian Dietrich Bonhoeffer. In a radio broadcast and public lecture as early as 1933 he protested against Hitler's rise to power through his criticism of what he called the "Fuhrer Principle." This concentrated people's longings and aspirations in one person who was regarded in quasi-religious messianic terms. In subordinating the responsibilities of an office to the authority of the leader, abdicating the responsibilities of followers to the leader's charisma, and rejecting the possibility that the leader is capable of disappointing and disillusioning his followers, the leader becomes a false idol rather than servant of God. Bonhoeffer was particularly critical of attempts to redefine ministry in the church in these ways.

The priestly and prophetic dimensions of Christ's threefold office in the Presbyterian model can be likened to the transforming kind of leadership articulated by James MacGregor Burns in chapter 1 above. Such leadership seeks to create a dynamic and mutual relationship between leader and follower so that the morality and performance of both are raised. Each is transformed through the act of leading and following, respectively. At the heart of the priestly functions of receiving confessions and serving as a mediator is empathy (compare Heb. 4:15). Likewise, transforming leadership is an approach that includes and recognizes the importance of empathy—that is, the ability to momentarily suspend one's own needs for the sake of followers by putting oneself in their shoes to gain their perspective. The priestly function naturally leads to the prophetic function. Having employed empathy in the priestly function to understand more fully the perspective of followers, a leader then moves to the prophetic function and calls followers to higher ethical and moral levels, which is the keystone of transforming leadership. The kingly function corresponds with the governing and direction-setting dimensions of leadership. A leader establishes a plan and takes action with the goal of raising the level of motivation and morality among his or her followers.

The Quaker alternative offers a different view of leadership, one we might be tempted to call nonleadership, in the sense that all who participate in a Quaker meeting lead and follow simultaneously. Yet the model points to the importance of breaking down hierarchies and displaying trust and respect. In addition, because all are involved in the decision-making process, there is a greater buy-in of all involved, which may in the long run save time at the implementation stage.

The Methodist approach brought back into the understanding and practice of leadership a strong focus on people's needs and location on the one hand, and on their empowerment and contribution on the other hand. This highlighted the centrality of serving others holistically, going to where people were rather than expecting them to come to you, and, given the right environment and encouragement, the capacity of ordinary people to effectively provide mutual help.

Pentecostals have traditionally had a difficult time knowing what kind of leadership to offer to the world Monday through Saturday. Because they believe that the kingdom of this world is in direct opposition to the kingdom of God, Pentecostals have traditionally opted not to get overly involved in the things of this world, including positions of leadership. At the same time, Pentecostals do bring to organizations a democratic approach to decision making by embracing the idea that each person should contribute to the final decision. Pentecostals take an emergent approach to leadership. In other words, they believe that the individual perceived to be the most influential, regardless of that person's title, will emerge as the leader of the group. These are valid approaches to leadership and fit well with organizations that are collaborative and less hierarchical.

The perspectives offered by these traditions provide rich insight into the multifaceted nature of leadership. Leadership can be viewed and understood from several vantage points, each of which is valid and necessary for a more thorough understanding of leadership. Each of these traditions has a unique view informed by its history, tenets, and key leaders. These ecclesiastical perspectives locate leadership in the context of faith convictions, and together they offer the core values of love, service, and high standards of ethical conduct.

These faith traditions reveal three common tensions that existed for leaders in the past and that are equally applicable to leaders today: the tension between (1) tradition and adaptation, (2) preservation and innovation, and (3) stability and change. These tensions represent critical questions leaders must face, such as the following: When may a leader seek a new, adaptive approach to leading an organization, especially when the adaptation calls for abandoning tradition? At what point is it appropriate to leave behind important traditions? The watch phrase of this age is "innovate or die." Is there ever a time when it is better for a leader to call an organization to preservation rather than to innovation? And how does a leader hold together the duality of stability and change? Both must be in place for an organization and, most important, the people to function at their best. These are but a few of the timeless and essential questions these ecclesiastical traditions raise that help to deepen and expand an understanding of leadership.

Conclusion

The biblical, historical, and denominational approaches discussed in this chapter open up some fundamental ways of understanding leadership. This is especially the case for people of faith who seek a more integrated understanding for their leadership practice.

The role of key metaphors in these approaches helps us better understand many facets of leadership. A metaphor is a powerful tool that sheds light on complex ideas or issues and opens up new perspectives. The power of metaphor lies in its ability to take knowledge from one domain and apply it to a completely different domain. Moreover, metaphor bridges the gap between familiarity and unfamiliarity. By comparing dissimilar things, we can comprehend the unfamiliar in familiar terms.[25] Such an approach increases insight and depth of understanding. In this case, metaphor increases insight into leadership and how it can be expressed in a biblically consonant way.

For instance, Paul suggested that leadership in the church resembles family life—mother and child, father and child, and child and parent. This metaphor for leadership stresses the affectionate relationship involved in leadership and the responsibility leaders have for leading people toward a deeper understanding of God and his love for each individual.

Likewise, the Benedictine tradition illuminates the role of the abbot using the metaphors of parent, physician, teacher, and steward. A leader of faith must lead like a parent who guides, like a physician who heals, like a teacher who facilitates learning, and like a steward who exercises good judgment over resources.

The leader as reformer is an excellent metaphor from the Lutheran tradition. It underscores the fact that leaders challenge static and confining ways of doing things and reform outdated practices into life-giving processes. Further, reforming leaders look to create multiple ways for followers to self-direct their efforts, thus creating greater freedom and personal responsibility.

Leadership can also be described using the metaphors of prophet, priest, and king—the threefold office of Christ from the Presbyterian perspective. As discussed above, the prophet proclaims, the priest reconciles, and the king rules or administers.

Yet leadership is not only about proclamation; it is also about listening, as the Quaker tradition reveals, using the metaphor of silence. Leadership is like silence: not an empty space but a holding space where what is important and necessary can be heard.

There is an emphasis on movement rather than position in effective leadership, as Methodism so strongly demonstrates. This means the style of leadership is shaped strongly by function and by representatives, who sometimes come from unexpected circles. These emergent leaders are recognized by their willingness to undertake leading and doing so more from experiential learning than from formal preparation.

Leadership is also like a vessel waiting to be filled with God's Spirit and empowered to do good works, as the Pentecostal tradition suggests. Leadership is like a gift received, and this gift comes with power to do good work in the name of Jesus. To receive this gift, the Pentecostal tradition reminds us, one must first be a good follower, open and receptive, and willing to respond and to be led.

This chapter is rich in metaphors that shed light on the practice of faithful leading. When leaders discover ways to integrate their faith into their leadership, the organizations they lead and the people in them experience clarity of purpose, an increased desire to serve with renewed energy.

Leadership has the power to affect people, projects, and contexts in significant and powerful ways. This reveals the importance of leading from wholeness and from a clear sense of one's identity in God. Metaphors are helpful in describing the attributes of leadership and even offer insight into what a leader actually does. But more is needed. Therefore, it is necessary to move a step beyond metaphor to ask, What actions should a faithful leader take to lead in ways consistent with his or her faith? In general, leadership that bears the imprint of faith includes the following characteristics:

- *Intentionality:* Leadership requires intentional action, and faith compels action toward spiritual integrity and ethical consistency.
- *Reflection:* This discipline leads to spiritual depth, greater self-knowledge, and organizational insight.
- *Self-evaluation:* Leaders who incorporate their faith ask: Is the person I see in the mirror the person I say I am and want to be? Leading from faith involves a willingness to receive feedback and course correct when necessary.
- *Covenant building:* Faithful leaders build alliances, create communities, seek partnerships, and promote teamwork.
- *Intellectual integrity:* This involves seeing the world as it is, not as one wants it to be. Such leaders never stop increasing their knowledge about human nature and the world.

- *Ethical integrity:* Upholding moral and ethical values in decision making, actions, and communication is one of the hallmarks of faithful leading.
- *Followership:* Leadership is never devoid of good followership. The faithful leader is a servant first, and from that emerges the desire to lead.
- *Inclusiveness:* This refers to drawing in a wide range of opinions, abilities, and people in order to define, equip, articulate, and ultimately undertake leading that welcomes all.
- *Perpetual learning and development:* Leadership is never mastered; it requires constant learning and development. Leaders of faith recognize that their role as a servant to an organization requires them to constantly hone their leadership talent.

These are some of the key hallmarks for faith-filled leading. Leaders of faith will find in these commitments the joy of service, the integrity of faith, and the fruitful results of honoring God through their leadership.

The next chapter further examines the contemporary discussion of leadership, focusing on leadership approaches that contain a spiritual dimension.

3

spiritual and religious dimensions of leadership: the ethical foundation

This chapter begins with a discussion of the intersection of leadership and ethics from the vantage point of religion and spirituality. Next, implicit signs of the growing concerns of leadership and spirituality are examined (Stephen Covey serves as a case study). Then we look at writings and people in which the spiritual dimension of leadership appears more overtly (Václav Havel is a prime example), and finally we look at two basic Christian approaches to leadership (offered by Patricia Brown and Max De Pree). As well as demonstrating the growing recognition that spirituality is integral to leadership, this chapter opens the door to a more detailed examination of faith-based approaches to leadership.

Religion, Spirituality, Leadership, and Ethics

Articulating definitions of religion and spirituality poses unique challenges of culture and context. For the purpose of this discussion, "religion" can be described as a particular system of faith or worship with reverential recognition of a higher or unseen power. The word "spirituality" can be traced to a reference by the apostle Paul in the New Testament (1 Cor. 2:14–15), where spirituality is used positively to connote a personal and affective relationship with God. By the twentieth century the word came to imply something that can be pursued in or outside formal religious traditions.[1] Spirituality can be defined as "The feelings, thoughts, experiences, and behaviors that arise from a search for the sacred."[2] L. W. Fry defines spiritual leadership as "comprising the values, attitudes, and behaviors that are necessary to motivate one's self and others so that they have a sense of spiritual survival through calling and membership."[3]

A review of the leadership literature suggests spirituality is discussed as a source of leadership motivation generally, and more specifically as a source of ethical grounding leading to virtuous behavior. Spirituality is also described as an aid for coping with difficulty and toxicity in the workplace for leaders and followers. Those who long for greater purpose, typically described as leading with soul, often find fulfillment from spiritual sources. A good deal has been written on work organizations as spiritual places where employees can easily integrate their faith with their work.

The spiritual and religious dimensions of leadership have only recently entered the leadership discourse and have received a lukewarm reception. This area of inquiry is fledgling at best and requires more extensive and empirical investigation.[4] Several questions concerning dichotomies remain, including the boundary between "religious" and "spiritual" as well as a concern for the private nature of religious/spiritual practice entering the public domain of the workplace. Some leaders identify as spiritual but not religious. There is a kind

of marginalizing taking place in this description, where religion looks askance at spirituality, and likewise spirituality rejects much of the so-called rigidity associated with religion; each perspective has marginalized the other.[5] Are leaders who speak of their spirituality more accepted when compared to those who identify with a particular religion? Further, the overlap of spiritual leadership with servant leadership and authentic leadership seems blurred; more refined definitions are needed. For example, it has been claimed that authentic leaders are more self-transcendent, are better able to create meaning in life and work, and engage in more self-sacrificing behaviors than less authentic leaders.[6] While these aspects can be associated with spirituality, how might they connect with broader aspects of leadership, such as vision and motivating others to succeed?

A Pew study found that 84 percent of the world's population identifies with a religious group, and nearly one-third of the world's population identifies as Christian. The Americas, Europe, Russia, sub-Saharan Africa, and Oceania are all majority Christian.[7] It is little wonder that nearly all the research on religion/spirituality and leadership has been conceived from the perspective of Western Christianity. This is clearly a bias of concern. What might the world's other religions contribute to a theological understanding of leadership?

The Intersection of Leadership and Ethics

Often the spiritual and/or religious dimensions of leadership are most accessible at the intersection of leadership and ethics. The ethical dimensions of leadership center on moral judgment, humility, and the capacity to think long term over short term. When leaders are exemplary in their leading, we often wonder, silently or out loud, what animates their ethics, and how is it that they are able to lead with a clear sense of values that are applied with consistency and authenticity. Many will claim faith or religion is not necessary for a leader to be ethical; at the same time, the words we use to describe values and ethics are borrowed from religion and applied to modern-day leadership. We can trace the roots of ethics back to timeless humanistic truths, many of which are also found in the world's major religions.

Until recently there was little interest in the spiritual dimension in leadership literature in general. This dimension was bracketed out by the largely value-free approach that dominated studies in many fields from the late nineteenth century through much of the twentieth century. Consideration of the ethical dimension of leadership was also affected by this approach. Over the past few decades, however, the growing interest in the spiritual dimension of life has opened up discussion of it in relation to work and leadership, and this can easily be found in the leadership literature.

The influence religion/spirituality has on ethical decision making and ethical leadership is significant.[8] For many, this is the most direct way in which faith/spirituality/religion influences leadership: by establishing a high threshold for ethical conduct and basing those standards on religious/spiritual principles. This area is ripe with possibility and in need of further investigation.

Whether religion/spirituality is foregrounded or backgrounded, it seems these constructs/ideals may act as an input for ethical leadership with the outcome being ethical action. Ethical action is the combination of these three elements:

- Ethical *commitment*, which is a combination of desire and will. Ethical commitment asks us to consider: How important is ethics to you in your personal life and in your professional life?
- Ethical *consciousness* (awareness). How conscious or aware are you of the ethical issues taking place in your daily life?
- Ethical *competency* (action). How competent are you at making ethical decisions?[9]

When considering ethical action and spirituality, an important question to consider is how religious/spiritual consciousness might inform ethical consciousness. What is the connection between these constructs, and how might religious/spiritual consciousness enliven ethical moral consciousness? All religions have a practice of developing awareness through reflection. How might contemplative prayer or mindfulness meditation, or other practices, lead to awareness that deepens ethical consciousness? Conscious awareness is very practical. It means to be awake in the present moment, to be fully alive, fully present to people and surroundings, rather than ruminating on the past or constantly planning the future. Thich Nhat Hanh says that to take care of the past or to take care of the future requires that one take care of the present moment.[10] Paul gets at the same idea in Philippians 4:8 when he writes, "whatever is true, whatever is honorable, whatever is right, whatever is pure, whatever is lovely, whatever is admirable—if anything is excellent or praiseworthy—think about such things."

Conscious awareness is like a muscle: it should be stretched regularly, otherwise the range will be quite limited. Leaders will need to be especially attentive to the use of contemplative practice to deepen and expand ethical consciousness. This is needed so that leaders may deepen their moral awareness in order to determine when a situation contains moral content, and when it does, how to consider that situation from a moral point of view.[11] In leadership there is hardly anything that falls outside of ethical consideration. Nearly every decision and every action taken as a leader has moral content because nearly every decision, every act, affects the lives of others.

Peter Pruzan argues that spirituality is the context for leadership. He bases this claim on his study of spirituality and leadership in the East, particularly India. He suggests the West can learn important lessons from the East. Because moral awareness depends on accessibility to moral frameworks, it is necessary to evaluate our moral frameworks. In the West, that framework is typically utilitarianism, which is an ends-based moral decision-making approach; more often than not, the goal is economic rationality, and the ends justify the means.[12]

By contrast, in the East, and in particular India, the moral framework is more deontological or duty-based. In this context individuals learn that they have a spiritual nature, from which emerges character and conduct in a seamless whole, which leads to an embrace of selflessness as well as the will to act without concern for outcomes—to act with nonattachment and not from ego but rather from duty to others. This approach resembles servant leadership, and indeed there are examples of this approach to leading even among leaders in the West. Research has shown that spiritual practices like contemplative prayer and mindfulness meditation heighten awareness of one's environment (including ethical issues) and one's self-awareness, leading to higher levels of moral reasoning associated with duty-based ethical decision making.[13]

Becoming a leader is no small challenge, Pruzan suggests. The self can be realized only by the person whose ego has been tamed, even ignored, who is truly selfless and does not seek rewards for his or her deeds. The selfless leader who is not attached to the fruits of his or her actions does not only achieve spiritual growth but also peace of mind and freedom from fear.[14] *YEP*

The point here is that ethical consciousness/awareness requires a kind of expansiveness, which is advanced through spiritual practice—expansiveness with regard to moral frameworks. Moral developmental theory has shown that advanced moral reasoning is more expansive and includes both ends-based (utilitarianism) and obligation-based (justice) approaches to ethical decision making.

To summarize these ideas:

- Ethical consciousness is the interpretive process of using one's awareness to determine when a situation contains moral content and then applying moral frameworks toward a decision that leads to ethical action.
- Religious/spiritual consciousness influences and informs ethical consciousness through reflective practices that serve to enlarge and deepen ethical consciousness.
- Thus ethical leadership depends on ethical consciousness, which is supported, informed, and perhaps dependent on religious/spiritual consciousness.

Implications for Organizations

Research has certainly shown that leaders with spiritual depth and ethical sensitivity are more likely to create organizations characterized as benevolent and virtuous.[15] Conscious leaders act as role models and shape the organization to embrace compassion. Research has demonstrated that when ethical/moral awareness is high in the organization, followers are more self-directed in their own ethical behavior, needing less guidance from their leaders. If we want ethical organizations filled with ethically conscious people who have expansive repertoires of ethical frameworks, perhaps that path begins with religious/spiritual consciousness. Something so noble must begin with something quite personal. Religious/spiritual consciousness is the ability to hold paradox and live with peace, performing work in a state of equanimity, able to conserve energy and avoid destructive stress. It truly is seeking one's divine purpose.

In organizations we often speak of community, but underneath that is really the concept of unity. We are interrelated at a deep existential level; we all share an identical core. This understanding can inspire compassion for people and the environment. Thinking such as this leads to nonviolence in thought, word, and deed; through meditation and prayer we shed feelings of hatred, anger, jealousy, and greed. True ethical leadership, true values-based leading, derives from a deep sense of spiritual consciousness—and such leadership is necessary for the sustainability of organizations.

Implicit Signs of Spiritual Concerns: Spiritual and Religious Themes in Popular Books

Writings on work and leadership by some well-known writers who do not expressly associate themselves with a religious perspective nonetheless contain interesting echoes of spiritual concerns. Among the most popular business books for 2014 was *Scaling Up Excellence: Getting to More without Settling for Less*, by Stanford professors Robert Sutton and Huggy Rao. In the book the authors describe the continuum from "Catholicism to Buddhism" to explain the mind-set behind business approaches, from standardization, which is exacting like a Catholic cathedral, to highly customized and even open-sourced approaches, which are like a Buddhist gathering, less formal and more improvised. The authors note that business leaders resonated with this religious metaphor.[16]

A very popular book in 2015 was *Overwhelmed: Work, Love, and Play When No One Has the Time*, by *Washington Post* journalist Brigid Schulte. She employs spiritual language when she writes about leisure as a place where we realize our full humanness, "a space for being fully human." She goes on to describe the contrast between contaminated time and contemplative time. Based on reviews, these themes resonate quite well with working parents and other busy readers.[17]

Case Study: Stephen Covey

Stephen Covey's *Seven Habits of Highly Effective People* has been one of the most widely read books since it was published in 1990;[18] translated into twenty-eight languages, over ten million copies sold, and people are still reading this book. It was followed two years later by his *Principle-Centered Leadership*,[19] which he has since followed with two cowritten books on personal and family development.

What makes Covey so popular is his effective use of metaphor; he is able to take what might seem complex and make it simple, with broad appeal. The timeless spiritual truths offered may implicitly indicate that he has done a masterful job of translating biblical principles to a broad audience, religious and nonreligious. There are several reasons for Covey's continuing popularity. His books combine several strands, each of which is appealing in its own right.

These include elements of popular management theory, fashionable morality, pseudo-science, universal spirituality, and technique. They appear to strike a chord with those in college and even middle-level bureaucratic positions in larger organizations who experience a lack of power and purpose in their work and are willing to swim in some of the prevailing currents of contemporary morality. For them, he provides a kind of "catechism" made up of formularized wisdom, spiritual resonance, and simplified management theory. The first of these, as one of the appendixes to a recent book shows, draws on Egyptian, Greek, Chinese, Indian, and Hebrew wisdom literature.[20] The second speaks to the lack of and the search for a spiritual dimension in the workplace and in the exercise of leadership.

Covey is a committed, lifelong Mormon who taught business management and organizational behavior for twenty years at Brigham Young University before becoming head of a large consulting firm and a well-known writer. In his books, however, he does not talk about his religious views. He speaks of God only in a generic way and refuses to acknowledge the particularly Mormon character of his approach. In his important article "White Magic: Capitalism, Mormonism, and the Doctrines of Stephen Covey," Alan Wolfe suggests that part of the reason for this is Mormonism's long-standing decision, going back to its founder Joseph Smith,[21] to suppress some of its views so as not to alienate the wider American public. It is also partly due to Covey's desire to appeal to the mainline culture of the United States as well as to a worldwide audience. Despite Covey's statements to the effect that the core principles and habits he identifies are those everyone knows to be true, Wolfe argues persuasively that the Mormon influences in Covey's work are incontrovertible. Wolfe does not argue that Covey's works contain a simple translation of Mormon beliefs, values, and practices into managerial language. What we find in them, he says, is a set of assumptions that, whatever their other influences and associations, have identifiable Mormon roots.

First, Covey conveys a faith in people's capacity to know and do what he prescribes. This faith in others is essentially the only kind Covey mentions. Unlike both Protestants and Catholics, Covey believes in the essential goodness of human nature. For example, Adam did not sin. He simply exercised his power of choice to eat from the tree of knowledge. This is why he could become God's son and even a divine being. He does acknowledge the presence of "bad habits" stemming from such forces as the appetites, pride, and ambition. Though he describes them as "character issues," he does not doubt the human ability to deal with them.

According to Covey, "natural laws" are intrinsic to every civilized society, just as physical laws are part of the fabric of the entire creation. Since, from a

Mormon point of view, human beings were present in the beginning with God, it is not surprising that these ways of operating were built into humans. At their best, people know them and operate by them. It is only because humans do not do so consistently that these ways of operating need to be transformed into habits that are automatically practiced. The notion of obedience to law is in accord with the central place of law in Mormon thinking and behavior.

Covey's seven principles are as follows: (1) be proactive; (2) begin with the end in mind; (3) put first things first; (4) think win-win; (5) seek understanding before being understood; (6) synergize; and (7) self-renew regularly.[22] Although Covey uses the language of truth in talking about these principles, they are more procedural than conceptual or moral in character. According to Covey, principle-centered leaders are characterized by the following: they (1) continually learn, (2) have a service orientation, (3) radiate positive energy, (4) believe in other people, (5) lead a balanced life, (6) see life as an adventure, (7) possess synergy, and (8) engage in holistic self-renewal.[23] The last two characterizations are identical with his last two principles. The remainder contain a mixture of attitudinal, educational, and lifestyle elements that touch on character but do not deeply explore it.

Though Covey uses the language of "moral compassing," he distinguishes between values, principles, and practices, arguing that the former are too general and the latter too specific. His seven principles primarily form a kind of procedural manual. As such, they have more in common with a daily ritual than a moral code. Covey's *First Things First*, a manual of "daily reflections," is consonant with this. Though he uses, indeed highlights, the language of habits, these too have only a secondary, at times marginal, reference to developing character. They relate more to aspects of self-development and lifestyle.

Covey's belief that anyone who so desires can put these principles into practice correlates with the Mormon view that humans have the necessary free will and willpower to fulfill their divine responsibilities. People are able to understand the principles embedded within them and to turn them into habits that influence behavior. The power of choice is a recurring theme in Covey's writings, and basic needs incline people to make positive use of this. Though resolve and willpower are not always enough, contractual arrangements with others with similar goals can help people do what is required. Accordingly, there is no need for grace to assist people or for the Spirit to empower them, doctrines that have little place within a Mormon framework. Though he sometimes talks about the importance of the "character ethic"—mainly in opposition to the "personality ethic"—the central elements of character are inadequately defined. Integrity, for example, is described as merely the value people place on themselves, and maturity is merely the balance people need to strike between courage and consideration. Love rates a brief mention, but Covey offers little texture and depth regarding what it involves.

When differences arise, tolerant and nonjudgmental attitudes should govern relationships between people. For Covey, the Golden Rule, or the law of reciprocity, as he calls it, is basic. Covey is influenced here by Mormonism's weak understanding of sin and atonement. As a result, there is little that is demanding, costly, and sacrificial in his view of relationships. Though he recognizes the need for people to move from accepting individual responsibility for their actions to developing interdependence with others, this is cast in terms of solidarity rather than genuine community.

In essence, then, as Wolfe says, "Mormonism's great contribution to the work of Stephen Covey has been to provide the unwritten assumptions for a secular version of what life means in organizations in which most people spend most of the time spinning their wheels."[24] The mixture of religious elements in Covey's writings—some genuinely spiritual ones springing from Mormonism's debt to its Jewish and Christian antecedents, and some more expressive of the natural religious instincts of the human heart—appeal to a wide range of people who have either lost touch with their religious heritage, do not know how to connect it to the life of work, or crave something they have lost in their adoption of more secular attitudes. It is precisely the "hidden presence" of this religious mixture that has proven so popular and successful.

I think this is stretching

Explicit Discussions of Spirituality in the Workplace

While some writers have incorporated hints of spiritual concerns into their writings, others have engaged in a more explicit discussion of spirituality and work. Of these, some have conducted specialized explorations of the link between spirituality and leadership. In these writings, the term "spirituality" has three basic meanings. All three sometimes appear in a single collection,[25] but individual authors usually tend to favor one over the others.

Definitions of Spirituality in the Workplace

Some writers define spirituality in humanistic terms: it has the capability—generally ascribed to the inner person or being, soul or spirit—to enable people to transcend their normal selves or to give expression to the multiplicity of selves within them. This approach draws on various traditions that speak about the soul, treating them basically as myths from which can be drawn important lessons for being and doing.[26] This view of spirituality rejects any religious connotations associated with the word, meaning any connection with the beliefs of an established faith.

Other writers define spirituality in more cosmic or interreligious terms, as the presence of some form of higher power or divinity that permeates all life and nature and into which people can tap to find resources for living and working.[27] Though this approach also avoids giving spirituality a traditional religious significance, it draws from a wide range of ancient traditions, especially Eastern, and forms of New Age spirituality.

What is interesting, however, is the way a number of key Greek terms from the New Testament have been increasingly drawn into the discussion of spirituality and the workplace. Terms such as *koinonia* (working in partnership toward a common end), *diakonia* (humble service in a significant cause), and *metanoia* (a radical change of mind and heart) now also appear in the literature. Alongside these we also find words common to the five world religions such as "love," "care," "forgiveness," "stewardship," and "trust."

Spirituality and Leadership

In a growing number of writings on leadership in particular, the same three approaches to spirituality appear: a humanistic approach, an integrative approach connecting leadership with spirit, and a transcendent approach. A mainly humanistic understanding underscores the first approach and is present in Lee Bolman and Terrence Deal's *Leading with Soul: An Uncommon Journey of Spirit*.[28] Though the authors draw on a diverse mixture of spiritual traditions, they also utilize philosophy, the social sciences, and poetry. They include certain extraordinary, not supernatural, aspects of spirituality but focus mainly on the human "spiritual center."

The second approach can be seen in Russ Moxley's work where he provides a more developed approach for connecting leadership and spirit in *Leadership and Spirit: Breathing New Vitality and Energy into Individuals and Organizations*.[29] Moxley, influenced by the writings of Parker Palmer, talks about how dispirited many workers are today, the fact that leadership often suffocates spirit, and the need for leadership that is not only inspiring but also inspiriting. His solution is that "we must learn to be our true selves and our whole selves," from which proceed new ways of doing leadership.[30] For Moxley, spirit is the life force that weaves through and permeates all experiences, defining a person's unique self and drawing him or her toward inner wholeness. It also connects people to everything that exists and draws them into communion with everyone with whom they come in contact. Spirit is "other" than whom people normally are. It is to be uncovered rather than discovered, appropriated rather than developed. Spirit is something prior to and different from a particular expression of religion. While religion can be a pathway to it or can complement it, spirit is in essence simply "being fully human."[31]

Though intangible, spirit is as real as anything else. People encounter it in the midst of the ordinary and the everyday, as well as through the extraordinary and the mystical. People sense it in busyness and activity as well as in solitude and touch it in moments of apparently random events as much as in unexpected synchronicities. The experience of spirit within comes in times of renewal, integration, and vitality. The experience of spirit between people occurs in moments of honoring others, treating them as ends rather than as means, and going beyond contractual or instrumental to covenantal or communal relationships. The experience of spirit in organizations happens through such specific practices as joint stock ownership, distributed leadership, and shared vision. Leadership that embodies and releases the spirit goes beyond being individualistic and coercive. It stresses partnership and balance of power, and knowing and embracing one's full self as well as affirming one's interdependence. It also recognizes the importance of calling and gifts, authenticity and wholeness. It nurtures itself through the inner disciplines of silence, meditation, and journaling, and through the outer disciplines of deep listening and sharing life stories, personal growth workshops, and learning through work itself.

A third and wider understanding that gives a more transcendent sense to spirit is found in the work of Peter Vaill called *Spirited Leading and Learning: Process Wisdom for a New Age*,[32] which contains connections with the process philosophy of Charles Hartshorne in his *Reality as Social Process*.[33] For Vaill, contrary to much thinking and training, "managerial leadership is not a secular enterprise. . . . It forces us to rethink the boundary between the secular and the sacred, between the natural and the transcendental."[34] Starting at the opposite end from Moxley, he first discusses the essential spirituality of organizations rather than of persons. Organizations are not secular entities, nor does their spiritual basis lie only in certain religiously minded individuals. Organizations possess an inherent divine foundation. Though recent decades have witnessed a widespread loss of meaning in organizations, they have an inherent coherence that enables their members to find meaning and credibility. This arises from more than leadership stability and institutional traditions—both of which are now in short supply—or from vision and mission statements.

In this way, Vaill opens up the possibility of organizations having a spiritual grounding that is located in the search for meaning. To do justice to this, people need "to search beyond what they can do *to* and/or *on* and/or *within* oneself,"[35] for it is the self itself that is inadequate. Only a turn to a transcendent source of meaning will open up people and organizations to greater possibilities. This is an ongoing process that amounts to "learning to think and communicate theologically—something, unfortunately, that is not presently contemplated by any known MBA program, though many do emphasize faith, spirituality and values," while some schools do offer dual degrees in business and theology/divinity.[36] What makes this search more difficult is the fundamental dislocation today between spirituality and everyday life. Yet unless spiritual life takes place within organizations, genuine life will not take place. Pursuing the spiritual life at a purely personal level within an organization is insufficient, though unfortunately, organizations that consciously set out to be more spiritual do not always succeed. Still, people do experience moments of quality work, loving teamwork, extraordinary leadership, united focus, and self-transformation in the workplace, all of which point to the existence of a spiritual dimension.

This is even more the case when an organization values such experiences. They can do so at the economic, technical, communal, adaptive, and transcendent or meaning-creating levels. Spiritual life is not restricted to the last of these but can be experienced in and through any of them. For example, at the economic level, spiritual awareness may be concerned with the meaning of waste, loss, ill-gotten gains, and windfalls. At the technical level, spirituality may involve notions of respect for materials, craft, and quality. At the communal level, it may revolve around a sense of genuine fellowship. At the adaptive level, it may concern forbearance and forgiveness. At the transcendent level, it may assist the discovery of meaning itself and finding the best language for it, to which others can orient their lives.

While a spiritual dimension to life is available to everyone in an organization, whether they have specific religious faith or not, it makes more sense to those who have faith in some kind of divinity. It is especially important for those at the executive level. Indeed, "to a large extent executive development for leadership in modern organizations is spiritual development."[37] We should therefore ask, "What are the implications for the spiritual condition and the spiritual growth of individual executives, and the need for them to foster vision, vitality, and spirit in the organizations they lead?"[38] For Vaill, executive formation must go beyond talking about the vision and mission of purposeful thinking and acting, for these deal with only externals. They do not take into account the personal qualities, core values, and deep passions that generate vision and mission. Such matters, particularly feelings, are too often suppressed or ignored in the intellectually-oriented training and operation of leaders. Only by encouraging people to engage in spiritual development will the necessary qualities, values, and feelings come into play. This development involves the following: (1) embracing new perspectives and the possibilities they open up; (2) exhibiting a passionate reason and faith; (3) developing an open value system with creative boundary management; (4) building a fellowship of kindred organizational spirits; (5) forging a new spiritual vocabulary and grammar that rehabilitate old theological terms, especially through conscious prayer; (6) appreciating the spirit in increasingly larger wholes; and (7) enhancing the ability to center one's attention and energies in the present, where spirit is mainly found. This entire area of spirituality, Vaill contends, raises "the most important contemporary problems in management."[39]

David Miller is an author who brings these approaches together as a coherent whole in *God at Work: The History and Promise of the Faith at Work Movement*, which offers a typology to capture the themes addressed by those who are participants in the faith at work (FAW) movement. Overall, Miller contends, people want integration with their faith and work through one or more of the four modalities identified: ethics, evangelism, experience, and/or enrichment. To be outside these four areas is to say that faith cannot or should not be integrated with work, and this leads to living a bifurcated life, by choice or by default.[40]

Those who seek to integrate faith at work from an ethics perspective will be especially attuned to operating from a virtue or values perspective: work is seen as an expression of God's order and as such these people hold self and others to high moral standards. Those with this orientation seek to expand the research of social and economic justice based on principles from their respective sacred texts.

Integration of one's faith with work through evangelism occurs mainly among Christians and Muslims, who see work as a calling to bring others into the family of faith. For Christians this may take the form of meeting in small groups for Bible study and prayer. The commitment to share one's faith in the workplace can be a central aspect of one's identity.

Understanding one's work as a calling describes those who integrate their faith in work through experience. Often one's work will have theological value and offer a sense of meaning and purpose. Certainly those of faith and those who do not embrace faith can equally find meaning and purpose in work, and indeed many organizations seek to create workplaces where meaning is found in and through one's work. The quest for meaning at work sometimes accompanies major transitions in life, where existential questions are examined or reexamined.

The final area in Miller's model, called enrichment, captures those who prefer to go inward for healing, prayer, or meditation. To this group, work is seen as healing or as a source of suffering and pain, where spiritual practice provides support. In addition to Christian FAW groups that fit this type of integration, there are other religious hybrids, like Christian Buddhists and Jewish Buddhists, along with secular spirituality groups, who seek enrichment which is the outcome of their FAW integration.[41]

We turn from this survey of spirituality in the workplace in general and in leadership in particular to a case study of explicit spirituality at work in the life of an international leader.

Case Study: Václav Havel

Václav Havel is an example of a figure who has connected spirituality with leadership. He possessed a profound religious faith that, while not Christian in nature, included many elements derived from or similar to those of Christianity, so much so that a leading Christian apologist devoted a book to him and encouraged his readers to view Havel as an exemplary role model of leadership at work.[42] After becoming a well-known figure in the artistic world of Prague, and as a result of his involvement in public demonstrations against the communist regime, Havel unexpectedly found himself thrust into the political limelight. In 1990 he became president of Czechoslovakia and in 1992, after the country's division, of the Czech Republic.

Born in 1936 to middle-class parents, Havel experienced both Nazi and communist rule. When he was twelve years old, his parents' property was confiscated by the state, and the family was forced to move to a hamlet where there was little employment and poor accommodations. In his mid-teens, after completing elementary school, he went to work as a laboratory assistant and attended night school in the city. Five years later he enrolled in a university, but his studies were interrupted by two years of military service. In his early twenties he developed an interest in drama and, with others, founded a regimental theater company.

In 1960 he started work at a theater in Prague, first as a stagehand and finally as a dramatist, remaining there for eight years. During that time he joined the Writer's Union and sought to hold its members accountable for their roles in society. Yet "the last thing the young Havel wanted to be was a leader. His heroes were playwrights whose genre was the theater of the absurd. Writers of this kind of drama do not take it upon themselves to change society."[43] His plays did not present heroes on whom people could project their hopes for action but rather encouraged them to face and do something about their personal and social misery. In Havel's view, the only real solutions are those that people discover within and for themselves. "Theater does not mediate that kind of help—it is not a church. Theater ought to be—with God's help—theater."[44]

In 1968 Havel became caught up in the dramatic events of the so-called Prague Spring, when the nation briefly sought to create what the world press called "the human face of socialism." He gradually got involved in debates, meetings, and declarations. After the Soviet tanks moved in, he focused again on his work in the theater, but within three years he found himself publicly branded as an enemy of the state and (unsuccessfully) indicted for subversion. He withdrew, as he says, into a kind of "internal exile." Then, in April 1975, he wrote a letter to the country's leader, Gustav Husak, describing the desolate state of the country and the entropic state of the government. Though his letter was widely distributed by the underground, for him it was more an exercise in "auto therapy" than a thoughtful protest.[45] A short time later he played a key role in organizing a well-orchestrated campaign to defend a group of musicians placed on trial for performing seditious songs.

In the late 1970s he was heavily involved in the production of Charter 77, a human rights petition that sprang from an emerging network of people and organizations committed to social and political change. Because he was the youngest of its spokespeople and also extremely mobile, because he owned a car, the authorities (wrongly) identified him as the key person behind it. He was arrested and held for eighteen months, released after being publicly disgraced, and then, after a brief period, imprisoned for an additional three years. It was only when he became seriously ill that he was released, though the authorities were also facing increasing international pressure to do so.

During his imprisonment, the spiritual dimension of his life found expression in letters he wrote to his wife. It was stimulated by a strong, mystical experience of standing "at the edge of the finite" and glimpsing transcendent "Being." This cast "a deep and obvious meaning" over his life, flooded him with a sense of "ultimate happiness and harmony," and resulted in his being "somehow struck by love."[46] Though Havel, for fear of overobjectifying the divine, often hesitates to call this Being "God," his definition "seems identical to a fully theistic God. All the characteristics are there, including personality."[47] This personal Being longs for all persons to be reintegrated with one another and with the divine. However "abstract and vague" such talk may sound, for Havel it signified a "vivid, intimate, and particular" relationship.[48] He had a sense that "in everything I do I touch eternity in a strange way." Though there were rumors of his conversion to Catholicism in prison, he responded that a full, inward acceptance of "Christ as the son of God" was a step he had not yet taken.[49]

In the years that followed he did not see himself as a leader of the struggle for change but as someone who had a gift for words and organization. His involvement was simply an extension of his work as an artist. As Havel explained in the 1980s:

> I've never taken a systematic interest in politics, political science, or economics; I've never had a clear-cut political position, much less expressed it in public. I'm a writer, and I've always understood my mission to speak the truth about the world I live in, to bear witness to its terrors and its miseries—in other words, to warn rather than hand out prescriptions for change. Suggesting something better and putting it into practice is a politician's job, and I've never been a politician and never wanted to be. . . . It is true that I've always been interested in politics, but only as an observer and a critic, not as someone who actually does it.[50]

The only kind of politics that attracted him was one from below, arising from everyday life and operating in a grassroots way. His general interest in public life sprang from a spiritual conviction that the world is "going through a great departure from God that has no parallel in history,"[51] and that it is only through a disavowal of this atheistic foundation and a spiritual renewal, involving a "global revolution in human consciousness," that a new world of meaning, values, and community could be built.[52] This explains the importance Havel attached to people's changing self-awareness, personal liberation, and social consciousness, to their growing hunger for truth, capacity to act more freely, and willingness to take greater risks. If people do not take this lead, official forms of leadership for change are either impossible or unproductive.

However, he did not see himself purely as a playwright. As he once said, "Though I have a presence in many places, I don't really have a firm, predestined place anywhere, in terms of neither my employment, nor my expertise, nor my education and upbringing, nor my qualities and skills."[53] He always felt something of an amateur in the various arenas in which he operated. He was certainly one of the most effective and respected participants in the events of 1989, especially in the formation of the Civic Forum, the first legal opposition in Czechoslovakia in forty years. As a result, after the fall of the communist government, he was approached about becoming president. This prospect took him by surprise. He did not feel naturally qualified or gifted for such a position. He had no formal political or bureaucratic experience. His arena was the world of culture and grassroots action, not public life and policy making. Nor did he regard himself temperamentally suited for the task. There were too many paradoxical tensions in his life.

For example, despite his activism, he said, "I long for nothing more than peace and quiet. I have an extraordinary love of harmony, comfort, agreement, and friendly mutual understanding between people; tension, conflict, misunderstanding, uncertainty, and confusion upset me." Despite coming across to many as confident, levelheaded, constant, and equable, "I'm very unsure of myself, almost a neurotic . . . tend to panic easily . . . am plagued by self-doubts." Despite acting (and in some measure being) rational, systematic, and disciplined, "at the same time I'm oversensitive, almost a little sentimental, someone who's always been drawn by everything mysterious . . . inexplicable . . . absurd, everything that escapes order and makes it problematic." Despite appearing a cheerful and sociable person who likes organizing events and bringing people together, "at the same time I'm happiest when alone, and consequently my life is a constant escape into solitude and quiet introspection." Despite being for many a constant source of hope, "I'm always succumbing to depressions, uncertainties, and doubts . . . on the lookout for some encouragement myself." Despite seeming steadfast and brave, if not hardheaded, "the fact is, I'm always afraid of something, and even my alleged courage and stamina spring from fear . . . of my own conscience, which delights in tormenting me for real and imaginary failures."[54]

Though at first he resisted the idea of becoming president, in the end he agreed. It helped, perhaps, that it was not the first time his country had chosen an intellectual for the position. Another factor was the unusual nature of the times. His country was going through a period of transition and needed a publicly identifiable and credible symbolic figure.

Overall, Havel's greatest contribution as a leader was probably his ability to articulate the hunger for meaning among the people in his country and to trace this back to its spiritual source. Doing so impressed many people in the West, for either they did not hear other national leaders giving voice to this, or, on the rare occasions that they did, the message did not come with the same clarity, passion, and credibility.

Basic Christian Approaches to Spirituality and Leadership

A number of writers on spirituality and work write from a more overtly Christian point of view.[55] In the past, discussions of the role of spirituality in leadership were found in autobiographies of individual leaders. Only in the past decade or two have such discussions appeared in general studies of leadership. Most of these authors have had leadership in large churches, denominational administration, and Christian organizations in view. One example is Patricia Brown's *Learning to Lead from Your Spiritual Center*.[56] Though her framework is Christian, she focuses mostly on God the Father rather than on Jesus, on humanity's original goodness rather than on the fall, and on the personal gifting of the Spirit rather than on the Spirit's wider presence or activity in the world. In other words, she draws selectively or one-sidedly from central elements of the Christian faith.

Brown argues that the cultivation of one's spirit is central to leadership and is intricately connected to a relationship with God and others. Leadership is fundamentally not something "out there" but something that proceeds from a Spirit-filled center. Honoring this entails taking "the journey in and down" and involves five key affirmations:

1. We are people of worth and live by the Spirit's power, not an official position, and by empowering others, not controlling them.
2. We work through our inner constraints and pains as well as through loving others in a mutual and reconciling way.

3. We are called to live out God's will faithfully and practically as we co-create and share authority with others.
4. We operate by trust, not manipulation, and out of a vision of wholeness, not a fear of failure.
5. We encounter the transcendent in all parts of creation and experience the fruit of the Spirit in building up character.[57]

These affirmations form the basis for leadership that emerges from who people are rather than what they do or aspire to. They enable people to evaluate whether they are exercising the best kind of leadership; to access their deepest dreams, intuitions, and desires; and to open themselves to new ways God can work in and through them. Grounded in these five affirmations, people engage in what Brown calls "Spiritwork." This involves:

- becoming more integrated and living in the present,
- reaching toward intimacy through heart conversations,
- connecting body and spirit, family and work,
- seeking spiritual guides and mentors,
- naming and handling reality in organizations.[58]

Max De Pree discusses the attributes of vital organizations and in doing so focuses on the spiritual qualities that give energy through deeply rooted and highly focused leadership.[59] These attributes enrich the life of an organization by encouraging faithfulness to the core values and mission, and enhancing its effectiveness in more than purely commercial terms. Such attributes always move an organization toward fulfilling its potential rather than simply attaining its goals. Indeed, they allow people to realize their own potential. Throughout his various writings on leadership, De Pree identifies the following key attributes:

Truth: Truth is personal, and truth is a quality of being, which means it leads to excellence, value, and worth in people and in the work they do. Truth is a difficult concept to pin down, but when we see it or feel it, we know we have encountered it. The great sadness of denying truth is that people become accomplices in their own spiritual demise. In the long term, this affects the welfare and effectiveness of an organization.

Access: This is a gift that needs to be shared. People should have access to work, a leader, learning opportunities, and medical care. They should also have access to a mentor as well as to faithful and healthy relationships within an organization.

Discipline: It is unfair not to delegate some of the important work. It takes discipline and courage to let go of important work, and it inspires discipline and hard work among followers when they are asked to operate with increased responsibility. A leader has a right to expect discipline from those in an organization and vice versa. Discipline among followers mirrors the discipline demonstrated by leaders.

Accountability: People need accountability, which is different from blame. Blame points the finger of shame; accountability helps people bear the weight of responsibility for outcomes that naturally come with tasks and assignments. Nonprofit organizations are good examples of accountability, for they are intentional about making themselves accountable to the people they serve.

Nourishing of persons: People are nourished by transforming work, growth, and learning and reaching their potential. Only by continuing to renew its members can an organization continually renew itself.

Authenticity: Vital organizations do not grant authenticity; they acknowledge that people (as created in the image of God) are authentic in their being.

Justice: The heart of justice is relationships constructed on right practice. Justice is always related to everyone in an organization; no one can be excluded from this practice. Justice has to do with participation and equal access, and it is related to the equitable distribution of resources, due process, rights, and responsibility. Justice opens the way for peace—peace and justice go hand in hand.

Respect: This is shown in an organization through civility, good manners, and appropriate language. Respect is evident when everyone is taken seriously. Respect becomes manifest in action.

Hope: Vital organizations generate hope through the way they approach and undertake work in light of their mission. Organizations that have a clear and compelling mission to which everyone holds themselves accountable create hope in their capacity to realize future dreams. Participation in a worthy mission makes work hopeful and hope-filled. There is a strong correlation between hope and the quality and character of relationships both inside and outside an organization. Organizations that are adept at building relationships that are strong, meaningful, and rich in character are places where hope permeates everything they do.

Unity: Unity transforms organizations into communities. A community performs on a much higher level than an organization because the people in it have a sense of belonging and commitment.

Tolerance: Tolerance is a function of wisdom, discernment, and acceptance. People do not have to think or act alike, but they do have to share a common vision and agreed-on goals for tolerant working relationships to exist.

Simplicity: This is a function of understanding the role of personal restraint in life. Vital organizations draw on resources of the Spirit that enable them to practice conservation and simplicity. These attributes are also essential to renewal and innovation—to take hold of something, a person has to let go of something else.

Beauty and taste: These two qualities nourish the spirits of people and organizations and are keys to creating vitality. Beauty and taste—the opposite of banality—have to do with aesthetics and creativity, poise and quality. People long for that which is beautiful and tasteful. The human spirit is nourished and delighted by beauty and creativity at several levels: in the physical environment, in the quality of the work, in the strength of the relationships in a community, in the poise with which people conduct themselves, and in the level of quality at which an organization operates.

Fidelity to a mission: People show fidelity to a mission through strict observance of their promises, which spring directly from their values. Such fidelity is the realization of commitment: It is words made flesh.

These attributes of vital, life-giving organizations—truth, access, discipline, accountability, the nourishing of persons, authenticity, justice, respect, hope, unity, tolerance, simplicity, beauty and taste, and fidelity to a mission—serve as a call to leaders and followers to create organizations in which people and those they serve can reach their fullest potential. These ideas may appear daunting and at times counter to the conventional wisdom on organizational success because they seem to focus on the "soft side" rather than on typical activities such as developing a strategy, improving work tasks, and building competitive advantage. In point of fact, these attributes pave the way for personal and organizational success, particularly in today's competitive marketplace. Perhaps these attributes can best serve as "fruits of the Spirit" for organizational life.

Conclusion

Though, as mentioned, Brown's approach is an overtly Christian one, its understanding of spirituality is limited and inadequate and fails to draw on the full range of biblical and theological resources that are available. Interestingly, Vaill, who has a less overtly religious view of spirit, is the one who highlights the importance of the theological as well as the spiritual dimension of leadership. De Pree gives flesh to a Christian approach to spirituality and leadership in talking about the attributes of vital organizations in a way that echoes but also translates for the contemporary workplace a number of core theological convictions.

The following chapter seeks to give more substance to the spiritual dimension of leadership as it considers writings that draw more fully or explicitly on specific religious perspectives.

faith-based approaches to leadership

Most writers on leadership do not look to religious sources or tradition for inspiration. Instead, they rely on established theories of leadership, on personal or observed experience, or on empirical studies of how leadership works. While they often include ethical maxims that stem from a particular religious tradition, for the most part they are not aware that separating a saying from its framework weakens its effectiveness. Recently, however, writers on leadership have begun to draw on religious traditions more broadly. A number have turned to Eastern and/or New Age spirituality.[1] Others, several of whom are discussed below, draw on Jewish and Christian sources.[2]

Some Popular Faith-Based Approaches to Leadership

David Baron: A Liberal-Jewish Approach

David Baron is a successful businessman and the founder of a liberal, as opposed to a more traditional Orthodox, Jewish synagogue in Beverly Hills that serves people principally in the worlds of media and finance. His book *Moses on Management: Leadership Lessons from the Greatest Manager of All Time* focuses on the pivotal Jewish religious leader Moses, drawing lessons from his life and work for the way leaders should operate today. In doing this, he identifies various parallels between the uncertainties and challenges of Moses's world and ours. His treatment contains a blend of Bible exposition, contemporary anecdotes, and humorous insights into the dynamics of leadership.

In the preface, Baron asserts that, contrary to popular belief, the Bible is all about business, and he declares that Moses was the greatest manager of all time. Though Moses suffered from what today would be regarded as significant drawbacks—he was reluctant, inarticulate, contradictory, sometimes impulsive, and occasionally overreached himself—he exhibited impressive strengths and achievements. He was not born to a leadership role, nor was he especially charismatic. He did not lead from the top, and he avoided control or manipulation. Though not the complete spiritual or moral role model, Moses was an inspired, hands-on, and effective leader who managed a consistently uncooperative staff and handled hostile outside competition. He grew into his role through a time of patient preparation and experience on the job, and his faith in God and humility before others were the cornerstones of his approach. He possessed such crucial skills as flexibility, quick thinking, confidence building, and the ability to forge unity out of a diverse group. He was also able to train and pass these skills on to others.

Next, Baron deals with issues of motivation and communication, Moses's tactics for mobilizing and energizing his people through their long journey, and the key ethical guidelines he laid out. He suggests parallels between the roundabout way Moses led Israel to the Promised Land and nonlinear approaches to business strategy, and between the role of the Ten Commandments in Israel's life and mission statements in organizations today. He summarizes Moses's success as a leader with the following ten phrases:

1. Accept the role of leadership
2. Assess the situation
3. Connect with God and the people around you
4. Deliver the results
5. Persevere through difficulties
6. Solve problems as they arise
7. Search out stimulating people and ideas
8. Enforce the organizations' rules
9. Endow your people with a legacy
10. Know when it is time to leave[3]

Baron recognizes some of the limits and weaknesses of leaders. He includes sections on learning to take reproof as well as mete it out, seeking help from within the leader's family, not being blinded by one's own power, letting others share the burden, being responsible for the hazards one creates, and making oneself as accessible as possible to those who take a different view. The ethical code he establishes goes beyond moral rules and includes such important items as being an advocate for one's people, speaking out against oppressors and wrongdoers, defending justice but not for the reward, blending compassion with accountability, creating a hospitable environment, and remembering the importance of small gestures.

One weakness in the book from a Christian point of view is his talk of Moses's "inventing" or "creating" a moral compass and strategic procedures for his people. Such language devalues the role of God in these two areas, though Baron does recognize the presence of divine revelation in the giving of the Ten Commandments. He regularly refers to God in discussing both Moses's and present leadership, but his discussion of the regulations of the covenant and holiness codes in the books of Exodus and Leviticus suggests that these came from Moses's own mind. As a result, Baron's approach contains a humanistic element that is at odds with the biblical material.

Laura Beth Jones and Charles Manz: A Paradenominational Christian Approach

Laura Beth Jones is the founder and president of the Jones Group, an advertising, marketing, and business development firm whose mission is "to recognize, promote, and inspire divine excellence."[4] She identifies her religious tradition as a mixture of Presbyterianism, Methodism, and ecumenical Christianity. Her book *Jesus CEO: Using Ancient Wisdom for Visionary Leadership*, which was twenty years in the making, is intended to be "a practical, step-by-step guide to communicating with and motivating people."[5] Her main interest is the types of skills involved in self-mastery, action, and relationships that Jesus utilized to train and catalyze his team. Throughout she weaves together the ethical principles and the general guidelines that were integral to Jesus's approach.

Jones labels Jesus's approach the Omega Management Style, distinguishing it from the Alpha and Beta Management Styles, associated with authoritative masculine and cooperative feminine uses of power. The Omega style is characterized by (1) the unparalleled success of Jesus's training of just twelve people, given the extent of his influence today; (2) the very human, unqualified, diverse, and fractious group he had with him; and (3) the applicability of Jesus's leadership style to any group of people involved in a common task. She believes that Jesus's Omega approach transcends the other two management styles, primarily because of the way it harnesses and empowers each person's spiritual energy.

Jones's concluding affirmations for leaders draw together the key elements of her book.[6] Aspects of them are highly revealing. For example, almost seventy affirmations begin with the word *I* (never *we*), and only seven contain a reference to God. This individualistic tone is strange given the book's focus on Jesus. Many of the principles she derives from Jesus's life and work are valid ones—being clear about one's mission, not requiring or seeking others' approval, looking at situations in new and different ways, having passion for a cause, holding others accountable for their actions, empowering others through one's example, and seeing the praise of others as the number one priority. She also specifically mentions the importance of seeing others as gifts of God and of recognizing that only God knows the total plan.

Yet some of her statements are couched in self-serving language. "I accomplish difficult tasks for my training and strengthening." "I release others so that I myself can fly." "I judge no one, knowing that judging others causes major energy leaks in my life." "I serve others, knowing that . . . I too will be well served." Also, Jones, drawing lessons from Jesus's so-called self-mastery to serve as a guide for one's own self-mastery, introduces a humanistic note that is not present in the Gospels. Jesus was wholly oriented to God, not self, as his clear statements about "doing the Father's will" (John 6:38) demonstrate.[7]

In addition, Jones's reference to transparency mentions only one's strengths, not one's weaknesses. Indeed, there is almost a complete denial of inadequacies and struggles, and it is only success, never failure, that receives mention. This is odd given the fate Jesus suffered on the cross, despite the ultimate outcome of his death. It is also one-sided for leaders to be told that "Jesus had no ambivalence about what he wanted to do"[8] given Jesus's request in the Garden of Gethsemane that the cup be taken from him (Matt. 26:39). Nor is it helpful for leaders to be told "to believe in themselves 100%."[9] Only an American could have written this affirmation: "I shape my own destiny. What I believe, I become. What I become, I can do."[10]

Another book that promotes an ecumenical Christian approach to leadership is *The Leadership Wisdom of Jesus: Practical Lessons for Today* by Charles Manz.[11] As the preface makes clear, Manz proposes a multifaith approach that, while it focuses on Jesus, seeks to transcend race and religion. Though many of Jesus's teachings do not directly address leadership, Manz is convinced that they offer a depth of ethical and practical guidance for leadership practice. He suggests that leaders should take account of the form as well as the content of many of Jesus's teachings, such as his use of parables. Because Jesus's framework is ultimately one of life beyond death, Manz recognizes that his injunctions are not necessarily intended to pay off in this life. Yet he believes that at some level all people desire to have a positive spiritual connection with others. Within this framework, he looks at leading others with compassion, leading others to be their best selves, how the seeds of greatness lie in the power of small things, and the importance of empowering others rather than being a visionary.

It is not improper to look to Jesus's person and work for guidance in exercising leadership, but one must see the full framework and nature of Jesus's approach to do this properly. Manz recognizes the indirect nature of some of Jesus's teachings about leadership as well as his otherworldly orientation. While not focusing too much on the person of the leader, Manz does see a positive spiritual orientation in both leaders and followers. He therefore fails to acknowledge the dark side of human nature. He also overlooks the differences in cultural conditions and even styles of speaking between first-century Jews and twenty-first-century Americans. This leads him to interpret some of Jesus's teachings in contemporary Westernized terms.

Max De Pree: A Reformed Christian Approach

Max De Pree, formerly CEO and chairman of the board of Herman Miller Furniture Co., draws discreetly but firmly on his Reformed Protestant religious heritage. Other influences on his view of leadership include his army experience during World War II, his work experience at Herman Miller, and people such as businessman Robert Greenleaf and artist Charles Eames.

Ultimately, De Pree's spiritual journey deeply shaped his core perspectives, values, and commitments. This is revealed in the language he uses, the policies he frames, and the procedures he designs. His approach emphasizes (1) serving, which involves making oneself vulnerable to others' points of view and criticisms; (2) abandoning one's ego and depending on the expertise of others; (3) creating environments in which people can grow and develop; and (4) communicating in a way that invites input and involvement.

In his key writings on leadership, De Pree identifies a range of attributes of good leadership.[12] Some of these have to do with gaining wisdom (e.g., intellectual curiosity and energy, discernment that brings insight and judgment). Others focus on developing relationships (e.g., having an awareness of people's cares, yearnings, and struggles; being present to them; having trust in their abilities; and having a willingness to be vulnerable). Others concern character (e.g., integrity, courage, dependability, and honesty). Several have to do with one's worldview (e.g., being comfortable with ambiguity; moving to and fro between future, past, and present; and having a sense of humor). Though largely implicit in his writings, it is clear that De Pree believes these attributes operate within a fundamental framework of belief.

A basic feature of his all-embracing theological framework is the conviction, derived from the book of Genesis, that everyone is created "in our [God's] image"

(Gen. 1:26). This means that each person reflects the Maker in a unique way and must be treated with respect and dignity. Leaders have the responsibility of helping people become who they can be and of opening themselves to learn from them. Since God creates diversity among people, leaders should endeavor to recognize and empower others so they can make a unique contribution. Part of this entails viewing each person as a whole person, not simply a worker, and valuing people over programs, systems, and bureaucracy. Because creativity and innovation lie at the heart of God's act of making people in his image, these attributes exist in every person, and leaders ought to enhance them.

De Pree also has a strong sense of God's operating by way of covenantal relationships. This was at the heart of God's bond with Israel. It involved more than a contractual arrangement through which each party set parameters and conditions regarding what they would do for the other. Such an arrangement, if broken, would lead to a termination of the link between the parties. Instead, God made an unconditional commitment to Israel and later to those who became Jesus's followers. Though both the Jews and Jesus's disciples had obligations, they stemmed from love, not law, and when broken did not necessarily end the relationship. De Pree saw his relationship with his employees as potentially a lifelong one and his responsibility as nurturing, enhancing, and supporting them through all kinds of circumstances. This created a space for his workers where they had a sense of belonging; could be and become themselves; were invited to participate in envisioning, designing, and implementing the company's future; and were held compassionately but professionally accountable.[13]

For De Pree, justice and equity are also strong values. These motifs appear often in the Bible, especially in the prophetic writings, Wisdom literature, and Gospels. Embodying these in the workplace entails (1) discerning the realities inside and outside the workplace and basing all that happens on truth telling; (2) striving to make decisions and policies that promote the common good of everyone in it; (3) being concerned about the poor and disadvantaged members of the organization; and (4) compensating and rewarding people in an equitable way. Employees should also be encouraged to help eliminate the needs and challenges of the wider society. Because the environment should also be dealt with in a responsible way, organizations should give careful consideration to the way facilities are built and settings developed, providing attractive and functional surroundings for employees.[14]

Finally, De Pree's view of leadership revolves around the core values of the Christian faith. First, trust in others is paramount, for without it an organization cannot function effectively. For employees, this involves developing a sense of loyalty when the actions of the company justify it. For employers, it means ensuring that the central values of the company are represented in its treatment of workers. Second, leaders should care about the welfare of their employees as workers but more fundamentally as people who have other roles and responsibilities. This includes giving them consideration and support when unexpected challenges, such as long-term illnesses or corporate downsizing, arise. Third, leaders should both articulate and embody hope, cultivating and exemplifying this through inspiring vision and creating synergy among their followers.

At the heart of these core values is integrity, which should govern all that takes place. This embraces fidelity to the mission of the organization, keeping one's word and fulfilling one's promises, and making only justified and defensible—not opportunistic or self-serving—compromises that are in the best interests of people. What flows from putting first things first is excellence at all levels of the operation and effectiveness in the organization's core business and outcomes.[15]

More Substantial Theological Treatments of Leadership

A Christ-Centered Approach to Leadership

Many books on leadership in the church focus on Jesus as the exemplary role model. For example, Andrew Le Peau's *Paths of Leadership*, referencing James MacGregor Burns's work on transforming leadership, focuses on Jesus as an exemplar of serving, following, facilitating, teaching, modeling, and envisioning.[16] A few books written by Christians include reference to activities outside the church but generally make little mention of people's work and workplaces. Leighton Ford's *Jesus: The Transforming Leader* does mention these settings more than most, even if only in a secondary way.

Ford's book offers a conversation between the portrait of Jesus in the Gospels and the model of transformational leadership articulated by Warren Bennis and Burt Nanus (discussed earlier). Ford bookends his portrait of Jesus by pointing out what was distinctive about him—namely, he was the unique Son of God, the Savior, and sovereign. In the intervening chapters, he points to nine roles involved in Jesus's leadership that are indispensable to transforming leadership. These are:

1. *The strategist:* In this role, Jesus had a sense of destiny, fulfilled earlier promises and hopes, had a consistent kingdom strategy and a long-range global goal, and leveraged the contribution of a few for a wider group of people.
2. *The seeker:* As the seeker, Jesus promoted kingdom values, served another's cause, taught another truth, accepted another result, awaited another time, and dreamed of another glory.

3. *The seer:* As the seer, Jesus experienced vision at key points. This vision had a divine source and was practical, compelling, personal, radical, realistic, and yet hopeful.
4. *The strong one:* In this role, Jesus showed his strength of character; external power and inner authority; firmness of purpose; force of speech; and gentleness, sensitivity, patience, and decisiveness. He was also accessible, yet needed to withdraw at times.
5. *The servant:* Jesus was on assignment from God; inverted the world's power scale; and showed the strength of servant power, the force of example, his mission to suffer, and the power of the cross.
6. *The shepherd-maker:* In this role, Jesus was the recruiter and empowered; shared life as the prime curriculum; formed a team with a common life and goal; enabled others to find meaning, equality, enthusiasm, and growth; and shared risks, a future, and power.
7. *The spokesperson:* As the spokesperson, Jesus was the prime communicator; modeled communication through clarity of purpose and confidence; was sensitive to words; respected means and ends; and evidenced focused speech, wise timing, and a sense of boundaries.
8. *The struggler:* In this role, Jesus discerned and transformed conflict; revealed strategies for fundamental, unavoidable, essential, and incidental conflict; handled rejection; and showed discretion and discernment.
9. *The sustainer:* As the sustainer, Jesus employed the key strategies of showing the way, shaping people, symbolizing values, setting the stage, and ultimately sharing the Spirit with others.

A look at this list reveals marks of Jesus's leadership that would not transfer to most organizations today, whether based on Christian principles or not.

- *Pursuing a kingdom orientation and strategy:* While there may be elements of such a strategy and orientation in some contemporary organizations, what is more important is looking at ways work and workplaces can reflect God's will through building community, seeking justice, and serving needs.
- *Having a mission to suffer:* While suffering may be a potential by-product of a faith-based approach to leadership, it is not part of its overt purpose and will not necessarily have a kind of "redemptive" effect.
- *Awaiting another's time and dreaming of another's glory:* While a sense of timing and a degree of modesty are key to effective leadership, to some extent,

leaders' schedules do not always leave them much room to maneuver. There are also stakeholders, and often stockholders, to take into account.

- *Experiencing divine vision at key points:* For ordinary leaders, vision is not purely an individual matter and does not come as clearly from a divine source. It tends to come in ways that involve the collaboration of others in its pursuit, evaluation, and framing.
- *Handling fundamental and unavoidable conflict:* Leaders are not as central or crucial to the life of organizations as Jesus was to the Christian movement. There is always the option of resignation if their—or the organization's—integrity is in danger of being compromised.
- *Strength of character and force of speech:* While both are admirable aspirations, leaders do not have access to the Spirit "without limit" (John 3:34) in the way Jesus did. Even in the Bible, some leaders were either in need of a colleague more gifted at communicating (Moses) or failed to possess conventional eloquence (Paul).
- *Inverting the world's power scale:* While believers seek to live in ways that are in tension with the way power is often employed in the world, leaders—even Christian leaders—have to operate in ways that correlate to some extent with the surrounding practices.
- *Shared life as the prime curriculum:* While a case may be made for theological students to be trained as they live together in a residential setting,[17] it is unrealistic for most work teams to have a common life as well as common work.
- *Sensitivity to and shaping of others:* The resources for developing insight into and properly handling others are not available to leaders today as they were to Jesus. This is also true of sharing the Spirit with people in comparison with modeling a life indwelt by the Spirit, or helping people to catch the spirit of an organization.

These differences between Jesus's leadership and that of leaders today do not mean that the work and setting of certain individuals do not in some ways parallel what Jesus did and experienced. Nor do they mean that leaders cannot learn from Jesus's life and approach. Because of Jesus's unique status and calling, however, the correlation between today's work and his own work is less than some writers suggest.

These same kinds of limitations are present in the books by Laura Beth Jones, Charles Manz, and Bob Briner mentioned earlier. They approach Jesus even more uncritically through the lens of modern Western assumptions, especially by individualizing the content and application of Jesus's approach. Even Ford is vulnerable, as his omission of Jesus's healing and miraculous powers indicates. Jones and Manz apply his teachings and practices without sufficient reference to actual work structures and processes.

One way to scrutinize the extent to which contemporary assumptions creep into such approaches is to check them against distinctly unmade characteristics of Jesus's way of operating. Take, for example, the classic book *The Peril of Modernizing Jesus*, by Quaker New Testament scholar Henry Cadbury. According to Cadbury, our age is perhaps more different from Jesus's time in its ways of thinking than in its ways of operating. "Manufacture, transportation, communication we know to be now quite different: but do we realize how different [are] mental processes, intellectual assumptions, forms of self-consciousness?"[18] He adds, "Not even the use of Jesus' own terms prevents an almost complete modernizing of him. In fact to use them in a modern sense only deceives ourselves and others into thinking that we are accurately representing him."[19] An extreme example of this is Bruce Barton's *The Man Nobody Knows*, according to which Jesus exemplified all the principles of modern salesmanship. "He was, of course, a good mixer; he made contacts easily and was quick to get *en rapport* with his 'prospect.' He appreciated the advertising value of news and so called his message 'good news.' His habit of rising early was indicative of the high pressure of the 'go-getter' so necessary for a successful career."[20]

Cadbury goes on to suggest some less recognized ways in which Jesus's general outlook and method of operating differed from those today. He has in mind the managerial mind-set and organizational culture that pervade modern society, the preoccupation with outcomes and success, and the preoccupation with structural change and reform.

First, Jesus's life was not as strategized or as organized as people tend to think. Modern culture's emphasis on making a living, carefully apportioning time, and planning for the future was largely absent from Jesus's world. "We can hardly make a picture of Jesus' life and that of his contemporaries that will be too casual for the facts. . . . Jesus was much more a vagabond or gypsy than many another in the land."[21] Indeed, "he reacted to situations as they arose but probably he hardly had a program or a plan. . . . The religious man in particular leaves planning to God and simply submits to the inevitable. He may foresee it, but that is not the same thing as courting it or planning it."[22] While Jesus's relationship with and submission to God certainly gave his life both a trajectory and a unity, his life did not involve the degree of creative planning and calculated prioritizing people tend to assume.

Second, we cannot read Jesus's teaching without considering "how far the traits of character or circumstances described tend to produce particular outcomes, for example, blessing or success." We "regard him as an experienced observer of the laws of character, which he states with insight and understanding of their inevitable results. I do not wish to claim that there are no such laws or that they are not in accord with Jesus' standards, but . . . for Jesus . . . the blessing is personally bestowed," that is, by divine intervention.[23]

Third, Jesus rarely if ever dealt with such institutions as work, private property, and wealth or with social groups along status or class lines. As far as social interrelations are concerned, "the modern mind tries to deal with both parties at once and to rise into a plane or principle of action which takes the interests, privileges, rights, or duties of both into view. Jesus appears to think conversely of one man at a time. . . . Even the Golden Rule . . . is merely advice for each man by himself."[24] Jesus did not universalize this so that it became a principle of organizational interaction.

Fourth and most striking of all, is the conspicuous absence in Jesus's teaching of the appeal to social motive.

> Sometimes he appeals to no motive at all, demanding a self-sacrifice that asks no return. . . . At other times he appeals to men's own sense of what is right. . . . In a few passages he is represented as urging a religious motive . . . or dedication to [his] person or cause. . . . Frequently the only motive is what we would now call a self-regarding motive, but nowhere—and this is my point—do I find unmistakable appeal to the rights or needs of the other party.[25]

Other Christian ethicists today have been influenced by John Howard Yoder and have come to more radical conclusions about the nature of Jesus's values and goals. The best known of these is probably Stanley Hauerwas.[26] These authors rightly point out the provocatively prophetic character of many of Jesus's actions and teachings, which only heightens the difficulty of casting him in executive leadership terms. They also highlight the important and seminal role of the Christian community as an exemplar for contemporary Christians.[27] Yet while their approaches are rightly critical of some of the uses to which Jesus is put in discussions of leadership, the differences between Jesus's mission and that of Christians today must not be overly emphasized.

Biblical Life-Story Approach to Leadership

In addition to concentrating on Jesus, other writers draw attention to a wide range of biblical figures who can illumine an understanding of leadership from a theological point of view. Numerous biblical stories feature leaders of God's people focusing on significant moments in their lives and work or providing extensive accounts of their development as leaders. Interesting examples of leaders with civic as well as religious responsibilities are David, Solomon, and

Hezekiah. John Goldingay, in his down-to-earth portrayal of David's reign in *Men Behaving Badly*,[28] describes in graphic and unapologetic terms the weaknesses and strengths, blind spots and awareness, compromises and integrity, failures and achievements of David as a man, head of a family, and ruler. In his book titled *Relational Leadership: A Biblical Model for Influence and Service*, Walter Wright focuses on the character and activities of some lesser-known biblical figures, such as Philemon, Tychicus, and Onesimus.[29]

J. Robert Clinton has given perhaps the most detailed attention to biblical figures in regard to leadership. In his work on developing a philosophy of leadership, he identifies a number of typical stages and tests through which effective leaders pass on their way to fulfilling their roles.[30] Not all leaders pass through all stages or in the same order. Indeed, Clinton's typology runs the risk of being overly systematized. Yet it offers some interesting insights into the process of leadership development.

While the Bible is at the heart of Clinton's approach, it is not the only resource he uses. Scripture, he says, is the leadership anchor, but it "does not speak directly to all issues of leadership," and "when it does speak there is freedom. It often gives general ideas or specific examples from which a leader must be led by the Holy Spirit to applications."[31] Clinton draws on a wide range of biblical examples, including Moses, Joshua, David, Jeremiah, and Barnabas. He also studies a large number of historical figures, mostly people in professional Christian ministries with a pastoral or missionary orientation, as well as some contemporary figures. He writes primarily for those in pastoral and missionary work, and his overall goal is to help potential and existing leaders organize what is happening in their lives, anticipate what may develop, understand new possibilities in past events, and better order their lives.

Clinton identifies the three components of his "leadership emergence framework." These are time analysis, process items, and patterns of response.

Time analysis concerns the general trajectory of a leader's development and provides the broader framework within which significant experiences in leadership formation take place. Time analysis refers to the chronological development of a leader and enables an emerging leader to see stages of development in relation to the whole, integrate experiences into a coherent picture, and help to set expectations for the future. Though each leader's time line is unique, the emerging patterns and overall lessons can be compared to a generalized ministry time line, which facilitates a wider orientation and evaluation of a leader's development. Such a time line moves through three stages.

1. A ministry foundation is established between the mid-teenage years and late young adulthood.

2. Next follows a growth in ministry, lasting anywhere from ten to twenty-five years, in which the primary thrust is the growth of the leader rather than ministry outcomes.
3. Finally, a person experiences a unique ministry, a time of effective work that generally comes in early to late midlife. This is usually preceded by a period of difficulty that opens the opportunity for a deepened relationship with God and greater character development.

Process items describe incidents in a leader's life through which God shapes him or her. Though each person is unique and each situation is specific, some common elements appear in the journey toward leadership.

Some incidents form character and involve the crucial role of "integrity checks." A successful story is the challenge to their food laws faced by Daniel and his friends (Dan. 1). A failure is Saul's refusal to fulfill God's directions in battle (1 Sam. 15). Variants on this are "obedience checks," such as are found in the story of Abraham's offering of Isaac (Gen. 22), and "word checks," which assess how much a potential leader has understood God. The classic example of this is Samuel's message from God (1 Sam. 3). In the early phase of work for God, people are generally confronted with two "ministry processes." The first is a ministry challenge, such as that confronted by Paul and Barnabas in Antioch before they received their main missionary call (Acts 11). A ministry challenge is a simple assignment that focuses on the job to be carried out as well as its effect on the leader and those associated with him or her. In the middle phase of maturing, a second ministry process involving ministry training often takes place, a good example of which is Timothy's recruitment by and accompanying of Paul (Acts 16). Discovery of a person's key giftedness often takes place during this time, as was Barnabas's experience in understanding the special contribution of Paul (Acts 9:27), which became pivotal for Barnabas's own future missionary role alongside the apostle.

Other process items have to do with what Clinton calls "relationship learning." These incidents in a leader's life teach valuable lessons about working with others and provide positive and negative insights into how spiritual authority functions. James and John encountered this type of incident when they requested status alongside Jesus (Matt. 20:20–28). Encounters with the changing dynamics of leadership, as with the shift of focus from Barnabas to Paul (beginning at Acts 13:13) as well as lessons about relating effectively to colleagues, also fit this category. Also relevant here is how to deal with ministry conflicts between subgroups, such as Greek and Hebrew Christians (Acts 6:1), and leadership backlashes, as Paul himself experienced (2 Cor. 10).

Another set of process items requires discernment in dealing with specific challenges relating to faith, influence, and prayer. According to Clinton, while these process items can be analyzed separately, they need to be correlated with such wider issues as development of leadership capacity and responsibility, expansion of effectiveness, and followership, all of which are basic to a biblical perspective on leadership.

In the final phase of ministry, leaders often face a set of experiences that are difficult to negotiate but open doors to more profound experiences of God. These include enforced isolation due to sickness, imprisonment, organizational pressures, or even self-evaluation. An example of the second is Paul's imprisonment in Ephesus. Leaders may also face significant crises, at times of a life-threatening nature, that help to form a mature character. Instructive here are the events Paul refers to in 2 Corinthians 1:8–11 and 4:7–12.

Because guidance has to do with the whole of a leader's life, the process items connected with it fall into different parts of the time line. Among these are the divine contacts God arranges, such as Paul's meeting Aquila and Priscilla (Acts 18), or mentors who have a profound influence on a person's life, as Barnabas did with Paul (Acts 11). Divine affirmation occurs when there is a special indication from God of his authoritative presence with a person, as with the miraculous answer to Samuel's prayer (1 Sam. 12:13–19). There is also what Clinton calls "dual confirmation," or two ways of receiving confirmation about a particular direction, such as Paul experienced first on the road to Damascus (Acts 9:1–9) and subsequently at the house of Ananias (Acts 9:10–16).

Patterns of response emerge from a comparative study of individual time lines. According to Clinton, at least twenty-five of these can be identified.

Four patterns may be classified as foundational, for they describe the backgrounds out of which leaders emerge. Three are transitional training patterns, which are connected with the move from one ministry phase to another through the course of a leader's life. Two testing patterns focus on faithfulness and character, and two on discovering and using giftedness. According to Clinton, "The time of development of a leader depends upon response to processing. Rapid recognition and positive response to God's processing speeds up development. Slower recognition or negative response delays development."[32] Several later patterns describe various levels of maturity and effectiveness. A destiny pattern spans a leader's entire lifetime and enables a person to see his or her key contributions in full perspective.

As already noted, Clinton does not argue that all these elements are present in the formation of every leader or that they occur in the same sequence. Yet his approach identifies and correlates a wide range of experiences that many people have in their formation as leaders. It also demonstrates that biblical stories, as well as stories about leaders throughout history, provide material that can be used to determine frameworks, processes, and responses involved in leadership.

There is, however, a danger associated with this approach. It is sometimes difficult to resist finding what one is looking for in light of previous studies. It is also tempting to correlate these factors in ways that homogenize experiences or patterns too much. A related tendency is to abstract them too much from particular life settings or types of personalities. It is also easy to structure them in a sequence that is too fixed. In reading Clinton's work, the sheer number of process items, the abstract nature of his descriptive terms, and the systematizing of his leadership data lead to a sense that the organic and diverse character of leadership formation has been too tightly classified.

The biblical narratives reveal the highly individual—at times even idiosyncratic—ways God leads and prepares people to fulfill his purposes. God's flexibility and versatility come through in story after story. The Holy Spirit—especially in the New Testament—also clearly has a role. Though Clinton affirms the role of the Spirit at the practical level, his view does not leave enough room for the creative and diverse ways the Spirit works. At times there is something bureaucratic about Clinton's approach, which is influenced by the modern predilection with analyzing, classifying, and organizing all experience and training.

Also, many figures in the Bible worked mainly in the "secular" rather than the so-called religious sphere of life that Clinton examines. Some of these, such as political leaders or bureaucratic advisers, carried out their work in civic or community roles and institutions. Others engaged in various professions and trades. Examples include Joseph, a prime minister; Bezalel and Oholiab, both master builders; Boaz, a city councilor; Daniel, an exiled bureaucrat; Esther, a royal consort; Nehemiah, a city governor; and Priscilla and Aquila, tentmakers who were also engaged in mission. Notable here are the diverse ways in which these people were drawn to what God wanted them to do. Unlike the biblical figures Clinton examines—for example, prophets such as Isaiah (Isa. 6) and Jeremiah (Jer. 1) or New Testament apostles such as Peter (John 21) and Paul (Acts 9)—these people did not receive a direct call to a particular kind of work or position. They did not experience an unequivocal personal vision or call. Instead, they were drawn, guided, or led by God into the kind of position that would fulfill his purposes. Consider some examples from Robert J. Banks's *Faith Goes to Work: Reflections from the Marketplace*.[33]

- Apart from his general dream of dominance over his brothers, Joseph experienced a succession of personal betrayals, reversals of fortune, periods out of public view, risky moral stands, delayed recognition, and unexpected calls on his services. Through these events God gradually and providentially moved him into the high position where he could best serve the future of the nation of Israel (Gen. 37–41).

- On account of their expertise as master builders, Bezalel and Oholiab were recruited by Moses to build the tabernacle. In doing so, they assumed responsibility for a large number of volunteers from diverse crafts and trades (Exod. 35–38).

- Boaz came into his role as a progenitor of Christ by an unusual route. As a relative of the widowed Ruth, he accepted his obligation to marry her and to continue his kinsman's line (Ruth 1–4).

- Daniel, on account of his looks and aptitude, was required to undergo a course of study and training to become a civil servant. Aided by some God-given academic and charismatic abilities, he was able to overcome a potentially unpopular moral course of action and ended up as the chief public servant in the land (Dan. 1–6).

- Esther, an exile, was drafted along with other young women into a beauty contest to see who would gain the king's hand in marriage. Because of her beauty and manner, she won, and through a series of risky and canny moves, she saved her people from genocide (Esther 1–9).

- Nehemiah, having retained a long-standing concern for his distant people and city, asked God for wisdom in finding a way back to them. As a reward for his service and reputation, the foreign rulers he served commissioned him to return and rebuild the city (Neh. 1–6).

- Priscilla and Aquila, a highly mobile and ethnically marginal couple, opened their home and offered work to a visiting apostle. This led to an invitation to travel with him and to engage in the work of church planting alongside their business of tent making (Acts 18–19).

By diverse means God drew these people to the places where he wanted them to be and the tasks through which they could make the most significant contribution to his wider goals. The word "call" is often used in regard to such leading.

Related to this life-story approach are the findings from a survey of the life experiences of almost two hundred Lutheran CEOs conducted by William Diehl and presented in his book *In Search of Faithfulness: Lessons from the Christian Community*.[34] Diehl undertook this in response to Tom Peters and Robert Waterman Jr.'s *In Search of Excellence: Lessons from America's Best-Run Companies* and focuses on faithfulness rather than excellence as the dominant Christian goal.[35] Using various indicators of faithfulness such as spiritual growth and understanding, active prayer life, commitment to the community, financial stewardship, concern for ethics and justice, and simplicity of lifestyle, Diehl found that roughly 30 percent of the executives consistently scored higher than the others, sometimes by a factor of two or three points on the scale. Endeavoring to find out what made the difference, he ran the data through his computer again and found only one common element. They all shared a sense of call, meaning they felt they were in the place God wanted them to be.

Although there are inadequacies in the life-story approach to leadership, it also broadens the biblical and theological framework for understanding leadership. While the trinitarian approach expands an understanding of leadership "upward" by seeking to integrate ideas based on the Godhead, the life-story approach expands an understanding "outward" by embracing the experiences of key figures among the people of God, past and present, who embody leadership through the Spirit's presence in their lives. This is a valuable contribution to the overall discussion of leadership.

Trinitarian Approaches to Leadership

Christian Schumacher, son of the widely read E. F. Schumacher, has advanced the idea of viewing the Godhead as a model for integrating faith and work. For him, the Trinity of Father, Son, and Spirit models the activities of planning, implementing, and evaluating that are part of any good workplace structure.[36] In some respects, his approach echoes Dorothy Sayers's *Mind of the Maker*.[37] In this stimulating book, Sayers develops an analogy between the Trinity and the act of creation involving the interrelationship of idea, activity, and energy.

At a more sophisticated theological level, Australian Christian ethicist Gordon Preece takes issue with those who view human work as connected primarily with the work of the Father, or of the Son, or of the Spirit.[38] He argues that human work is in some sense an expression of all three—the creative and providential activity of the Father, the servant and redemptive work of the Son, and the charismatic and transformative work of the Spirit. Preece is indebted in part to the thoughtful, if somewhat abstract, theological discussion of human work in *Work in the Spirit: Toward a Theology of Work*, by Miroslav Volf. Volf, in turn, was influenced by his mentor, influential Protestant theologian Jürgen Moltmann, who drew attention to the relevance of the Trinity for understanding government. Put simply, the Trinity does not support what Moltmann calls a hierarchical or chain of command approach but rather a perichoretic and collegial approach.[39]

Catherine Mowry LaCugna's *God for Us: The Trinity and Christian Life* discusses the Trinity in a way that illuminates an understanding of the nature of persons and the ethics of relationships in organizations.[40] For LaCugna, inclusiveness, community, and freedom are the ethical values that find their origin in the interrelationality within the Trinity. These three ways of relating should characterize human relationships in organizations and are especially important for affirming those who work within them.

Inclusiveness speaks to accepting and welcoming people into a group or organization. Leaders who practice inclusion accept people in their uniqueness and create a sense of belonging by showing interest in discovering their particular character and gifts. By providing a hospitable space for people to actively participate, a leader unleashes a flow of resources and possibilities into an organization.

A community seeks to acknowledge interrelatedness at every level of reality and contradicts the forces destructive to genuine community, especially the misuse of power and discrimination. In recent years, much has been written about Peter Senge's idea of the learning organization.[41] According to Russ Moxley, from the Center for Creative Leadership, the learning organization and building community go hand in hand.[42] The same principles that generate the learning organization—interdependence in decision making and problem solving, dialogue, and acceptance of differences—also create a sense of community for its members. Leaders play a key role in creating organizations in which everyone can contribute, learn, and develop, both personally and professionally. This offers people a context for participating not just in a company but in a community.

Freedom refers to personhood in a community; it allows people to contribute uniquely and authentically, to express creativity, and to operate within a safe environment of trust and hope. Max De Pree writes that "leaders owe people space, space in the sense of freedom. Freedom in the sense of enabling our gifts to be exercised, the need to give each other the space to grow, to be ourselves, to exercise our diversity."[43]

According to Peter Block and Peter Koestenbaum, in *Freedom and Accountability at Work: Applying Philosophical Insight to the Real World*, to embrace freedom is to accept accountability, and with accountability comes guilt, and with guilt comes anxiety. And so we seek to "escape from freedom," as Erich Fromm puts it,[44] so that we might escape the anxiety that comes with freedom. We escape through conformity, disrespect for individual differences, and dominating regimes.

To create the space for freedom will at times require initiating and leading change. To many people, such change feels more like an act of intrusion or disruption than of personal or organizational liberation. However, it is an act of love because it brings people in the organization and the way the organization operates closer to the essence of the inner life of God in the Trinity. Leadership that creates freedom requires a movement beyond the overly rigid boundaries most organizations seem to have. Such a movement—motivated by love—opens up for the leader and the followers the experience and the practice of freedom in the workplace. The inclusive and communal character of the interrelationships within the Trinity, when lived out in an organization, serves the people in spiritual as well as practical ways.

Stacy Rinehart's *Upside Down: The Paradox of Servant Leadership*[45] focuses primarily on leadership in parachurch movements or Christian organizations and stresses that relationship is at the core of the Godhead. The basic spiritual principles of leadership are enshrined within this divine relationship. The members of the Trinity work together in developing the plan of redemption, exhibiting interdependence, unity, and diversity. There is role differentiation, but the members share authority. Lessons leaders can learn from this include the following:

- There should be unity and diversity among leaders. Leadership should be a group function with shared authority.
- Leadership should be relational, not hierarchical or organizational. Relationships, not the task of an organization, should bind leaders to followers. Power struggles, jealousy, and competition have no place. Each person has a unique and complementary role and contribution.
- Mutual respect and dependence are spiritual requisites of leadership. As people listen more carefully to one another and discern more clearly the value of one another's contributions, leadership begins to take place through more than one person. Leadership rotates according to whoever is pointing the best way forward at a particular time.[46]

Rinehart argues that such a model of leadership also has servanthood rather than mastery over others at its center.

A more developed trinitarian perspective on leadership is present in *Oriented Leadership: Why All Christians Need It*, a book on leadership in both the church and the world by Benjamin Williams and Michael McKibben.[47] These coauthors write out of their managerial and consulting experience and have the everyday world as well as official religious work in mind. What makes their contribution interesting is the way it draws on Orthodox rather than Protestant or Catholic traditions.

Williams and McKibben's basic concern is that believers "have fallen prey to a myriad of leadership theories, experiments, and philosophies which are, at best, only partially Christian." Similar to Robert Greenleaf, they view leadership as in some measure "the responsibility of all and the charge of some." They describe leadership in action as "perceiving and articulating the vision of the kingdom of God and effectively defining and communicating its incarnation, following Christ's example of service." They see a reflection of this in Christ's community, the church, the body of Christ.[48]

Having a clear sense of who one is, which comes through developing intimacy with God, is where leadership begins. Knowing oneself is the key to one's effectiveness as a leader. Because we are created in the image of God, we reflect something of the life of the Trinity. Because leadership takes place within the Trinity, it is in essence "a divine attribute" that is at the very heart of our being. It is a God-given dynamic in our nature and therefore a basic dimension of being a person. This is a democratic understanding of leadership. As the authors say, "Our leadership positions may vary and our positions of leadership may be different, but that doesn't alter the fact that we are all called to be leaders." The goal of leadership is "enabling persons to become all that they were created to be."[49]

Vision is at the root of discerning and implementing this understanding. A proper vision entails having a clear mental picture of how things should be, regardless of what they are now. It involves loving God and the creation and desiring to live a life of thanksgiving for all that God is and has done. As a result, people with this vision accept the responsibility of stewardship, which involves the human management of God's gift of the world. Such a vision gives aim to daily life, guides commitment, stimulates motivation, informs speech and behavior, clarifies expectations, and develops unity.

The Father is the source of the vision, Jesus models its implementation, and the Spirit generates enthusiasm and empowerment for it. The unity, love, and harmony among the three members of the Trinity exemplify and catalyze the process and structures involved in a vision coming into being. As people work together to discern and implement a vision—working through the mission, goals, objectives, projects, activities, and procedures involved—they are engaged in a trinitarian exercise that issues in incarnated action in the church and the world. The Persons of the Trinity act together, in unique but inseparable ways, and never do anything apart from one another. Leaders must seek a similar kind of participation in organizations. The goal is consensus, not merely agreement but a common position reached as people possessing varying levels of authority engage in conversation.

It is clear that for these authors the Trinity is not a doctrinal abstraction but a divine paradigm of what leadership involves. Trinitarian dynamics, therefore, have practical implications for how leadership functions. First, it should never be authoritarian, coercive, or dictatorial. Love and service, not command and control, characterize relations within the life of the Godhead. A trinitarian view of leadership also navigates between hierarchical (top-down) and egalitarian (leaderless team) styles of leadership. In the Trinity, the Father is the source of its life, but all three members of the Trinity act in a unified, loving, and harmonious or conciliar way. Leaders must strive to fuse these apparent opposites. According to Williams and McKibben, the former has more to do with the structure of decision making, the latter with its communication, both of which are needed for effective leadership and mutual accountability.

The authors identify other theological motifs as a framework for understanding and practicing leadership. First, leaders should view all of life as sacramental so that every activity can become a participation in and a reflection of divine life at work. Leadership can be viewed as a sacramental activity because "it includes the opportunity and responsibility to serve and to be *the channel* for communion, love, and grace."[50] Second, leaders should view Christ as the servant leader par excellence, reflected especially in his washing of the disciples' feet, his role as the suffering servant, and his self-emptying sacrifice on the cross. It is important to note, however, that the model of servant leadership Jesus provides is based on his following the Father. Leading and following, therefore, are two sides of the same coin. A leader is a first among equals rather than a person on the dominant side of an unequal relationship. Such leadership involves authority, but authority that flows from love, and function revolving around service rather than positions and power.

Rinehart's approach rightly puts relationship at the heart of the Trinity and draws appropriate implications for leadership. Leaders should demonstrate interdependence, exhibit unity in diversity, recognize people's unique contributions, and express shared authority. Yet by ruling out a hierarchical element by stressing the equality of those in leadership, he makes the Trinity too egalitarian. He also bypasses an identifiable human authority in favor of emphasizing the ultimate leadership of the Godhead, thereby overlooking the need for leadership to be represented symbolically if not actually in human representatives.

Williams and McKibben's approach goes further, taking some of these inadequacies into account and providing a more nuanced trinitarian perspective. Still, their treatment has a few problems.

- Their terminology is not always user-friendly. Part of the reason for this is that the book comes from an Orthodox setting and the authors have a desire to address people with Orthodox convictions. In addition, the Orthodox worldview, even when it is engaging with aspects of daily life, often seems a little disengaged from many of the realities of contemporary challenges in the workplace.
- Their failure to interact with the contemporary discourse on leadership in the workplace limits the value of their work.
- They include little recognition or discussion of some of the harsher pressures and realities of working life. This too limits the value of their discussion.

Despite the inadequacies in the Trinitarian approaches to leadership, they do provide an illuminating alternative to understanding roles, work, and leadership. By exploring the multifaceted relationships within the Trinity, it is possible to glean insight and new models for shared power, relating to others, and leading. The nature of God, expressed in the Trinity, offers a superb representation of unity within diversity, community, freedom, and a collegial approach that is nonhierarchical. Since we are created in the image of God, we are drawn to a way of leading that honors the nature of God as expressed in the Trinity. People begin to experience the sacramental nature of leading when leadership takes on the nature of God. Indeed, many women have drawn on the themes of collegiality and models of shared leading as they seek to express their own leadership in ways that are theologically informed.

Women and Leadership

An important aspect of the growing interest in leadership today concerns women in leadership. In their book *Megatrends 2000*, John Naisbitt and Patricia Aburdene predicted that in the 1990s women would cease to be a minority in the marketplace. They write, "To be a leader in business today, it is no longer an advantage to have been socialized as male. Although we do not fully realize it yet, men and women are on an equal playing field in corporate America."[51] Naisbitt and Aburdene's prediction was accurate to some extent: today women make up half the workforce worldwide and comprise 50 percent of managerial positions; however, at the senior level only twenty-three companies in the Fortune 500 are headed by female CEOs. There is still more work to be done if women are to hold half the senior-level positions in organizations.

The Organization for Economic Co-operation and Development recognizes the engine women create when they go to work, stating, "Women, which constitute half of the world's human capital, are one of its most underutilized resources."[52] An assessment of the economic impact resulting from an increased number of working women by the year 2020 could boost the economic output of various countries by as much as 27 percent in India, 9 percent in Japan, 11 percent in Italy, and 5 percent in the United States.[53] This impact means there is an immense opportunity to manage the leadership development of women worldwide in order to address labor shortages and realize global economic improvement.

More women are entering universities: the average global university enrollment is around ninety-three men for every one hundred women; in the developed world 60 percent of college graduates are women. In Saudi Arabia 51 percent of students are women, and in China women account for 42 percent of the student population.[54] A study conducted by the PEW Research Center tracking the percentage of high school graduates who enroll in college the fall term after graduation found among students of color more women are entering college than men: Hispanic (76:62), black (69:57), and Asian (86:83).[55] More women than men enter graduate programs in education, public administration, and social and behavioral sciences, and about an equal number in law; in business programs women comprise 43 percent of entrants.[56] Overall women account for 60 percent of master's degrees and 52 percent of doctorates awarded in the United States.[57] Even with the increased number of women entering academic programs, women report feeling less prepared for their careers and experience lower morale than male students.

Organizations recognize the value of women's leadership; indeed, the business case on the value women add to organizations is well documented. Catalyst has distilled much of the research and offers that women's leadership impacts organizations' financial performance, talent management, and positive reputation, and increases innovation and team performance.[58]

Though a woman may feel called to express her gift of leadership in the marketplace, she may also encounter resistance. For women of faith, the issue of workplace equality also intersects with the question of vocational calling. The voices of women at the senior levels of leadership are still few, and it takes a great deal of courage and a clear sense of calling for women to make it to the top, where key organizational decisions are made.

Female leaders of faith see their leadership as an expression of their faith in the workplace. From this vantage point, work is sacred, and leading is an expression of service. Faith-based leaders find meaning and purpose through their work and help others to do the same. In the book of Matthew, Jesus was asked which was the greatest commandment, to which he replied: "'Love the Lord your God with all your heart and with all your soul and with all your mind.' . . . And the second is like it: 'Love your neighbor as yourself.' All the Law and the Prophets hang on these two commandments" (Matt. 22:37, 39–40). Muhammad commanded his followers to "do goodness to relatives, parents and neighbors." The Dalai Lama teaches that compassion is not "religious business, but human business." Buddha admonished people to "light a lamp for others." Indeed, through time and across cultures, religious teachings stress loving others as ourselves. These sacred texts and directives suggest that women of faith not only can balance spirituality with the practice of leadership, but some may even consider it a way to obey the tenets of their faith.[59]

Conditions in the marketplace are aligning with women's leadership in important ways. For some time, the term "knowledge worker" described the value in the workplace measured by an individual's ideas and intellectual generativity. But that phenomenon is actually changing quickly because knowledge is now a commodity; everyone has access to the same information, and thus knowledge is no longer a matter of competitive advantage. Because of this shift taking place, we are moving from an era of "knowledge workers" to "relationship workers." An examination of the best companies to work for in America reveals a common theme: the best companies create the means for people to build strong, numerous, rewarding personal relationships at work. Women are superbly adept at building relationships. Work is a relationship, not a transaction. Going forward, it will be more and more difficult for companies with transaction-based cultures to attract the best talent.

The skills needed to bring out the best in others are practices often motivated by faith and spirituality—the ability to listen deeply, show respect, and demonstrate fairness, patience, open communication, and a reverence for the humanity of all. The research on leadership describes this style of leading as transformational. Research has shown that women are slightly better at showing transformational leadership because they know how to perceive the motivations, thoughts, and feelings of others, picking up on subtleties in team interactions. Organizations today value collaboration, encouragement, and support over command-and-control leadership.[60] Moreover, women's participation in groups has been correlated with higher collective intelligence,[61] and teams led by women show improved performance. It seems that women's style of leading fits well with contemporary organizational demands. Many organizations are examining ways to advance more women into leadership positions in order to reap the organizational benefits that come from improved performance. For the faith-based woman, leading from authentic collaboration has significant implications for creating organizational community.

When considering the need to position more women in positions of influence, the discussion necessarily touches on diversity and change. In her book *Thinking in the Future Tense: Leadership Skills for a New Age*, Jennifer James states that diversity "is more than a policy. . . . It is our national identity and our unifying creed." We are "one nation of many cultures," and this is a "precursor of what lies ahead—one world of many cultures. . . . How well we accommodate diversity is indicative of how well we handle future change." Quoting essayist Asta Bowen, James suggests that within our country, "we are engaged in a pioneer effort to 'tune democracy to its finest tolerance,' and as leaders of faith, we are compelled to embrace and accept difference." More broadly, "we must make ourselves into global citizens, able to celebrate differences." She further calls for dispensing with the us-them mentality and indicates the need for individuals and organizations to develop "high diversity IQs."[62]

Culture change goes deep into both individuals and organizations. To effect long-term, meaningful change, "we have to rely on our own courage, [and] the best place to look for insight into managing diversity is inside yourself."[63] We could certainly add faith to the list. It takes courage, insight, and faith to embrace change and diversity. Female leaders of faith operate from a worldview of transformation. As God's intent is to bring about genuine change in the world through people of faith, it follows that faith-driven female leaders will seek ways to transform systems so that diversity is recognized, honored, and celebrated. We might call this an aspect of the redemptive work of faith-based leadership.

Questions of Power

Any discussion of leadership and faith must include the idea of power and how best to use power to move people, projects, and processes toward the accomplishment of goals. Janet Hagberg offers a well-integrated approach to the expression of power that works for both women and men of faith. "Personal power is the extent to which one is able to link the outer capacity for action (external power) with the inner capacity for reflection (internal power)."[64] This idea brings together power and reflection so that a leader of faith can act thoughtfully, something that groups, teams, and organizations need.

Hagberg describes power as something that one grows into and that develops over time. Power tends to follow six distinct stages:

1. *Powerlessness:* At this stage, leaders can be described as secure and dependent, possibly trapped, helpless but not hopeless; fear holds them back from finding their true, authentic power. At this stage, such people lead by force and inspire fear.
2. *Power by association:* This form of power comes about as leaders learn the ropes. There is some dependency on supervisors; to grow, leaders must move out on their own, take risks, and develop competencies. Such leaders lead by seduction and inspire dependency.
3. *Power by symbols:* At this level, power is a controlling affair, and the people exercising it are often described as ambitious, competitive, charismatic, and egocentric. Not knowing they are stuck in this controlling stage of power holds them from going forward to the next stage. They lead by personal persuasion and inspire a winning attitude.
4. *Power by reflection:* Leaders at this stage use influence as a way to express their power. They are known for being strong, reflective, competent, and

skilled at mentoring. They show good leadership by modeling integrity and inspiring hope.

5. *Power by purpose:* Leaders who express their power by purpose are known for their vision and can sometimes be called "the irregulars." This is because they are not ego-oriented. They are quick to give away power and let others lead. They are self-accepting, calm, humble, confident of life's purpose, and spiritual. The hallmark of such leaders is empowerment, and this inspires love and service.

6. *Power by gestalt:* The final stage of power is expressed as wisdom. Leaders at this stage might be called the souls of the earth, for they are comfortable with paradox, unafraid of death, quiet in service, and ethical. In a sense, their power is almost invisible, and they seek to inspire inner peace in those around them.[65]

This model shows that the exercise of power moves from leader-focused power to other-focused influence. It allows leaders to see the promise of power when it is integrated with reflection in the service of others and not self. Leaders of faith can find in stages 4 through 6 the balance between the exercise of power and the personal integrity of faith.

Conclusion

An effective and comprehensive biblical theology of leadership must draw on the person and work of Christ, the way biblical figures were led by God, and the nature and activity of the Trinity to develop into effective coworkers with Christ. Paul's understanding and practice, as discussed earlier, should also be taken into consideration. It is also important to extend and supplement what we can learn from the Bible with other wise reflections and practices in the area of leadership, including approaches from a wide range of theological traditions. In this chapter we applied these ideas to the topic of women in leadership. We need discernment to sort out what is true and false, fitting and inappropriate, abstract and practical, timely and outdated. The general presence of God's image in people, the general revelation of God's truth in the world—however limited or distorted it may sometimes be—and the general activity of the Spirit in life give us encouragement to do this. In the following chapters, this is what we seek to do.

5

practicing
leadership through
faithfulness,
integrity, and service

Finding a valid starting point for reflecting Christianly on leadership is one challenge. Translating reflection into day-to-day working life is another. Doing so entails developing an approach to leadership that involves the whole person and translating that approach into action. Addressing the whole person highlights the role of imagination, emotion, and wisdom, as well as understanding. More basically, it highlights the importance of a leader's character.

Toward More Holistic Leadership

In his book on the need for managers to do things differently, David Clutterbuck makes a plea that more attention be given to the catalytic role of the imagination.[1] This, he argues, makes a real difference in how people see issues and tackle problems. It also involves creative behavior, which he describes as "walking around corners backwards." He sets out how effective use of imagination can make a contribution to such diverse aspects of an institution's life as celebrating its successes and dismantling its weaker elements. He also identifies its importance in choosing from unlimited organizational shapes, generating a spirit of adventure, and struggling against "normalization."[2]

Increasing recognition is now being given to the essential role imagination plays in understanding. Metaphors do not just illustrate our ideas but are indispensable for any thinking at all. They provide us with a more concrete frame of reference than abstract thought and suggest connections we need to develop new ideas. People's behavior and understanding are largely governed by them as well.[3]

Not only individuals but also organizations require images. They depend on them to tell the stories of how they came into being, what they are now doing, and where they see themselves heading. Images compete for attention, and organizations have to choose between them, or invent new ones, to tell their institutional stories. This is one of the key roles of leaders.[4]

In his well-known books, Daniel Goleman declares that, in addition to IQ, emotional intelligence, or EQ, plays a critical role in work in general and leadership in particular.[5] Indeed, cognitive intelligence, at least in the form of academic achievement, is a reliable predictor in only 20 percent of cases of how effective a person will be in leadership. Since leadership is fundamentally about leading people, there is a need to understand, relate to, and draw the best out of them. Without EQ, other capacities a leader brings to the job, however highly developed, are too easily short-circuited.

Goleman describes the five key elements of EQ as personal awareness, self-regulation, motivation, empathy, and social skills. Expression of these, combined with what Goleman calls highly aware role mapping—a perceptive understanding of the way people undertake their responsibilities with fellow workers—gives rise to what Carlos Raimundo describes as "relational capital."[6] This term describes resources in an organization that are derived from the quality of its human interactions. The presence or lack of relational resources is as much a factor in organizational growth and effectiveness as the presence or lack of financial resources.

At the same time, we should not minimize the importance of wisdom. Alistair Mant's survey of exemplary leaders reveals the presence of practical intelligence, which is more than the relevant information they need to operate effectively.[7] Such practical knowledge is broad rather than narrow. At its core is the ability to think systemically, determine chains of cause and effect, and understand the role of smaller units within larger networks. The outcome of such well-grounded intelligence is timely judgment—the ability to size up a situation quickly and to act decisively.

At the heart of Mant's approach is what he calls ternary leadership. Binary leadership focuses chiefly on direct leadership of a transactional kind that places interpersonal influence and persuasion at the center. As such, it is characterized by a fight/flight, win/lose, and power/survival way of operating. Ternary leadership can be either direct or indirect and is oriented more to transformation. Here relationships are governed by the purpose and object of the enterprise in which people are engaged, and alongside a relational and consensual style this demands more thought. Failures in leadership frequently spring from a lack of such practical intellectual firepower. What is needed, John Dalla Costa adds, is not more specialist expertise but more integrated across-the-board wisdom.[8]

The centrality of wisdom for leadership has been most recently stressed by Mark Strom. He defines wisdom over against the purely either/or character of law, formulas that view a portion of life as only definable in terms of in/out, best/worst, right/wrong. Wisdom views life as a whole, is unremittingly contextual, and arises from attentive observation, which discerns patterns, links, analogies in behaviors, personalities, and character that lead to basic insights. These patterns define reality, unlock its truth through conversations, work primarily through influence to captures others' minds and hearts, and shape character more than just personality. Wisdom is not afraid of complexity and ambiguity. It prefers fashioning stories and detecting others' unique contribution to abstract propositions and promoting general cleverness. It is marked by a sense of promise and grace rather than expectation and demand. Wisdom continues to learn from experience and lives out what it discovers with integrity and care.[9]

The relevance of imagination, emotion, and wisdom to leadership has a vital biblical basis in its depiction of the way God works and relates. He is the one who is constantly doing something innovative or new. He is full of passion and compassion. His profound understanding of events and people is constantly affirmed. These qualities regularly appear in those who excel in serving his people. Paul, for one, thinks and works outside the box, expresses deep feelings, and displays keen discernment in dealing with his communities and fellow workers. Each of these three aspects of leadership has a role to play in bridging the gap between aspiration and performance, but they tend to overlook a dimension without which they are likely to fall short. This is the area of character. In philosophical discussions during the past two decades, several leading thinkers have contended that a focus on making ethical decisions assumes that working out what to do automatically involves possessing the ability to do it. Yet we cannot take this for granted. Christians recognize that, as a result of the fall, knowledge does not necessarily result in action. As Paul puts it, "I have a desire to do what is good, but I cannot carry it out" (Rom. 7:18).

In recent years, several writers have highlighted the importance of character for exercising leadership. In discussion with the author of a book on the subject, Patricia La Barre argues that the basic defect in current views of leadership is the neglect of character-building conversations that open up the possibility of real change.[10]

The average person is stuck, lost, riveted by the objective domain. That's where our metrics are; that's where we look for solutions. It's the come-on of the consulting industry and the domain of all the books, magazines, and training programs out there. And that's why books and magazines that have numbers in their titles sell so well. We'll do anything to avoid facing the basic, underlying questions: How do we make truly difficult choices? How do we act when the risks seem overwhelming? How can we muster the guts to burn our bridges and to create a condition of no return?[11]

People in leadership must be committed to grappling with what it takes to change deeply ingrained habits relating to how they think, value, manage frustration, and act. Here lies the zone of fundamental change and strength. As James Kouzes and Barry Posner write, "character counts!"[12]

Throughout the centuries, Aristotle's philosophical approach tended to be the most influential in ethical reflection. This approach gave primary attention to how people gain the capacity to carry out their aspirations, determinations, and responsibilities. It focused on virtue ethics—that is, how to become the kind of person who would make the best choices—as opposed to decision ethics—that is, how to determine the most important factors that result in the best choices. In recent times, Alasdair MacIntyre has become the leading philosophical exponent of this approach to ethics, while in theological circles Protestant ethicists such as Stanley Hauerwas have developed a similar approach. So have some Catholic writers.[13]

Parallel to this virtue-oriented approach is the character-centered approach of the often-overlooked Old Testament Wisdom writings, whose importance is now being increasingly acknowledged. These recognize that personal formation precedes as well as accompanies good choices. Character makes a person more capable of implementing a decision and also shapes the quality of the decision being made. It plays therefore both a performative and an informative role.

Since growth in character includes affective as well as volitional and cognitive development, it enhances leaders' emotional and relational abilities. It makes them more aware of how they operate at these levels and how better to work with and for others. Though character has less effect on their skills development, it can help them to deploy their skills more appropriately and consistently.

Development of a leader's character is not only a personal matter but also is influenced by the kind of relationships he or she has with others as part of a family, at work, and in the wider community. While not determined by these relationships, it is partly shaped by them, but not always in a straight-line way. Whether a person's surrounding communities are full of or lacking in the qualities that make for character, they can help to propel or retard a leader's personal growth.

A further important contribution is made by Michael and Deborah Jinkins in their book *The Character of Leadership: Political Realism and Public Virtue in Nonprofit Organizations*.[14] They argue that a leader's effectiveness is also partly determined by the character of his or her work community and the organizations to which he or she belongs. This is why personal character, even of the highest quality, is not in itself enough. Unless a leader's character has a relational and organizational edge or dimension, shaped by engagement with the people and structures around that person, he or she will be unable to encourage either in a fruitful direction.

The discussion that follows focuses on three key aspects of character relating to leadership: faithfulness, integrity, and service.

Leadership and Faithfulness

When religious people, especially those who are Jews and Christians, talk about connecting their convictions with their work, discussion commonly focuses on the contribution their "faith" makes to the role they play. This is also true of literature stemming from these sources—studded with phrases like "faith in the workplace," "believers in business," or "faith and leadership." Organizations established by such groups or people also generally highlight the word "faith" in their names or mission statements. An interesting exception to this is the Center for Faithful Leadership at Hope College in Holland, Michigan.

As a leader, however, it is not enough simply to have faith or to be perceived as a person of faith in the workplace. That is, faith means more than holding religious beliefs or standing up for them publicly. Faithfulness is required as well as private or public faith. This means more than maintaining a consistent personal relationship with God or talking about one's faith with others. It also means more than obedience to an employment contract or a workplace superior.

Faithfulness entails a closer and more extensive connection between beliefs and behavior. Forging such a link requires a certain kind of character. Possessing this requires having certain principles that form into habits. Today, from Robert Bellah's analysis of some *Habits of the Heart* to Stephen Covey's *Seven Habits of Highly Effective People*, there is more recognition that inner priorities and values must be embodied in regular practices.[15] People in the workplace increasingly want leaders whose behavior is shaped not just by company policy, political correctness, or individual preferences but also by character. However, the understanding of character in these books contains some limitations.

- Too often it sounds as if developing the right kinds of principles and habits at work is simply a matter of working harder. Yet according to the New Testament, faith, and therefore faithfulness flowing from it, is more a gift than an achievement (see Eph. 2:8–9).
- The principles and habits discussed in most popular books do not go deep enough. Fairness, honesty, service, and excellence do not cover the full range of Christian qualities (as in Gal. 5:22–23). For example, justice involves more than fairness, goodness more than honesty, sacrifice more than service, and faithfulness more than excellence.
- On their own principles are too dry and abstract to motivate people to practice them. They first require the dispositions from which principled behavior flows. These develop largely through being on the receiving end of divine or human life-changing experiences and gratuitous acts of kindness. These are the kinds of things that generate lasting personal transformation.

In the Bible, faithfulness is always concrete, never just an attitude or an ideal. It recognizes that, because life is complex, faithfulness may vary according to circumstances. There are no simple answers or formulas that fit all occasions. Yet it is not enough for a person to have his or her heart in the right place. Faithfulness always involves practical decisions and actions.

Leaders must learn to live *out* as well as to live *by* faith, to *keep* as well as to *have* faith, and to be faith*ful* as well as to be *full* of faith. Such actions have advantages for both leaders and those who work with them. Faithfulness leads to a clearer understanding of organizational goals and values, better morale, and a higher degree of trust. According to Max De Pree, "Trust grows when people see leaders translate their personal integrity into organizational fidelity," when followers see "that leaders can be depended on to do the right thing."[16]

When leaders clearly and consistently express their faith through faithfulness in the workplace, they gain credibility. James Kouzes and Barry Posner claim that credibility is the cornerstone of effective leadership.[17]

As well, faithfulness enhances an organization's potential for growth. In for-profit organizations, faithfulness spills over into supplier and customer loyalty, increased cost advantage through improved productivity, and stronger long-term investor commitment.[18] In nonprofit organizations, it creates greater buy-in of members, more vigorous initiative and effort, and more permanent financial support.

Faithfulness also has advantages for the wider community. An organization that models the way faithfulness can function raises trust in society and presents a model of organizational fidelity from which other institutions can learn.

Faithfulness in action may also open up people to discovering the fundamental role of faith in life in general.

With Respect to the Mission

Leaders who exhibit faithfulness have a clear sense of what they are doing and are able to deliver it. They either start or emerge in organizations that create value for employees and members, partners and allies, customers and clients. For example, stating a mission is an act of faith. A mission statement expresses a commitment to being as well as doing something. It is important for those in leadership positions, at any level, to be faithful to their organization's mission. What does this mean in practice?

First, these leaders continue to believe that what they have embarked on is achievable, and they seek to operate in a way that is consistent with the practicing-leadership content of the mission statement. This does not mean that when unanticipated difficulties or hurdles appear, they downplay them or pretend they do not exist. In and through these they maintain the viability of the mission and continue to uphold it, especially for those who are anxious. For example, Lee Iacocca's faith in the ultimate success of the faltering Chrysler Corporation was critical to restoring the confidence of a demoralized workforce and federal financial support. Second, leaders should behave, relate, and operate in a way that reflects the character of the mission. If it puts customers first, they must put customers first. If it promises extraordinary service, they provide the same. If it is committed to quality, they create an environment that supports and stimulates this. Third, faithful leaders seek to clarify in terms of the mission why they have adopted a certain process for decision making, devised a particular structure for change, or taken a specific course of action.

With Respect to Promises

Over a period of time, leaders generally make promises to those who work with and for them. Unfortunately, there seems to be a growing disparity in both private and public life between the promises leaders make and the actions they take. Nowadays, most people seem to regard a promise as the expression of a hope rather than the creation of an obligation.

Though, because the marketplace is complex and unpredictable, promises cannot always be kept, as far as possible faithful leaders endeavor to keep their word. They do not make contradictory promises to people inside and outside the organization. When they do so, questions soon arise about their integrity.

Nor should they make casual promises. Faithful leaders honor their promises despite altered circumstances.

With Respect to Mistakes

Like everyone, leaders make mistakes, but frequently they are better at hiding them, protecting themselves from the consequences, or turning them to their personal benefit. Faithful leaders acknowledge their mistakes, aim to minimize future errors, and seek to learn from them. At the same time, they know that the future does not belong to those who make the fewest mistakes. They are aware of the need to encourage experimentation and innovation. A leader who exhibits faithfulness holds people accountable for their mistakes but also forgives them and helps colleagues to improve their performance.

With Respect to Loyalty

In these days of job shift rather than job security, most organizations find it difficult to guarantee lifelong employment. How do leaders exercise faithfulness in such a climate? First, they can commit themselves to building or maintaining an organization that will last, despite the changes that take place. Second, they seriously consider committing long term to an organization rather than pursuing better positions elsewhere. Third, they also seek to influence decisions that will enhance an organization's long-term capacity.

Here is an example. When he became CEO of Herman Miller, Max De Pree promised training for people who suffered from cutbacks to help make them more marketable. He set in place a process that assisted them to find new positions. He assured them of a salary until they received an offer comparable to their present positions. In doing this, De Pree displayed a creative reformulation of organizational loyalty.

There are other ways in which faithfulness can lead to loyalty. Leaders can provide organizational stability, share the profits, identify and empower the use of gifts, grant employees a role in decision making, and give them incentives to come up with creative ideas, for which they are honored and rewarded. When these actions become standard operating procedures, then image and reality, ideals and practice, statements and behavior become one, creating a stronger loyalty between employees and leaders.

Leadership and Integrity

The words of R. Buckminster Fuller, born from experience, that "Integrity is the essence of everything successful," have often been quoted. "Integrity" is the one word that crops up with increasing regularity in organizations' mission statements. According to international studies, it is one of the main three characteristics that employees admire most in their leaders. Leadership research indicates that there is a direct link between ethical integrity and organizational moral culture, even if in some cases it takes considerable time for this to appear.[19] Psychological studies have confirmed that integrity in leadership matters, not just because of the positive effects that can flow from it but from the harm those in leadership positions can do. Integrity in the leader of an organization, studies suggest, is more important than lack of conscience, self-control, or tolerance of an individual, acting alone.[20] On many sides today we hear calls for greater integrity in personal, professional, and public life. But few pause to reflect for long on the word's full meaning, the complex challenges facing anyone who seeks to act with integrity, and what is involved in its everyday practice.

Occasionally people give the impression that integrity is a simple matter. A key figure in an attorney general's department with whom we met declared that in all his years of drafting legislation he had never experienced a moral challenge. Consequently he believed that living with integrity was quite straightforward and did not require discussion. Others believe that, at least in certain occupations, integrity is impossible. In such cases, people must close their eyes to much that happens or make so many compromises that they cannot maintain ethical rectitude.

A handbook on business ethics written by Gordon Pearson, *Integrity in Organizations: An Alternative Business Ethic*, argues for a position between these two extremes.[21] He rejects the unrealistic recommendations about organizational integrity in most writings on the subject as well as the approach that sidelines ethical behavior. Utilizing Lawrence Kohlberg's stages of moral development from childhood to maturity, Pearson accepts the less-than-normal ethical behavior and lack of concern for social responsibility required in the early days of a business for it to survive and compete. He therefore rules out from the start heroic individual efforts to operate in a thoroughgoing ethical way. Over time, however, an organization can adopt different standards that gradually attain higher levels of organizational integrity. While allowing that both leaders and organizations develop in their capacity to act with integrity, Pearson's equating of organizational and individual moral stages of development confuses categories. The law rightly treats organizations as adult corporate selves. In addition, leaders in organizations are not at an infant-like level of moral development and should seek to elevate their understanding and behavior.[22]

There are, then, those who tend to be too naive, those who tend to be too skeptical, and those who inadequately defend a position between the two. The challenge is to recognize the insidious challenges to acting consistently with integrity and to endeavor to do so with a reasonable hope of attainment. While Christians acknowledge that at times our human frailty makes living with integrity difficult, it does not render it impossible.

But what precisely do people mean when they call for greater integrity in leadership? As Stephen Carter, in his fine book on the subject titled *Integrity*, says, "Everybody argues that the nation needs more of it . . . but hardly any of us stop to explain what we mean by it." "Indeed," he adds, "the only trouble with integrity is that everybody who uses the word seems to mean something slightly different."[23]

When the word "integrity" is used thoughtfully, it generally refers to a trait possessed by individuals and organizations who act in a principled way in all situations. The focus is on acting in accordance with high moral standards and being willing to publicly defend those actions when they lead to controversy.

The meaning of "integrity" is filled out by considering certain related terms. The word "integral," for example, speaks of what is inherent to or at the core of a person. Having integrity is not the same as developing a certain skill. It refers to something more organic. Losing integrity does not just lead to having less of *something*; it means becoming less of a *someone*. "Integrity is not so much a virtue itself as a complex of virtues, the virtues working together to form a coherent character, an identifiable and trustworthy personality."[24]

As the terms "integrate" and "integration" show, integrity also involves consistency between various aspects of a person and their roles. Acting with integrity is more complex than simply fulfilling moral obligations. The question of standards, how to act rightly in one's work, involves more than asking, "What should I do?" in a particular situation. When integrity is present, there are no discrepancies between the way a person acts in one situation and another or in one of his or her roles versus another. There is a consistency and congruence about the way he or she carries out responsibilities. In a person of integrity, "there is a *togetherness* about his or her personality" that some might describe as "wholeness" and others as "holiness" of character.[25]

One indication of the renewed interest in integrity is the rise of professional ethics. Too often, however, professional ethics focuses on only moral principles without raising questions about the kind of character needed to implement them or the larger vision and mission that inspires them. Decision making is also sometimes viewed too individualistically, ignoring the core institutional values and ethos that shape the dilemmas individuals face, often taking place in an allegedly value-free context in which religious or ideological frameworks are excluded. As a result, the principles expounded do not have a ground of support that justifies their selection over that of others.

Challenges for Professionals

Some of the challenges that confront professionals are outlined by Donald B. Kraybill and Phyllis Pellman Good, the coauthors of *Perils of Professionalism: Essays on Christian Faith and Professionalism*.[26] They include the following:

- Serving the interest of a profession rather than the people it is designed to serve and rating accountability to it higher than accountability to them
- Demonstrating the ability to create a professional service rather than meeting a demonstrable need in the community
- Protecting the secrets of professional work rather than sharing them with clients so they can deal with certain problems themselves
- Manufacturing a need that only a specialist can satisfy when there are simpler or more systematic ways of dealing with it
- Overstepping one's position by performing services that tend to control the client rather than assist and empower them
- Using inside information gained from a client to advance the professional's interests in some way
- Overcharging clients for services rendered

At the root of these bad choices in the workplace lie three factors: the flawed personalities of the people involved, intractable values or practices in organizations, and complex situations making it difficult to discern what is really at stake.

What is at the heart of acting with integrity in any situation?

One way to determine this is to consider the meaning of integrity in various biblical passages. Several passages in the Psalms place it in parallel with words like "uprightness" or "righteousness" (Pss. 7:8; 25:21) or in contrast to references to "wicked schemes" and "bribes" (Ps. 26:10) or to "duplicity" and "perverse" speech (Prov. 11:3; 19:1). Integrity can also be explored in the lives of key biblical figures such as Joseph, Moses, Rahab, Samuel, David, Nehemiah, Jonah, and Daniel. A prominent example is Job, who is described as "blameless and upright, a man who fears God and shuns evil . . . [and] still maintains his integrity" (Job 2:3; cf. 2:9; 27:5; 31:6). Or Abraham, in whose life it means more in the nature of sincerity and straightforwardness (Gen. 20:5).[27]

Another way to approach the issue of integrity is by asking the following questions:

- What is the best moment for raising a significant question or issue?
- In discussing options, is there a concern for truth in the way facts are treated and translated into deeds?

- Do both the process followed and the decision made display the virtue of patience?
- Was there a recognition that a choice was involved and an avoidance of talk about "I had to do it"?
- Did the approach balance organizational survival with taking risks to achieve long-term vision?
- Has the outcome integrated the concerns of those from diverse sociocultural backgrounds in the organization?
- Will the action exhibit a proper regard for all the people involved as well as a loving concern for them?
- Is it likely to lessen evil and extend justice, especially for those who are most vulnerable?
- Does it cohere with the bedrock identity of the organization and its signature ways of operating?
- Can the decision be altered if circumstances change and another option opens up?

A Specific Approach

A contemporary approach to acting with integrity focuses on three connected perspectives: an ethic of critique, of justice, and of care. The ethic of critique considers the distribution of power and privilege and who defines what is going on in a situation. In circumstances where power and decision making are restricted to a few, it may be easier to compromise. The ethic of justice considers who may participate, how policies are determined, whether rights are involved and for whom, and by what criteria resources are allocated. This allows a leader to consider issues of fairness and to invite participation in policy formation and resource allocation. The ethic of care concerns relationships and includes issues of dignity, human potential, and empowerment.[28]

Max De Pree committed himself to listening to the concerns of employees and created regular ways for this to happen. He was once asked why he didn't value adoptive births as much as natural births. He replied that he valued both equally. The female employee countered, "No, you don't. If you did you would offer the same benefits for both." De Pree had assumed that company policy made no distinctions in this area. When he discovered this was not the case, he changed the policy to provide equal resources for both situations.

This example points to the sharing of power between CEO and employee (ethic of critique), the value of the individual and the desire to improve his or her quality of life (ethic of care), and the changing of a policy so that everyone in the same situation could have access to the same resources (ethic of justice). When these three perspectives are used to balance and support decisions, the result is integrity.

In addition to using these perspectives, leaders can decide and act with integrity when they approach situations in the following ways: in a spirit of prayer, through which God may reveal fresh possibilities; with a willingness to consult with others in a vocational or communal group; and by aiming at a win-win rather than a win-lose situation. They should also be aware of their own capacity for self-deception and realistic about the frequent resistance they will encounter to their commitment to core convictions. But in all this, as a recent book suggests, they can be sustained by belief that their organization will develop a more human culture and a greater unity of process and direction across its component parts and subcultures. Further, depending on its size and purpose, its influence will reach beyond the boundaries of the organization into related regional and global structures.[29]

The Role of Compromise

Though the opposite of integrity is often said to be compromise, the reality is not so simple. Compromise must not be confused with two processes that are at times too simply equated with it. First, there is a difference between compromising and strategizing. The latter involves working out a long-term, often complex, set of tactics for reaching a desired end. This may involve moves and countermoves, unexpected demands and apparent concessions that appear to obscure the goal of the exercise. Such strategies are a means to an end, temporary positions that are part of the larger exercise that is being played out, and may be appropriate or inappropriate. Second, there is a difference between compromising and negotiating. There are legitimate and illegitimate ways of negotiating, but the process of negotiating does not itself involve compromise.

What, then, is compromise? Mostly the word has a negative connotation. For example, it can be used to describe a decision or an action that entails a lowering of standards on the grounds of expediency or to relieve pressure. When persons fail to act with consistency, they are said to have "compromised their integrity." To make or accept a compromise is to cross a moral line and therefore betray one's core convictions. Yet the word can also be used in a positive way, as when we talk about making "a good compromise." This may involve finding a middle ground between two options based on different principles or the same principle.

Life is full of situations in which it is not possible to do all or even most of what one wants. Such is the case with politics, which is often described as "the art of the possible." So too in the world of commerce, when both parties reach an agreement that gives each sufficient of what they desire. In such fields, resources, supplies, time, and personnel are often in short supply, and choices have to be made about who will receive them. Since participants practicing leadership often have deeply held conflicting opinions, it is only through trade-offs that a good and sustainable compromise can be reached.

A case can be made for legitimate compromise by examining the many biblical stories in which it is encouraged. A classic example is that of Naaman, the adviser to a foreign king who, on a visit to Israel, was healed by a leading prophet of the day. Because on his return he would be the lone believer so long as he continued to give his allegiance to the true God, he was permitted to bow his head in an act of pagan worship in his own country (2 Kings 5:15–19).

Another example is the meeting of Paul and Barnabas with the apostles and elders in Jerusalem to discuss the validity of the gentile mission. If Greek and Roman converts would agree to avoid certain actions that Jewish Christians found offensive (Acts 15:23–29), it was agreed that the latter would endorse Paul's initiative without requiring Greek and Roman believers to be circumcised. Consider also Paul's practice of circumcising one of his coworkers, the half-Jew Timothy, but not another, the Greek Titus. On the one hand, his actions reflected his stated practice of becoming "all things to all people so that by all possible means I might save some" (1 Cor. 9:22). On the other hand, he would not move an inch when he felt that doing so would jeopardize a central Christian truth. For example, he disagreed with Peter at Antioch when he encountered what he considered a betrayal of basic gospel principles (Gal. 2:11–14).

Biblical stories touch our imaginations as well as our minds and evoke a range of possible applications. In the same way, biblical metaphors, images, symbols, and models can help us to understand appropriate compromise. The biblical metaphors "salt" and "light" are guides to how God's people are called to operate. So too are images describing God's people as being "aliens and strangers" yet also a "royal priesthood" among others in the world. There is also the powerful symbol of "taking up the cross" daily in the workplace. We must be careful, however, not to straitjacket these metaphors, images, and symbols into a moral framework that is too confining.

If we think only in terms of black and white, good and bad, right and wrong, we overlook the emphasis on wise or unwise, fitting or unfitting, appropriate or inappropriate in the Old Testament Wisdom writings, such as Proverbs. For example, in the presence of a superior who is at times hostile, it is not simply a matter of whether what one says is true or false but whether it is a good time to speak, how much should be revealed, and in what way (Eccles. 8:2–6). There are times when it is better not to press for something that is good simply because it would bring about an unproductive reaction. On other occasions, it is better to wait for a more opportune time.

If such a decision is the best in a particular situation, is it not the will of God even though we may feel we should do more? For example, when Jesus was unable to heal in a certain place because the people's faith was lacking, it was not a negative compromise on his part. Similarly, if we have only a limited amount of time or number of resources, our options are limited, and while we might feel regret, we should not consider this a failure. Helpful here is Dietrich Bonhoeffer's distinction between ultimate (i.e., "ideal world") and penultimate (i.e., "real world") realities, the latter constrained by actual events, situations, and people. Sometimes, as he says, the constraints we operate under require us to "sacrifice a fruitless principle to a fruitful compromise."[30] In other words, we will achieve more by maximizing what is possible, even if it is not all we would like to do, than by holding out for an ideal we are incapable of realizing.

To make compromises that have integrity, leaders should have the following in view:

- Because behavior flows from a sense of who leaders are and where they are heading, they should have a profound biblical grasp of the way God shares his character and purposes with his people.
- They should be aware of how their own life stories fit into the ongoing purposes of God and allow them to be shaped by relevant biblical images, metaphors, and stories as well as basic beliefs and principles.
- Since good compromises are more a product of good character than good decision-making capacities, leaders should continue to give priority to who they are seeking to become, not just what they would like to do.
- To have a proper perspective of the particular issue at hand, they should keep the big vocational picture in mind, both for themselves and their organizations, while never letting go of basic aims and purposes.

As Richard Higginson concludes:

If compromise is to be understood in this way, it is important to affirm the element of tension. Where this is lacking, compromise easily degenerates into uncritical conformity, a complacent acceptance of the *status quo*. The best compromises are those which take the "promise" part of the word "compromise" seriously. In other words, they are creative, and hold out hope for something better in the future.[31]

Leadership and Service

A Seminal Discussion of Servanthood

Robert Greenleaf, during his time as a manager at AT&T, introduced the idea of servanthood into the discussion of leadership. A Quaker by background, Greenleaf encountered the writings of the famous German novelist Herman Hesse at a critical point in his life. Especially influential was a story in Hesse's novel *Journey to the East*.[32] This story, influenced by Eastern thought, gave Greenleaf the idea of the servant as leader. In his writings, however, this idea is placed in a broader Christian, specifically Quaker, framework.[33] While Greenleaf occasionally refers to the presence of servant-leader motifs in the lives of such figures as Lao Tzu, Buddha, and Confucius, he mainly draws attention to the fact that "the idea of servant is deep in our Judeo-Christian heritage. Servant (along with serve and service) appears in the Bible more than thirteen hundred times."[34] Greenleaf did not have any formal theological or ethical training, but as Anne Fraker comments, alongside his workplace experiences and meditation, "He developed a sense of ethics from his own Judeo-Christian upbringing and later Quaker affiliation."[35] Others also acknowledge "the importance of Quaker values in shaping [his] orientation."[36]

While he does not often explicitly mention Jesus, Greenleaf regards him as the archetypal leader, focusing primarily on Jesus's distinctive teaching and behavior. Some of Greenleaf's favorite stories are of Jesus washing his disciples' feet and his encounter with the woman who had committed adultery.[37] Jesus as a sensitive, moral, and compassionate leader particularly catches his attention. For Greenleaf, Jesus's inspired and creative contribution was obscured by the codifying and co-opting work of the church in subsequent centuries.[38] The early Protestant Reformers and their more radical Anabaptist counterparts removed some of the accretions and enabled us to see the original Jesus again. Although Greenleaf regards Quaker leaders such as George Fox and John Woolman as operating in a spirit similar to that of Jesus, he is also critical of them for failing to develop an adequate structure for "a society of equals in which there is a strong lay leadership."[39]

Greenleaf advocates the relevance of servant leadership for the market-place, not just the church. This runs counter to the power-seeking, take-charge, command-and-control stance so commonly associated with leadership. For him, servant leadership means placing the good of others and the organization over the leader's self-interest. While this contradicts the abuse of power, such leadership does not avoid its responsible exercise and influence. Servant leadership is not a kind of antileadership, for leading takes place through foresight, courageous action, and accountability, even though such actions happen in the context of shared decision making among rather than over others.

From Greenleaf's writings, Larry Spears has identified the following critical characteristics of servant leadership. It is the ability to:

- listen to others and discern the will of a group,
- have empathy with one's fellow workers,
- help make both others and oneself whole,
- rely on persuasion rather than coercion and positional authority,
- think and act beyond day-to-day realities,
- hold in trust and be a good steward of an institution, and
- build community among one's colleagues and fellow workers.

These characteristics, however, are by no means exhaustive.[40] In his list of key working principles of servant leadership, Walter Wright — influenced by both Greenleaf and De Pree—notes that leadership is about influence and service, vision and hope, character and trust, relationships and power, dependency and accountability.[41] Some adherents of servant leadership further stress its compatibility with valuing diverse opinions rather than conformity, creative rather than disruptive conflict, and exhibiting tough rather than purely supportive caring.

The Later Variant of Stewardship

A more recent variation of the servant leadership model is one revolving around stewardship developed by Peter Block, building on his earlier work titled *The Empowered Manager*.[42] As shown in the subtitle of his *Stewardship: Choosing Service over Self-Interest*, the idea of service is central to his approach.[43] For Block, stewardship is the "umbrella idea" for achieving change in the way institutions are governed, especially in the challenging areas of the distribution of power, purpose, and rewards. This goes beyond more technical fix-it style programs by highlighting the importance of seeing one's role as primarily that of a trustee who adds value to something valuable one is passing on to the next generation. Stewardship "is the willingness to be accountable for the well-being of the larger organization by operating in service, rather than control, of those around us."[44] This runs counter to the attitude of self-interest that so often drives leaders.

Block's preference is to retire the language of leadership in favor of the language of stewardship. Doing so involves moving from patriarchy to partnership and from security to adventure. To achieve this, leaders must move beyond dominance and the wish for dependency and be willing to make full disclosure and develop more open and inclusive managerial practices, offer choice to and build capability among employees, and build widespread financial accountability throughout the organization. This results in the creation of a balance rather than a hierarchy of power within an organization, a commitment to the entire community rather than to individuals or teams, empowerment of all to help define the organization's purpose and ethos, and an equitable rather than an unbalanced distribution of rewards. The ultimate proof of the effectiveness of such an approach is whether it passes the test of the marketplace while at the same time continuing to incorporate the concerns of the Spirit.

According to Block, while putting an emphasis on service and stewardship would result in "the end of the era of leaders," it "would not eliminate leaders."[45] People would still function in significant roles and positions, but they would operate from among rather than over others, seek participation more than make a presentation, establish connections before expressing content, and ask questions as much as give answers. They would also recognize that change emerges as people are encouraged to make unique contributions and as conversations take place within various parts and levels of an organization.

Though this view has been criticized for being otherworldly and not facing the hard realities of life in the marketplace, companies that have adopted this philosophy of servant leadership have done extremely well. Among them are Herman Miller, ServiceMaster, and TD Industries, all of whom have been featured in lists of highly profitable corporations and the best companies to work for. The cross-cultural potential of this model of leadership has also been advocated.[46]

Still, this model has limitations and difficulties at both the religious and the practical levels. Greenleaf focuses on Jesus as a moral example, falling under the critique of Ken Blanchard, who says that "when people talk about servant-leadership, Jesus is often a model, without even referring to his ultimate sacrifice."[47] And while at times Greenleaf places a strong emphasis on the Spirit—as in his remark that the "Spirit is the driving force behind the motive to serve"[48]—he tends to place too little stress on the specific content of the Spirit's character and role. This might also explain his more generic rather than specifically Christian references to the Spirit,[49] probably a result of the Quaker emphasis on "the inner Spirit" or the influence of Hesse's mystical interests. Advocates of servant leadership have sometimes quoted Jewish mystics and Buddhist masters as well as Jesus and the Hebrew prophets.

For some people in leadership positions, the language of servanthood has negative connotations. As Shirley Roels has pointed out, servanthood is sometimes understood in terms of overly self-effacing and other-determined ways of operating. These have more to do with servitude than with service. The word is particularly open to abuse when applied to those in a position of disadvantage or forced inequality, such as many women and minority groups. In these cases, the word does not retain its biblical sense: the status of servants was based on the positions and responsibilities of the people they served. Gone, then, are the loftier biblical overtones of being a servant of the One who is above all others, namely, God, and of having the responsibility of keeping his purposes and ways of operating firmly in view rather than others' commands or wants.[50] Susan Nelson Dunfee goes further and advocates friendship rather than servanthood as the better model for encouraging wholeness to those who are still generally regarded as having a second-class status.[51] While not taking up this proposal, there are good grounds for taking Roels's concerns into account in speaking about servant leadership where female leaders are in view.

In his book *No Longer Servants but Friends*, Edward Zaragoza agrees with the critics of servant leadership just mentioned. He goes further, however, in asserting that this paradigm wrongly values the individual rather than the community, doing instead of being, and giving up power over empowering others. Because this demands that leaders become more than they can be, it ends up making them less than they really are. For these reasons the model of friendship is preferable.[52] As Siang-Yan Tan argues, however, Zaragoza confuses servanthood with servitude. Genuine servanthood values the community as well as the individual, being as well as doing, empowerment as well as yielding power where relevant, and does not deny an element of friendship in the leader's relationship with colleagues.[53]

While Greenleaf did insist that a leader is a servant first and only in the wake of that service a leader, many who describe themselves as servant leaders continue to give prominence to the second word over the first. In their dealings with others, they may be more approachable, but they still retain close control of what happens, supervise most of what takes place, and reserve the right to make basic decisions on their own. Ultimately, for all the appearance of being consultative and responsive, they operate in ways that are not much different from those of traditional leaders. Such people have co-opted the language of servant leadership for their own agendas and purposes. Sad to say, this has often been the case in the church and in many religious organizations.

Overall, the word "servanthood" is in danger of being viewed through the distorting lens of its contemporary misuse by those in authority. It is also in danger of being viewed too little in terms of its full Christian meaning. The trouble with the phrase "servant leadership," therefore, is that though it moves away from inadequate views of leading others, it still gets the order of the words wrong. "Leadership" remains the key term and "servant" the qualifier. What we need today are not, as is so often suggested, more *servant leaders* but, properly understood, more *leading servants*.[54] We need people who will serve the mission, structures, and members of an organization in a way that goes beyond their peers and points the way forward for others.

It is not always easy to work out how to make the notion of servanthood operational in organizations. Too often the call to be a servant has an idealistic ring about it that does not sit well with the challenges and compromises of so much daily work. Yet clues to what it entails are evident. One can look at the contribution of those in an organization who are regarded as its most appreciated servants. It can be seen in those who do not delegate difficult matters to others but rather take full responsibility for them. Servanthood is evident in those who depend on others for wisdom instead of relying purely on their own resources, those who take a stand on matters even at the cost of their positions, and those who are willing to suffer voluntary loss for the good of their organization.

Some years ago, one of us visited a monthly breakfast attended by twenty-five Christian businesspeople from a range of churches. After eating, it was their custom for a member of the group to explain a pressure or difficulty in his or her work. On this particular day, the case in question revolved around the issue of mandatory downsizing. The senior manager presenting the case had to fire one of his two assistants. Both were highly competent associates. One had more experience and worked longer for the company. The other was going through a time of marital stress and loss of confidence and was not performing as well. The presenter felt that seniority should probably be the prime consideration. Yet he also sensed that firing the junior assistant would put that person's marriage and self-esteem under even greater stress.

Discussion continued for some time, and as the breakfast drew to a close, the presenter said that as a result of the group's deliberations, he had a growing sense that he should keep both assistants, promote the senior assistant to his own position, and fire himself. Though this entailed considerable risk in an increasingly problematic job market, he was willing to take this in seeking alternative work. This was a striking example of someone who was willing to sacrifice himself for the sake of his colleagues.

Such an approach to leadership is not only applicable to those at the top of an organization; it can also take place at any level. Especially significant, however, are the abilities to faithfully articulate, embody, and extend the mission of the organization and to draw in and empower others to implement and enhance it.

Conclusion

The qualities of faithfulness, integrity, and service discussed in this chapter are most perfectly embodied in Jesus, the ultimate role model not only for life but also for leadership (Heb. 12:2–3). They are also modeled in the life and work of Paul, whose faithfulness to his calling in the midst of difficult challenges and circumstances, quest to display integrity while remaining sensitive to situations and flexible in practice, servant heart, and actions—in promoting Christ rather than himself and developing the leadership gifts of everyone around him—stand out so impressively. This highlights two things. First, leadership is about who a person is before and alongside what he or she does. It grows out of personal wholeness as well as wholeness in the sense of breadth and balance of life. Such wholeness is not so much a mark of leadership as a precondition and a catalyst for it. Only by possessing it can people avoid the intrusion and the effects of the shadow side of leadership. These include always needing to be in charge and have everything under control, inflicting pathology and inadequacies on others, falling into the messiah trap with its attendant danger of workaholism, becoming a mere persona rather than a genuine person, and failing to overcome the inability to share weakness or face failure. Second, because leadership is ultimately about who a person is as a whole, it is fundamentally about followership before it is about leadership. It is only through the gift on the cross of Jesus's life and the gift of the Spirit that people have any chance of developing into the kinds of people who have the capacity to serve and therefore lead others well.

Eugene Peterson catches the flavor of these two points when he notes that leaders influence followers far more by the context out of which they live—body language, personal values, social relationships, dress, consumer choices, and chosen companions—than the text they articulate. Leadership is not primarily a skill, although it employs skills. It is a way of living that suffuses everything we do and are. Leadership is a way of being in a family and marriage, a way of being among friends, a way of going to work, a way of climbing mountains, but most basically a way of following Jesus. And so, in a culture that accords enormous attention to leadership, it is essential that we take a long, hard look at what is prior and foundational to it—namely, "followership" (Mark 1:17). *Followership* gets us moving obediently in a way of life that is visible and audible in Jesus, a way of speaking, thinking, imagining, and praying that is congruent with immediate realities of "kingdom" living. Following enters into a way of life that is given its character and shape by *the* leader. Following involves picking up rhythms and ways of doing things that are mostly unsaid. Following means that one cannot separate what the leader is doing and the way she or he is doing it. For those of us who are in positions of leadership—as parents, teachers, pastors, employers, physicians, lawyers, students, farmers, writers— our following skills take priority over our leadership skills. Leadership that is not well grounded in followership—following Jesus—is dangerous to both the church and the world.[55]

6

leader development: leaving a legacy

Leader development is the sine qua non of leadership. Leadership is for a lifetime and requires that leaders be engaged in learning and developing over the duration of their careers and lives. While the context of one's leadership will change over the course of time, still personal discovery is the precursor to leadership development at every stage of life. Thus developing as a leader begins with developing the inner life. In this way, leader development is a process of increasing self-knowledge and self-awareness of one's strengths and challenges, one's blind spots and cravings. Moreover, development ought to move the leader to higher levels of moral awareness and spiritual development, and this requires cognitive ability and the motivation to lead with maturity. The signs of moral maturity in a leader include humility, self-management, decorum, being temperate, having poise, generosity of spirit, accepting responsibility with no blame toward others, and a sense of expansiveness.

An important distinction is leader development as different from leadership development. Leader development is inward focused and seeks to develop self-awareness, skills, and talents, and operates with the premise that increasing self-knowledge leads to improved leadership capacity. Leadership development can be thought of as inclusive to the team, organization, community, and company, and it seeks to expand the capacity for leadership all throughout the enterprise.

Because leadership is very contextual, the leader must continually develop and adapt to new, evolving, and unknown conditions. Just when you think you've got it, it changes—and so must you. Increasing readiness for change on the part of the leader is important for leader effectiveness. How then is it possible to think about relevant leader development when change is the constant? Indeed, this requires developing the inner life and soul of the leader in order to prepare for the outer expression of leadership. Change itself is instructive if one is able to quickly synthesize new information and adapt to new conditions.

A pressing question that quickly surfaces is which approach to leader development is most effective. There are many forms and means to developing leaders; the most common are outside-in approaches, including 360-degree feedback, mentoring, and coaching. By contrast, inside-out approaches involve assessments plus reflective practices, such as journaling, to increase self-awareness; often retreats are used to accelerate this process.

Many argue that the only way to learn how to lead is to actually lead; experiential approaches are frequently used to give emerging leaders a chance to lead and refine the skills necessary for effective leadership. Experiential learning projects engage potential leaders in solving real-time organizational challenges and provide valuable feedback leading to increased leadership capacity. In order for rich learning to result from experiential learning, the aspiring leader is encouraged to engage in mindful awareness—that is, being fully engaged in the present moment. Mindfulness practice enables leadership learners to be fully aware of what they are doing and what can be learned from the leadership tasks and challenges encountered. Accountability with respect to mindful awareness is important—simply being asked on a regular basis "What have you done in the past two weeks and what have you learned from your experiences?" increases the impact of experiential learning.[1]

A comprehensive approach to leader development involves at least four skill areas: technical, relational, conceptual, and ethical.

Technical Skills

Many begin the leadership journey through the process of developing a particular area of expertise, such as accounting, teaching, or counseling. Developing technical expertise is the foundation for developing as a leader. Technical skills provide the basis for knowing and applying methodologies and frameworks for how to approach tasks and projects. Mastery of one's technical area(s) of expertise leads to seeing oneself and being perceived by others as competent. Important questions to consider include the following: Am I using my skills and abilities in ways that add value to others and to the organization? Do others, especially senior leaders, see my contribution as generative and essential?

While competence in one area does not necessarily translate to the same level of competence in another area, still, mastery in at least one area leads to confidence and garners respect. While technical expertise is fundamental to one's ability to work well and accomplish goals, technical mastery is not enough to qualify one for leadership. More is needed, especially relational and conceptual skills.

Relational Skills

As one advances to higher levels of influence, one must utilize one's relationship skills as the conduit to acquiring referent power, leading to influence, and the ability to get work done through others. While one's technical knowledge is important and necessary, it becomes less important as one moves to higher levels of influence. Psychologist and Harvard professor Robert Kegan has this to say about relationships: Who comes into a person's life may be the single most important factor of what that life becomes—who comes into our lives is a matter of our ability to recruit and to be recruited by others.[2] This idea of recruiting and being recruited speaks directly to the ability to build and sustain meaningful personal and professional relationships across the landscape of one's leadership. Each person must ask: Am I the type of person others want to recruit into their lives and organizations? And am I recruiting others into my life and organization who are capable and possess moral and spiritual maturity?

Today we see an important shift happening, one mentioned earlier: we are moving from knowledge workers to relationship workers. When we examine companies at the top of the list of the best companies to work for and ask what is it about those companies that makes them exemplary, the answer is rather simple: it's relationships. The best companies create the means for people to build strong, numerous, rewarding personal relationships at work. This shift is especially important for women, who are adept at building relationships. Because work is a relationship, not a transaction, going forward it will be more and more difficult for companies with transaction-based cultures to attract the best talent. The top reason people leave organizations is fractured relationships with bosses or coworkers. Leaders who are adept at building strong and positive relationships create a firm foundation for organizational success. According to *Fortune* magazine,[3] the new corporate MVPs are not those with the best ideas; the most valuable players are those who can harvest the best ideas from others. Effective leaders use relational skills to help others give birth to their most creative ideas.

Conceptual Skills

Leadership is often associated with vision, strategy, and problem solving; these are examples of the conceptual responsibilities of leading. To some extent, developing conceptual problem-solving skills involves learning from doing, and this includes failure. Learning what works in a particular situation may also be a matter of learning from what does not work.[4] Developing an approach to solving complicated challenges hinges on the capacity to embrace complexity and to search for the simplicity on the other side of complexity. In such cases it is often far more useful to discover what is working well in the system or situation rather than searching for the root cause of the problem. Taking an appreciative-inquiry approach involves studying the conditions that lead to success and replicating them to increase the probability of better and more productive performance individually and as a group. An appreciative approach is far more generative and positive, and leads to an increased sense of well-being; this approach can be used to discover what is the group or organization's highest aspiration or most inspiring vision for the future.

Vision can be thought of as a story. Who are the characters, and what is the journey of challenge and overcoming obstacles to reach the desired destination? The centerpiece of the story is an inspirational purpose. Why does this vision matter and to whom? Dr. Martin Luther King Jr. was a masterful orator of vision as storytelling, most notably demonstrated in his "I Have a Dream" speech, in which he proclaimed, "And so even though we face the difficulties of today and tomorrow, I still have a dream. It is a dream deeply rooted in the American dream. I have a dream that one day this nation will rise up and live out the true meaning of its creed: We hold these truths to be self-evident, that all men are created equal. Now is the time to make justice a reality for all of God's children."[5] Dr. King connected the laws of a nation to laws of God—equality for all.

Vision often calls for change and requires a strategy for leading change toward the vision. In the current reality of constant shifts to which organizations and individuals must adapt, leading change is the hallmark of organizational leadership. Leading change and strategy is an advanced leadership skill requiring a great deal of conceptual understanding of the context of the organization and the future that is not yet seen. With increased levels of responsibility, leaders depend mainly on their relational and conceptual skills to lead people and organizations through change, which requires a strategy to move toward an inspiring and compelling vision.

Ethical Skills

Leaders of faith will want to consider their moral and spiritual development as part of their ethical leader development.

Moral Development

Moral development can be understood as the foundation for ethical and moral decision making in leadership. Research has suggested there are at least two moral developmental paths—a concern for justice and a concern for care—and these tend to be gendered in some respects. C. Gilligan and J. Attanucci found that both men and women demonstrate concerns about justice and care, and tend to focus on one of these moral domains over the other.[6] Further, in discussing moral dilemmas women tend to utilize a care orientation, and men tend to utilize a justice orientation. They concluded that indeed there are two moral orientations, justice and care, and that for some in their study, these two domains overlap; one-third of their subject population dealt with the moral dilemmas using both justice and care as criteria for moral decision making. J. G. Smetana, M. Killen, and E. Turiel have suggested that the moral constructs of justice and care coexist in individual reasoning among men and women, and that the ways these constructs are applied depend on the context and the personal importance of the issue(s) being considered.[7]

Values Development

Researchers see a strong connection between values and leadership behavior; indeed, most researchers would agree that values are predictors of behavior, and this includes ethical leadership.[8] Jean Piaget suggested that morality and action share an intimate relationship, that action logically follows morality.[9] "Values have always been regarded as important because they are assumed to play a major role in behavior."[10] Theorists note that the relative importance one places on a particular value will determine the degree to which that value influences action.[11] M. Rokeach understood the power of values and their influence in guiding human behavior. Values are commonly linked with behavior, such that values are demonstrated in the leader's priorities, decision making, and actions taken.[12]

Research has suggested that values develop over the life span, and important developmental sources of values include relationships with parents, peers, teachers, and mentors.[13] Certain contexts facilitate values development, such as the cultural setting of one's upbringing, including social/political influences, educational settings, and of course religious/faith contexts. Significant life experiences, especially those that are challenging—marriage, starting a family, and the death of a loved one—play a key role in the development of values, such as professional roles.[14]

Highly prioritized values for female leaders are benevolence and achievement. These values represent self-transcendence, which motivates people to accept others as equals and show concern for their welfare through benevolence. Often benevolence is animated by one's spiritual life. Achievement represents a self-enhancement value, motivating people to pursue one's own success or ambition by demonstrating influence over others.[15]

Further, as described earlier, the literature on women's moral development and women's ways of leading maintains that women operate from an "ethic of care" supported by an emphasis on relationships that foster growth and offer mutual empathy and empowerment—which seems to describe benevolence. The classic literature on leadership effectiveness, using Robert Blake and Jane Mouton's managerial grid, confirms that effective leadership exhibits both a concern for results (achievement) and for people and relationships (benevolence).[16] Last, the model of transforming leadership, proposed by James MacGregor Burns, affirms that effective leadership begins with a moral motivation to enhance followers' self-worth and support their dignity as human beings.[17]

Perhaps benevolence and achievement are complementary values needed for effective leadership, where benevolence values mediate achievement values in the direction of service to others rather than service to self.[18]

Men tend to emphasize security and self-direction values. Security is the motivation to create stability and safety for self and others, including one's family, and values belonging and reciprocity. Self-direction values represent creativity and exploration, along with autonomy, freedom, and independence as well as choosing one's own goals and exercising control that leads to mastery. Overall self-direction values openness to change.[19] These values seem to align with the literature on moral development, which suggests men's development emphasizes individualism and separateness.[20] As mentioned earlier, men tend to utilize a justice perspective, in which fairness and formal rules of conduct are important, since people's interests and prerogatives often conflict. Thus a rule of justice is needed to adjudicate differences. To solve moral dilemmas, one turns to the rules of justice. Justice responds to a world that is experienced as hierarchical with relationships of dominance and subordination, where problems are an opportunity to determine the rights and claims of individuals.[21]

What shapes values also shapes one's leadership. The developmental sources of values and the moral orientation toward justice and care guide leadership actions. What is emerging is an increasing belief that values and ethical leadership are intricately tied together and always have been, even if this close association has not been acknowledged directly.[22]

Moral Stress

Ethical leadership has an inherent paradox. Dedication to consistency with regard to moral commitments often creates conflict due to competing commitments, resulting in a particular type of stress. This challenge is captured well by L. K. Trevino, L. P. Hartman, and M. Brown. They note that we want our leaders to be both moral managers and moral persons.[23] Ethical leaders are morally attentive to the moral content of events embedded in the multiplicity of the leader's roles, functions, and relationships; therefore, moral decisions are ever-present in the world of leaders.[24] The moral will that drives a leader to act with moral integrity in the many aspects of leading sets up the conditions for conflicting goals, creating outcomes where simultaneous moral commitments cannot be met. This paradoxical state creates a particular kind of stress called "moral stress."

Developing as an ethical leader requires increasing one's capacity to deal with moral stress. S. J. Reynolds, B. P. Owens, and A. L. Rubenstein have defined moral stress as "a psychological state (both cognitive and emotional) marked by anxiety and unrest to an individual's uncertainty about his or her ability to fulfill relevant moral obligations."[25] Moral stress appears when managers and leaders experience conflicting claims, typically between self and stakeholders, when moral obligations personally and professionally collide, resulting in a "right versus right" decision.[26] Moral stress results from enduring conditions that are not easily remedied, "where no effort or resource can remove the conflict."[27] Prolonged moral stress can have deleterious effects on moral reasoning, leading an individual's resolve to be weakened and creating the potential for immoral behavior. The question arises: How might the negative effects of moral stress be mitigated? Sustainable resilience offers one possible adaptive response to the consequences associated with moral stress.

Leader Development and Resilience

By way of definition, the concept of resilience can be explained in a variety of ways. Resilience is the adaptive capacity to rebound, to demonstrate buoyancy or recuperative power, to continue forward in the face of adversity.[28] The Latin root *resilient* means to jump back or recoil, and applies to both physics and human endeavor. Physically, synonyms include pliability, flexibility, elasticity, and suppleness; symbolically, resilience includes spirit, hardiness, toughness, strength, and resistance. Broadly construed, resilience is a process, an outcome, a defiant steady state, and something one comes to know is present only after the fact.[29]

Resilience can be understood as a response that takes two forms: recovery in the wake of an acute stressor and sustainability in response to chronic difficulties. The human attributes that support resilience in both forms may be quite similar, and the differences are worth noting. Recovery is the returning to homeostasis, to a more balanced state following an acutely stressful experience. Sustainable resilience is called for in response to chronically stressful times, particularly those that give rise to choices concerning values and priorities. Sustainable resilience asks how people sustain well-being "in a dynamic environment characterized by ongoing challenges that threaten to disrupt engagements that give life meaning and purpose."[30]

How might sustainable resilience enable ethical leaders to maintain moral behavior while enduring moral stress? Sustainable resilience is characterized by heightened awareness and a sense of one's own identity. Reynolds, Owens, and Rubenstein suggest that for each role played in society, there is a sense of identity. Often described as a source of meaning, the identity of each role also includes expectations for action. Sustainable resilience builds on the action capacity of identity—whereas moral stress can function as a way to shut down action, sustainable resilience acts to sustain action in the face of enduring difficulty.[31] Moreover, sustainable resilience animates the willingness to make moral choices toward preserving values and purposes associated with the leader's ethical identity and role responsibilities. While moral stress seems to be concomitant with ethical leadership, sustainable resilience provides an adaptive coping mechanism for meeting the challenges of making moral choices in the context of leading. Ethical leaders who find within themselves sustainable resilience will be more likely to uphold moral commitments while enduring moral stress.

Much of the research undertaken to grasp the dimensions of resilience emerges from the fields of psychology and health; additionally, the topic has found wide appeal in the social sciences, including management and leadership. As Diane Coutu points out, resilience is something that can be measured and is highly sought after in recruits and employees identified as having high potential for advancement in large organizations.[32] Whatever one thinks about resilience, it is a "multifaceted construct with economic, historical, political, and sociocultural dimensions."[33]

Much has happened in our world in recent times to bring the topic of resilience to the foreground as we collectively strive together toward a more compassionate world. Of interest to this discussion on leader development is the question of how resilience develops in leaders. Religious traditions—including Christianity, Judaism, and Islam, all Abrahamic in origin—offer wisdom on developing resilience in leaders and organizations.

Judaism, Christianity, and Islam have each preserved resilience narratives that ground the individual or the endeavor into a deep understanding of identity and purpose that encourages listeners to persevere and overcome their present adversities. Collectively, interpretations of Wisdom literature from religious/spiritual traditions form a rich conceptual basis from which we can readily acknowledge resilience as an important quality of leadership sustainability. More emphatically, it is a necessary quality of character in order to cope and overcome both the inevitable challenges within the person and the assaults from the outside. But where does it come from, and how is it formed? The Hebrew Bible and its sages draw lessons of resilience from Psalm 1:3: "He will be like a tree firmly planted by streams of water." The scriptural metaphor of a tree, developed throughout the Hebrew Bible, gives a reference point to ground the faithful in the image of stability and renewal; the tree draws nourishment and renewal from water, a life-giving source, thus increasing its stability and resilience. Such a tree is much more likely to endure hardship and challenge because it remains in close proximity to the source of its replenishment. Likewise, the story of Hijrah in Islam also fosters images of resilience. This narrative takes Muslims back to the roots of their fifth-century beginnings, when Muhammad left Mecca and emigrated to Medina. From the historical recounting, specific active meanings are extrapolated and retold. To the early Muslims Hijrah meant giving up all forms of paganism, submitting to the will of Allah, respecting one another, achieving peace, overcoming superstition and ignorance, pursuing knowledge, respecting the mind, ceasing fighting over resources, working for the common good, and achieving unity and harmony. As one commentator writes, "Hijrah replaced fear with hope, aimlessness with purpose, statelessness with freedom and confidence in the future."[34] Christians also draw from metaphor, history, and narrative to contextualize their challenges in order to be inspired to carry on. One example would be Paul, when he wrote the following to the Corinthians:

> We do not want you to be uninformed, brothers and sisters, about the troubles we experienced in the province of Asia. We were under great pressure, far beyond our ability to endure, so that we despaired of life itself. Indeed, we felt we had received the sentence of death. But this happened that we might not rely

on ourselves but on God, who raises the dead. He has delivered us from such a deadly peril, and he will deliver us again. On him we have set our hope that he will continue to deliver us, as you help us by your prayers. Then many will give thanks on our behalf for the gracious favor granted us in answer to the prayers of many. (2 Cor. 1:8–11)

Within such language are notions of community, obligation, faith, belief, and hope, and the spiritual disciplines of prayer and gratitude. These elements form an interrelated dynamic that is visible in much of the historical narrative and teachings of the New Testament. Christians have a rich resource from which to draw.

The social sciences have also contributed to our understanding of the dynamics of resilience. Laura Reave's "Spiritual Values and Practices Related to Leadership Effectiveness" is an example: a helpful review of 150 studies that propose a spiritual leadership paradigm.[35] Jerry Patterson's "Resilience in the Face of Adversity" is another example of efforts to unpack, clarify, and apply this concept.[36] Included within this body of research is recognition that resilience may best be understood as part of a spiritual dynamic connecting leadership and resilience to spirituality.

Spiritual Development

Spiritual development becomes a necessary component of ethical leader development in the journey to expanding the capacity for resilience. Indeed, spirituality, defined and explored in detail earlier in this book, is vitally connected to resilience and is further developed through a heightened sense of conscious awareness and reflection.

Conscious leaders have the capacity to identify multiple levels of self-observation,[37] including centeredness, self-motivation, coherence, insight, creativity, inspiration, and transcendence.[38] As such, it has been shown that conscious leaders possess a clear purpose in life and in work. It is well documented that spiritual practices such as prayer, meditation, and contemplation greatly assist in the development of consciousness.[39]

Spiritual development for leaders entails helping them to understand the deeper connection between moral values and ethical leadership actions, and decisions made on behalf of the organization and society. Spiritual development as part of leader development requires a good deal of self-reflection and meditative thinking, with the capacity to assess personal/organizational congruence. Parker Palmer states that action and contemplation, while at first appearing to be contradictory ideas, actually inform each other, not as opposites but rather as two ends of a continuum that seek the same end: to celebrate life.[40] The active and the contemplative are paradoxical, held together by honoring the desire to lead and simultaneously maintaining the integrity of one's identity. Leading with resilience spiritually is a choice to live the creative tension inherent in the paradox of action and contemplation.

In the life of activity lurks a kind of frenzy and violence. The demands of modern life seem to threaten and bewilder us at every turn. In the contemplative life resides the opportunity for deep reflection, learning, and renewal. "The function of contemplation in all its forms is to penetrate illusion and help us to touch reality."[41] We all carry positive and negative illusions about ourselves and our world, and contemplation is a gentle but substantive way to confront such illusions. The self-confronting nature of contemplation brings us to integrity and authenticity, thus making our leadership more honest and real. Palmer makes this recommendation: leaders must learn to sit in solitude and community, exploring not strategies and tactics but their own inner lives. There is an inner teacher who has guidance to offer—but we need both inward stillness and other people to help us hear its voice.[42] The "voice" Palmer describes also lives in literature, poetry, stories, and sacred texts, all of which serve as a means for approaching spiritual insight through contemplation. To live fully embracing both action and contemplation is to seek the hidden wholeness—and when we do this "we begin to learn compassion for all human beings who share the limits of life itself."[43]

Through reflective practice common in religious and spiritual traditions, conscious leaders are keenly aware of the deeper meaning of their leadership and its impact on multiple stakeholders. Because conscious leadership has a connection to religiosity and spirituality, these constructs (religion and spirituality) enrich an understanding of effective leadership. Spiritual development as a component of leader development is gaining mainstream acceptance as a means to create more ethically centered leaders. Moreover, as work becomes increasingly complex, demanding higher-order thinking, workers are seeking meaning and significance from their employment.

Spiritual development involves increasing acceptance across differences. Religious pluralism is commonplace in many secular and faith-based organizations; as such, leaders would do well to surface common-ground concepts, such as the Golden Rule, to create community and undergird the moral foundation of work. Indeed, through time and across cultures, religious teachings stress loving others as ourselves.[44]

Religion continues to affect ethical leadership over the course of life. James Fowler suggests that many young adults shift from an uncritical acceptance of their religious heritage to a more critical evaluation of previously accepted beliefs and practices.[45] This may include reexamining one's belief system or experimenting with alternative religions or spiritual practices. Cross-sectional and longitudinal studies suggest a general increase in the importance of religion in the latter years of life.[46] James Loder proposes four phases of spiritual development: (1) the awakening, often precipitated by a deeply unresolved conflict, whether with another or oneself; an awakening regarding the conflict involves the intense realization of an "aha" moment, a sudden, clear, existential insight regarding oneself and one's relation to God with regard to the conflict; (2) the purgation, the passionate movement toward a closer and more intimate relationship with God; (3) the illumination, which leads one to a deeply interior place toward an understanding of the depth of love God has toward all people and in particular to oneself; (4) toward unification, which is the unification of one's illuminated spiritual awakening with the entirety of one's life to create unity and integrity.[47] Loder comments that the middle years of life are a period of turning inward in a spiritual journey in search of meaning "to give coherence to the vast array of experiences"[48] lived in one's lifetime. The deepening of spiritual development can coincide with the desire to lead more authentically.

Paul's Idea of Leadership Development as Legacy

The apostle Paul created an approach to developing leaders that Whittington and his colleagues refer to as self-perpetuating, with the intent of leaving a long and enduring legacy.[49] Paul's intention was to develop leaders to carry on the work of spreading the gospel. In this way Paul served as a teacher of leaders. It has been said that teaching others to lead is the highest level of leadership.[50]

The leadership lessons of Paul are timeless and offer a comprehensive approach to leader development that serves as a model for us today. Paul's exemplary approach to developing the next generation of leaders includes, first and foremost, careful attention to his own leadership, so that he might serve as a role model to all, someone worthy of imitation.[51] Paul's mission to build and grow the church throughout the Roman Empire required that he lead so as to create future leaders, and to do this he led with authenticity and transparency, so that his leadership practice might be easily adopted by others. To this end, Paul practiced leadership as an influence process without asserting his authority. In the spirit of servant leadership, he was a servant first and then a leader, follower-centered and not self-centered. As an authentic leader, Paul showed sincere affection and emotion toward his followers.[52] At the same time, he was bold when faced with opposition, holding steadfast to his values and convictions. In this way he demonstrated moral authority.[53] Central to leaving a legacy through one's leadership is being perceived by followers as an exemplary leader worthy of imitation.

governance: practicing faith-based leadership

This chapter addresses the need for better, more faith-informed leaders at the senior and board level, where strategic decisions are made. The leadership literature has offered very little on the topic of senior governance and Christian leadership. A good deal has been written on board development and board responsibility, but too little has been written on senior board level leadership from a faith perspective. This chapter aims to close this gap.

Leadership at the top of an organization is somewhat mysterious. Often those in the organization are quite removed from the board members, who serve to ensure the long-term health and sustainability of the enterprise. "Boards of directors can be characterized as elite decision-making teams that operate in complex environments and produce output that is mostly cognitive in nature."[1] Criticism of boards is frequent and direct when organizations and the leaders in them fail ethically or financially. "Surely the board knew" is a well-worn phrase and infers the board could have or should have done something to prevent the collapse from happening. This raises the question: What is the leadership responsibility of a board of directors?

For nonprofit board members, the qualities necessary for effective leadership include the following:

- *Integrity:* demonstrating zero tolerance for unethical behavior, both for themselves and their colleagues.
- *Passion:* real enthusiasm for the mission of the organization.
- *Organizational skills:* qualities that add value to the organization, such as marketing, finance, or human resources.
- *Independence:* having no unique business, financial, or personal relationships with the organization.
- *Mature confidence:* speaking out and actively participating in board and committee deliberations.
- *Corporate manners:* recognizing the difference between productively participating in discussions and counterproductively dominating deliberations through the volume or length of comments; must be able to work productively with the CEO of the organization without micromanaging.
- *A sense of context:* making relevant, informed comments focused on the specific aspect of the issue being considered.[2]

Leadership qualities for board members of for-profit enterprises focus on technical expertise, primarily industry knowledge, followed by strategy and financial or audit capabilities. The skills most often lacking among board members are technology, human resources–talent management, and international or global understanding.[3] These skills are critically important as board members are expected to make substantive contributions to one or more typical standing committees, which include (1) audit, (2) compensation, (3) executive, and (4) governance and nominating. The personal qualities of sought-after board members are high personal integrity in one's personal and professional life, strong communication skills, and interpersonal adeptness, plus sound judgment.[4]

Boards that add value to an organization and secure its long-term sustainability are forward looking and include members who have the expertise to scan the external environment and respond to changing conditions appropriately. Populating the board with capable and competent members begins with knowing what current and future experience gaps exist. "An incoming chair should try to imagine what his or her board might look like, ideally, three years from now. What kinds of skills and experience not currently in place will help fulfill the company's long-term strategy?"[5]

Defining the boundaries between the board and chief executive and management staff is critical to minimizing misunderstandings. Establishing role clarity on an annual basis is a productive exercise. Board members who spend time understanding the organization and its partners and constituents, competitors and customers, are more informed and better able to engage in strategic decision making. A high level of engagement as a board member leads to increased meaning, purpose, inspiration, and the opportunity to enhance one's reputation as a board member and to extend one's personal network.

Securing a seat on a corporate board is a function of networking, possessing the right skills, and having previous board experience. Service on a nonprofit board is often the best place to develop board-level leadership experience. While current and former CEOs are the most sought-after board recruits, the role is open to others willing to serve.

Strategic Focus

One of the most important functions of the board of directors is to work closely with the CEO or executive director to determine the strategic focus of the organization. Max De Pree's directive to define reality as the first responsibility of leadership captures the starting point for strategic thinking and planning.[6] Strategy formulation begins with developing a clear picture of the internal and external environments of the organization. The results of this discovery process are the essence of defining reality. The board will focus its attention mainly on factors in the external environment that have an impact on the organization's viability. Both for-profit and nonprofit organizations can be impacted by external domains, such as changes in the industry, shifts in the size of the targeted market segment, conditions in the economy, access to financial capital, number of and threat from competitors, legal-regulatory and political changes, demographic shifts in key client or customer groups, changes in the physical environment, cultural and technological changes in the broader society, and the availability of a well-trained pool of potential employees or volunteers. Defining reality for the organization relative to the impact of these external environmental sectors is critical to the sustainability of the organization.

According to R. M. Burton, B. Obel, and G. DeSanctis, changes in the external environment can be evaluated along two scales: complexity and unpredictability. The rate of change in a given sector indicates the degree of unpredictability for that sector relative to the organization. Complexity refers to the number of sectors affecting the organization and the degree to which those sectors are interdependent, such that a shift in one sector leads to a shift in another.[7] For example, think of a long-standing food bank in the process of defining its changing reality. The food bank owns the building where it has served the homeless and working poor in a large urban downtown area for more than twenty years. The food bank has outgrown its facility as the number of clients seeking the services of this ministry has increased, and programs offered through the food bank have ventured into youth programming. At the same time, gentrification in the food bank's physical location is pushing the poor and homeless population farther out of the city center; the food bank is realizing its clients are now living in locations where fewer resources exist to serve their various needs. As the food bank officials scan the external environment, senior leaders are seeing significant shifts in the demographic make-up of their client base: more and more younger people are homeless due to a recent economic downturn, and the food bank's clients are migrating out of the city. There is a cultural shift happening too; the downtown area is transforming into a gentrified modern habitat for urban professionals seeking to live near their places of employment in the city center. Moreover, policy decisions are impacting funding streams for this ministry. This nonprofit organization is defining its external environmental reality as moderately to moderately highly unpredictable and highly complex. The board of directors and the executive director are considering a major strategic focus shift that would include selling their building for top value to a developer, relocating the organization to the area to which the homeless are migrating, and expanding their services to include more comprehensive care, including a pantry, youth programs, skills development and job training, and housing services. This will require hiring staff with capabilities in these areas of service.

The Perils of Success

One difficulty for boards of directors in corporate America—as a result of the organizational troubles that surfaced in the 1990s and early 2000s—is finding qualified, ethical leaders who are willing and able to accept the responsibilities of serving as senior leaders. The ethical sustainability of the organization rests in large part on the board and other senior leaders; indeed, much attention is given to preventing ethical misconduct. While a good deal of attention is placed on preventing ethical failure, little attention is given to dealing with the perils of success. Organizations and the board members who oversee them would do well to consider how to prepare leaders for success.

The life of King David offers a portrait in how success of a top leader can lead to disastrous results. In their discussion of the virtue and public and private morality of leaders, D. Ludwig and C. Longnecker highlight the challenges of success. In their explanation of what they call the "Bathsheba syndrome," the authors show how success carries its own set of ethical challenges. When senior leaders reach the pinnacle of their professional careers, there is a tendency to become complacent, and even the most admired leader can lose strategic focus. Leaders at the top are obligated to act with restraint when handling privileged access to information, people, or other resources, to do otherwise leads to a slippery slope resulting in organizational disaster. The failures of King David certainly reinforce this principle. Finally, leaders who have achieved success can develop an inflated belief in their ability to manipulate or control outcomes. A kind of delusion takes hold whereby leaders believe they can cover their unethical tracks and never be found out.[8] Like King David, senior leaders with a great deal of positional authority are dangerously close to their own perils of success. Current and aspiring leaders must realize it could happen to them. Several steps can be taken to mitigate against a personal Bathsheba syndrome: (1) live a balanced life; (2) remember that you are a steward of the organization, that your primary role is to serve the organization by helping the enterprise achieve its aspirations and goals; and (3) compose an ethical team of peers who will inspire you to lead at your best and who will confront you if your actions drift in a direction that calls your character into question. The key here is to develop humility and maintain accountability.[9]

Servant Leadership

Senior leaders would do well to consider a service approach to leading by utilizing servant leadership. At the core of servant leadership are a set of attributes senior leaders are encouraged to embody, these include the way one conducts oneself with others: with humility, vulnerability, and awareness of the human spirit. Leaders at the top have significant demands, and servant leaders meet these challenges with a particular kind of depth described as courage, discernment, and a strong intellect. Finally, the senior leader who leads as a servant must consider her impact on the organization by serving as a role model, demonstrating presence, comfort with ambiguity, and most importantly, stability.[10] Leading can be conceived as occurring along a continuum from managerial control on the one end to spiritual holism on the other end. Inexperienced leaders often demonstrate their leadership as a managerial function, utilizing a very transactional way of leading. As one grows and matures as a leader, one's values begin to take on greater clarity and centrality and the expression of leadership moves from transactional to more transformational. Eventually the leader embraces the responsibility and vision to engage in changing cultures within organizations and/or society. Finally, at its end point, leadership is a spiritual endeavor.[11] Moving from one end of this spectrum to the other involves giving up control in favor of serving people and directing systems toward moral ends. This is quite similar to James MacGregor Burns's idea of transforming leadership, which occurs "when one or more engage with others in such a way that leaders and followers raise one another to higher levels of motivation and morality."[12]

Servant leadership fits very well with a spiritual or Christian approach to building an organizational culture of inclusivity, trust, and partnership.[13] Moreover, servant leadership, as a values-based approach, aligns with the important board function of articulating an organization's guiding values. Proper governance requires the delineation of values that guide the board's leadership. However, simply creating an undifferentiated list of inspiring values provides too little guidance for the actual work of governance. Dividing values between those that inform purpose and those that guide the methods to achieve the purpose is far more useful. In this regard, the board is essentially speaking to itself about the values that inform the governance process at the level of officers, committees, and individual board members.[14] Such a process enables a board to directly link servant leadership characteristics to specific governance actions, for example, devising concrete ways to genuinely listen to and seek input from the management, staff, and constituents of an organization.

Politics at the Top

Spiritually rich organizations enjoy the free flow of information and place high value on participation. It would seem such organizations have figured out how to reduce the perception of politics often expressed "as uncertainty, ambiguity, and, [frequently], worker insecurity."[15] If indeed organizations are political in nature, as Henry Mintzberg suggests,[16] and since leadership at the top of the organization is political, how might a faith-based leader embrace servant leadership in the politically charged context of board leadership? Political skill has long had a negative connotation, implying ruthless manipulation and using people as a means to an end. Indeed, historically, political ability has been defined as the use of influence, persuasion, and manipulation.[17] However, more recently, political skill has been redefined to align more with emotional intelligence, using one's ability to understand others as a means of influence. Characteristics of political skills from this vantage point include sincerity, honesty, integrity, self-awareness, social and emotional intelligence, interpersonal influence competencies, and social capital.[18] Using this definition suggests the possibility of employing political skill in the service of organizational strategy while maintaining an intact moral value system.

Religious Perspectives on Senior Leadership

Perspectives from religious traditions can offer insight into faith-based strategies for leaders at the senior level of organizations.

Buddhist Radial Economics

According to Buddhism, the central characteristic of human life is suffering or inadequacy. This spiritual tradition originates from the northern part of India in the fifth century BC and was founded by Gautama Siddhartha, who liberated himself from suffering through his unique spiritual practice of meditation. After his supreme enlightenment, he taught his doctrines of compassion, wisdom, and calmness of mind for more than forty years.[19]

In the Buddhist tradition, suffering is a condition common in life, in some cases brought on by overattachment and the craving of material things and power. At other times suffering results from loss, sickness, aging, and death. The instrument or means to escape from suffering is the Noble Eightfold Path, which is the core of the Buddha's teachings. It sets the foundation for an understanding of right behavior and has eight elements in three divisions: wisdom, virtues, and spiritual practice (concentration).

Wisdom
1. Right view
2. Right decision

Virtues
3. Right speech
4. Right action
5. Right livelihood

Spiritual Practice (Concentration)
6. Right effort
7. Right mindfulness
8. Right concentration[20]

The Noble Eightfold Path is an ongoing spiritual development, a virtuous spiral that leads to liberation, or the final cessation of suffering, which is the foremost goal of Buddhism.

Liberation from suffering is facilitated very specifically by following five precepts that spell out how to conduct one's life in alignment with the virtues set forth in the Noble Eightfold Path. The five precepts (also called the five mindfulness trainings) resemble the Ten Commandments and present a Buddhist perspective of a global ethic. One need not be Buddhist to practice these principles.

The five precepts are as follows:

1. *Reverence for life:* Practice compassion, do not kill or harm, and do not let others kill or harm.
2. *True happiness:* Practice generosity in thinking, speaking, and acting; refrain from taking what is not given.
3. *True love:* Cultivate responsibility and learn ways to protect the safety and integrity of individuals, couples, families, and society; refrain from sexual misconduct.
4. *Loving speech and deep listening:* Practice loving speech and compassionate listening in order to relieve suffering and to promote reconciliation and peace in oneself and among other people, ethnic and religious groups, and nations; refrain from false speech.
5. *Nourishment and healing:* Determine not to try to cover up loneliness, anxiety, or other suffering by losing oneself in consumption; refrain from taking in toxicants.[21]

If a Buddhist perspective were applied to the strategy of an organization, the result would be a radical realignment of the economic goals of the company. According to Laszlo Zsolnai, a Buddhist economic practice has five distinguishing characteristics, which provide a model of Buddhist economic strategy:

1. *Minimizing suffering:* An economic enterprise is worthy if it aims to reduce the suffering for every stakeholder and furthermore ensures good-quality basic necessities for humans with the lowest resource consumption.
2. *Simplifying desires:* Rather than cultivating or multiplying desires, an economic enterprise should simplify desires, ensure contentment, and encourage moderate consumption.
3. *Practicing nonviolence:* The reduction of violence to the lowest possible level is identical to the reduction of market forces to a small, adaptable scale for the benefit of every participant.
4. *Genuine care:* This is the opposite of the instrumental use, treating stakeholders as goals and not as tools in themselves, with significant economic outcomes.
5. *Generosity:* People are "homo-reciprocants," tending to behave gratefully and reciprocate favors.[22]

An excellent example of these practices in action is the company Patagonia, started by Yvon Chouinard in 1972 and currently led by Rose Marcario, who has practiced Shambhala Buddhism for twenty years.[23] The company has run ads with themes such as "Don't Buy This Jacket" and initiated practices to discourage overconsumption. Their "Better Than New Worn Wear" program actively encourages nonconsumption by offering to repair jackets and gear at their Reno, Nevada, factory. They also send their biodiesel truck around the country offering free repairs for garments and gear. They state, "One of the most responsible things we can do as a company is to make high-quality stuff that lasts for years and can be repaired, so you don't have to buy more of it."[24] The company is relentless in finding new and better ways to make products from recycled materials and in aiming that none of their products ever makes it to a landfill. They actively work with suppliers to do the same. The result is an economic wonder: as a benefit corporation, Patagonia is in business to make the world better through grants totaling $61 million and in-kind donations to more than one thousand organizations over the past thirty years.[25]

Islamic Virtuous Leadership

In the Qur'an the Prophet Muhammad is described as one possessing character and virtue. In a key verse in the Qur'an (68:4) God describes him as follows: "And you [Muhammad] stand as an exalted standard of character." R. I. Beekun says, "This verse describes the very core of Muhammad's leadership." The Arabic term *khuluq*, used in this verse, means "character." In verse 26:137 this same word has an additional meaning, that of an acquired or learned "custom" or "habit."[26] This suggests character is something that can be acquired and built over time by anyone who wishes to lead a virtuous life. Muhammad's character was virtue-centric and is consistent with the Qur'an. This model of Muhammad is also consistent with Aristotelian thought, in which ethics centers on virtues, and virtues derive from character. Long before Muhammad received the revelation, he was known as trustworthy and truthful; indeed, he "modeled core virtues that defined his character and his behavior: truthfulness and integrity, trustworthiness, justice, benevolence, humility, kindness and patience."[27]

Muhammad's character-centric style of leadership is a demonstration of transformational leadership.[28] He was able to raise people's awareness of the folly of worshiping many gods in favor of understanding God as One and thus uniting Arabia under a single monotheistic religious polity in Islam. "Muhammad spent his lifetime teaching and mentoring his followers in the core Islamic virtues and values and stressed the universal brotherhood of mankind, enjoined benevolence, kindness, and justice and argued against the egoism that permeated the times."[29] Moreover, he valued intellectual stimulation, a component of transformational leadership, by offering his followers a new worldview. In addition to raising their spiritual awareness, he urged them to engage in learning and to excel in whatever field they pursued. Followers were encouraged to search for and acquire knowledge not for self-aggrandizement but rather to get closer to and to serve their creator. Taking this to heart, Muslims developed some of the first universities and led in many scientific areas for centuries.[30] Muhammad also showed components of servant leadership in his commitment to service before self; he stated that "a leader of the nation is their servant."[31] Clearly, his character-centered leadership modeled the virtues he preached, and he is unique in that he blended elements of transformational and servant leadership styles.

Based on five principles critical to Islam—intention, awe, gratitude, consultation, and accountability—Muhammad's example provides a leadership approach for senior leaders. Intention is important when discerning the intent guiding the behavior of other people, including other leaders. Virtuous leaders have reverence and awe for God, holding the leaders to high standards. Such awe maintains an inner consciousness and sense of duty to God. Gratitude is a key element of Islam and a reminder of the boundless generosity of God toward humankind. Without such gratitude one is likely to become arrogant and self-centered, but upholding gratitude enables one to remain humble. Consultation is the practice of seeking the counsel of others, especially in decision making; this is an important attitude for senior leaders, as it stresses consensus building. Accountability ensures one is true to one's word with regard to tasks; it ensures integrity, justice, and trustworthiness because the leader's actions will be judged by somebody else. Muslims believe everyone will have to account for their actions on the day of judgment—leaders notwithstanding.[32]

Eboo Patel is the founder of Interfaith Youth Core (IFYC), a nonprofit dedicated to promoting interfaith cooperation by building interfaith advocates across college campuses. A practicing Muslim, Patel embodies the five principles of Islam and translates these into his leadership. Recognized as a global leader of the interfaith movement, Patel has extended the discussion about faith and religion into the public square in an effort to promote peace and collaboration by helping young people build on their commonalities across various religious and nonreligious identities.

Eboo's core belief is that religion is a bridge of cooperation rather than a barrier of division. Indeed the work of IFYC shows how gratitude for those who hold different religious beliefs fosters acceptance and dismantles ignorance. IFYC has built a nation-wide interfaith collaboration of students staff and faculty across secular and faith-based college campuses with the intent that interfaith dialogue will spread to the broader society. Patel is inspired to build this bridge by his faith as a Muslim, his Indian heritage and his American citizenship.[33]

Patel has written books and articles and has spoken to numerous audiences, among them the United Nations and the Technology, Entertainment and Design conference.[34]

Christian Shared Leadership

Shared leadership is an approach to governance that fits well with the model of servant leadership. C. L. Pearce and J. A. Conger define shared leadership as "a dynamic, interactive influence process among individuals in groups for which the objective is to lead one another to the achievement of group or organizational goals or both."[35] This influence process is peer to peer, and the title "leader" is not specifically assigned. Even the board chair is considered first among equals and does not have formal authority over members of the board. When power is shared in this way the board of directors can be thought of as a system of leadership.[36] Shared leadership suggests individual board members must be accepting of one another's temporary leadership and equally adept at followership.[37] This is a fluid process in which "directors continuously switch between 'leader' and 'follower' roles based on desired capabilities and expertise given the situation at hand."[38] Designing organizational structures where leadership and power are shared aligns well with lateral shared leadership and the stewardship component of servant leadership.

On inclusion and shared leadership, Mark Strom makes the case that Paul is one of the strongest advocates in classical literature for equality of women with men. Intentionally, Paul avoided the vocabulary of leadership, choosing language to "ignore rank and subvert status."[39] For example, he used the word *phronēsis* ("virtuous thought"), particularly in Philippians, to convey the idea of everyone having the same mind. In so doing he is taking a sharp departure from the conventional mind-set of hierarchy prevalent at that time; not everyone can be of the same mind because there is a very distinct and commonly understood class system. Paul replaces this class system with an egalitarian mind-set that is radical in its relational emphasis.[40] Paul called for radical egalitarianism, writing that there is neither Jew nor gentile, neither slave nor free, neither male nor female (Gal. 3:28). Against a backdrop of leadership by rank and social status, Paul modeled a new social order of antileadership, recasting influence as the result of service: "in humility value others above yourselves, not looking to your own interests but each of you to the interests of others" (Phil. 2:3–4). Moreover, we learn from Paul's writings that early followers of his teachings met in small groups using shared leadership to discuss and explore new ideas. This radical model of shared governance and leadership was perpetuated throughout the region, forming a movement that continues today.

The Orpheus Chamber Orchestra, although not a Christian institution, embodies the goals of egalitarian leadership. Often called the leaderless orchestra, Orpheus has perfected the art of leading through community. Unlike most orchestras, Orpheus does not have a conductor; instead, responsibility for conducting music is shared among the players. The designated leader for a given piece of music is responsible for giving the downbeat and "leading" the orchestra to the completion of the piece while at the same time maintaining his or her role as a performing musician. A core group within the chamber orchestra takes responsibility for a first set of thoughts on how each piece should be interpreted and performed, which is brought to the larger group, where everyone in the orchestra has an opportunity to provide input—something unheard of in a standard conductor-led orchestra. Power and influence are shared; everyone contributes, and thus each one has a voice and a sense of responsibility for the outcome.[41]

This strong egalitarian culture permeates the entire Orpheus Chamber Orchestra organization, from the business side to the board of directors to the musicians. But when the founder of this radical approach left, in 1999, the orchestra struggled to keep the culture of shared leadership alive. A departure from shared governance on the business side of the operation brought the organization to near collapse.[42] However, with the help of a new board chair, the orchestra returned to the structure that fits its culture: more egalitarian and shared responsibility, less boss. Essential in shared leadership is that the influence process sometimes involves peer, or lateral, influence, and at other times involves upward or downward hierarchical influence.[43] At the core of this approach is thus a focus on leadership rather than leaders, and the acknowledgment that leadership is a socially constructed phenomenon that is not strictly confined to a formal or assigned leader.[44] Orpheus is a beautiful and poignant example of what is possible when a group of people understands that leading is not so much about role and rank, but much more about an outcome made possible by the collective contribution of all.

christian leadership in action: some exemplary case studies

This concluding chapter looks at a number of significant figures who exemplify different facets of Christian leadership and in the process challenge some common assumptions about what leadership in general involves.

Are Leaders Always Ahead of Those around Them?

According to most writers on the subject of leadership, one mark of leaders is that they are always out in front of others—their colleagues, subordinates, and competitors. Leaders are not *above* others as much as *ahead* of others. Linguistically, this is what "taking the lead" means. Being ahead of others can take many different forms, such as discerning a need that cries out to be met, identifying business trends before anyone else, experimenting with new methods and approaches to familiar challenges, undertaking creative research and development, forming and heading a pioneering enterprise, creating innovative structures and delivery systems, or finding new ways to add value to a product or a service.

All things being equal, success is said to come to the person, group, or organization that is able to get ahead of others in any of these ways. Even if circumstances require a temporary halt, stepping sideways to move forward, or a strategic retreat to rethink priorities, leaders are the first ones to realize the necessity for such a move. They may consult with others before deciding what to do and may seek others' help in explaining proposed changes, but in and through all of this, what marks leaders is their knack for seeing things in advance of others and staying ahead of the pack. While this quality is a part of what leadership involves, it is not always necessary for good leadership. Indeed, it is sometimes more important for leaders to be behind rather than in front of those around them.

Frank Buchman: A Leader of a Global Movement

Frank Buchman was born in 1878 in a small pietistic Lutheran town in Pennsylvania. His family later moved to the nearby burgeoning city of Allentown. After assisting in a church in a mixed neighborhood in Philadelphia, Buchman, around the age of thirty, became the YMCA secretary at Pennsylvania State College. Over the next five years he had a significant religious influence there, and his gifts in communicating and organizing became known to college ministers around the country. He was offered a teaching post at Hartford Theological Seminary and from there undertook several speaking tours in Asia. Though when speaking he was sometimes prone to self-advertisement, from early on he looked for ways to bring others into the limelight while he stood by and supported them from behind. As one observer commented at the time, "I have been interested in watching this man Buchman all day. He is always in the background, pushing others into places of leadership and responsibility." According to his biographer, while he was "an ardent advertiser of his own activities, he was also surprisingly self-effacing. . . . Extrovert in his manner, he was at heart profoundly reserved."[1]

Through his travels, Buchman had a growing sense that God was calling him "to remake the world" through encouraging dramatic personal change in the lives of key individuals. He had already begun to display an unusual gift for personal relationships, especially with people of a higher social standing or in significant positions of responsibility. Realizing that this task was too large for a heroic-type leader, he began enlisting a diverse group of people to join him. By his early forties, he had drawn together a number of inexperienced but dedicated people from America and Britain who were willing to travel as teams to colleges and other institutions. Wherever they went, these teams gathered people together for several days in a relaxed atmosphere to consider fundamental life decisions. After two years of coordinating such teams, Buchman resigned his position at Hartford, the last paid position he would ever have, and threw himself into what would become his lifework.

What he started contained the seeds of what became known in the late 1920s as the Oxford Movement and a decade later as Moral Re-Armament. His declared aim was to change leaders and to create the leadership that would alter present conditions. This led him into an unceasing itinerant life, one that was nurtured and guided by his practice of waiting on and listening to God for an hour each morning. As the work grew, he became increasingly aware that people were attracted to events by the quality of the team members rather than by his personal presence with them for a limited time. He decided, therefore, to create and train a highly disciplined team that would remain together for a longer period of time. This original group multiplied and, with his encouragement, individual teams began visiting other countries. As he entered his fifties, Buchman shifted his focus to preparing new team members for this expanding work. He always felt it was better to give time offstage to ten people who would do the work than to try to do it center stage himself.

During the 1930s, as international conflicts intensified and the specter of war threatened, Buchman concentrated his efforts on encouraging peace among national leaders. He and his teams worked hard in Europe to prevent the growth of Nazism and, after World War II, sought to bring conflict resolution to troubled and volatile situations. Because all these efforts took place behind the scenes, they rarely received attention in the media. Outsiders frequently viewed Buchman's activities as secretive and sectarian and consequently often criticized or opposed them. These developments led Buchman to move even further into the background. It is a testimony to his approach that, after his death in the early 1960s, the movement continued to operate through the exercise of collective rather than single leadership.

The tantalizing question about Buchman is this: Without binding anyone by a vow, contract, or financial guarantee, how did he gather so many diverse full-time and part-time colleagues who worked with him during his lifetime and continued to work with one another after his death? Even after observing him for ten years, Arnold Lunn, the well-known author and onetime critic of Buchman, failed to find a satisfactory answer: "He has no charisma that I can see. He isn't good-looking, he is no orator, he has never written a book, and he seldom even leads a meeting. Yet statesmen and great intellects come from all over the world to consult him, and a lot of intelligent people have stuck with him, full-time without salary, for forty years, when they could have been making careers for themselves. Why?"[2] Henry van Dusen concluded that the answer lay partly in his prevision, his understanding of human nature, and his confidence in his method of working. But above all, it lay in "the absolute deliverance of self—his hopes, his necessities, his reputation, his success—into the direction of the Divine Intention."[3]

In other words, it was primarily his focus on, or his abandonment to, what he perceived as God's work that was decisive.[4] "I had nothing to do with it," he once said. "I only obey and do what He says."[5] This meant, of course, that he was often the first to see what needed to be done and to test it. Those attracted to his movement were encouraged to emulate his actions rather than simply fall in behind him. Convinced that "he was wonderfully led to those who were ready" for this challenge, he believed that they were capable under God of more than they realized. He did not feel that he had any ability that others could not experience themselves. His operating principle was to "accept people at any point at which they are willing to arrive, and not urge them to do anything they are not led to do." Otherwise, he said, "I should be surrounded by a group of parasites rather than people who are taught to rely on God and let Him direct them individually."[6] Despite his pivotal role in the movement, Buchman viewed leadership as "the task of the whole fellowship."[7]

Implications

Leaders who place themselves behind others do not just give others room to take the lead but also personally back them as they do so and provide whatever resources—material, financial, and institutional—they need to succeed. Some cultures understand the importance of this dual way of operating better than others. One summer a few years ago, Robert and his wife were driving north over the border into British Columbia. On a high mountain pass, they stopped at a gas station to refuel. The station also housed a restaurant and a small museum. Inside the museum, which was a simple one-room affair, were artifacts, pictures, documents, and stories associated with the local Native American tribe. One of the stories caught his eye.

A member of the tribe had become separated from it. He looked everywhere for tracks but could not find them. In the course of his wanderings, he came across a member from a neighboring tribe. After they greeted each other and caught up on local news, he asked the following questions:

"Have you seen my people?"

"How many of them were there?"

"When was this?"

"Where were they?"

"In which direction were they headed?"

"How fast were they going?"

Much to his relief, the wandering tribesman received the answers he was seeking. After thanking his informant, he said, "I must find them—I am their *leader*!"

The most interesting aspect of this story is that it reveals how great a leader this man was. He had trained the members of his tribe so well that they had left him behind. Though it is right and proper for leaders at times to be ahead of those around them, at other times it is just as important for them to be behind them. They can do this by actively promoting and supporting people so they can make the best contribution possible. Leaders who are preoccupied with being out in front are in danger of neglecting this responsibility. Then they wonder why their people find it so difficult to keep up with them. When leaders give others the backing they need to develop, it is not long before some of their protégés begin to outdistance them in certain areas. When this happens, leaders find themselves behind those around them in another way. Yet this should not cause them alarm but deep satisfaction, for it frees them to move ahead into new areas, leaving those they have trained in charge of what they have left behind.

Does a Leader Need a Certain Kind of Personality?

Many organizations have an ideal type of leader in mind. The ideal often has to do with experience, abilities, and skills. But often, consciously or unconsciously, there is a preferred personality. This may be based on the character of an earlier leader who was greatly admired, a leader in another organization who is considered the best in the field, or the typical characteristics of a leader according to the training programs members of the organization have attended. A notion of an ideal type of leader also appears in connection with particular occupations. The top businesspeople are tough, social workers are caring, lawyers are hardheaded, salespeople are aggressive, accountants are unemotional, and psychologists are sensitive. Sometimes it is possible to choose between two types that are equally acceptable: teachers may be strict or sympathetic, judges may be grave or acerbic, artists may be soulful or flamboyant.

People also have expectations about the kind of personality leaders should have when their roles involve a high degree of public visibility, as in civic or political life. Such people should be confident and assured. They should be willing to engage in self-presentation and promotion. They should be significantly motivated by self-advancement and fulfillment.

Overall, it is widely believed that there is a general correlation between personality and position. That fit may differ from occupation to occupation, from organization to organization, and from culture to culture. It may be flexible rather than tight, allowing for a range of possibilities or variations. It may vary according to the changing nature of an occupation, organization, or culture.

It may depend on the degree to which the person or institution concerned is going through a critical phase. But there is still an inclination to believe that certain types of personalities mesh better with certain types of positions.

We are not suggesting that personality and position have nothing to do with each other. What we want to challenge is the assumption that there must be a consistent and significant relationship between the two for good leadership to take place. In the end, a good match depends on what a particular situation demands.

Søren Kierkegaard: A Public Intellectual

Søren Kierkegaard was born in 1813 to bourgeois parents in Copenhagen. He suffered from a curvature of the spine that left him with a permanent stoop. This gave him, according to some contemporaries, "a gnome-like appearance." But it was clear from an early age that he was extremely intelligent and psychologically observant. He developed into a gifted conversationalist and had, on occasion, a sarcastic wit. These gifts soon made him well known to the intellectual and literary society in Copenhagen, though he preferred the company of friends, ordinary folk, and children.

In his early twenties, Kierkegaard's first articles appeared in newspapers. This was during a period when he turned his back on Christianity. In his twenty-fourth year, however, he committed himself fully to God and resumed study for a master's degree in theology. After a deeply romantic attachment to a young woman, Kierkegaard suddenly broke off the engagement, causing a furor among social circles in the city. In 1843, at age thirty, his first major work, *Either/Or*, was published under a pseudonym. It represented his journey from an aesthetic to an ethical stance toward life and was a literary sensation in Copenhagen. Two more personal works immediately followed (*Repetition* and *Fear and Trembling*), spurred in part by his doomed love affair. In these and the books that followed, Kierkegaard led his readers beyond aesthetic and ethical approaches to life to one that was overtly religious.

His next publication, *Philosophical Fragments*, indirectly asked, "What is Christianity?" and "How does one become a Christian?" Another book (*The Concept of Dread*) probed in a profoundly psychological way the nature of original sin. A year later, the last of his pseudonymous writings, *Stages on Life's Way*, continued the account of his spiritual journey. This was followed by his greatest work, *Concluding Unscientific Postscript to the Philosophical Fragments*. During this prolific four-year period, Kierkegaard found his vocation as a writer and, in addition to the works mentioned, composed seven volumes of what he called "edifying discourses," thoughtful devotional reflections on what was involved with being a Christian. Since, as a layman, he could not preach from the pulpit, he used books to communicate with a wider audience.

In the late 1840s Kierkegaard was criticized as a writer in a weekly scandal sheet called *The Corsair*. Though he was not named outright, highly insulting cartoons made it clear that he was the object of attack. The criticism was directed at his motives and character as well as his writings and continued for the best part of a year. Other papers followed suit, and as a result, Kierkegaard could not appear in public without facing ridicule from even the ordinary citizens of the city. He was pilloried as both a pathetic egotist and a comic figure, the village idiot of Copenhagen. He was even featured as the main character in a successful farce that played in theaters all over Denmark. Only once did he issue a public reply, and then he lapsed into silence. With this, all hope of his having a significant impact as a writer was gone. Even the name Søren, the most common name in the country, fell into disfavor.

In spite of everything, Kierkegaard learned to view these events as part of God's plan for his life, and he remained convinced of his vocation as a writer. He began to come to terms with being a prophet who was misunderstood, not only among the literati but also by the general population. Unexpectedly, the king of Denmark continued to seek his advice during the time of public attack and even offered him an annual gratuity to cover publication expenses. Kierkegaard politely refused, stating his need to maintain independence and to demonstrate that his only allegiance was to God. When, in his thirty-fourth year, he began writing his devotional trilogy (*Edifying Discourses*, *Works of Love*, and *Christian Discourses*), he laid aside all attempts to speak indirectly about Christ, a step that was strengthened by a deep spiritual experience that he described as a kind of "second conversion."

While he continued to produce devotional works, in his late thirties he focused especially on the complacency and superficiality of conventional Christianity. A critique of institutional Christianity had been implicit in his writings for some time. Now, in a trilogy (*The Sickness unto Death*, *Training in Christianity*, and *For Self-Examination*), this came to the forefront. In the first, he accused the church of giving people religious tranquilizers rather than helping them to undergo radical surgery. In the second, he criticized the church for obscuring the genuine character of Christianity and making it too easy to be a believer. (Instead of converting pagans to Christianity, he said, Christianity had itself become a form of paganism.) In the third, he attacked the church for objectifying the Word of God so much that people were relieved of the obligation to make it personal and live it out. He held back half of this volume from publication lest it bring pain to the primate of the state church, Bishop Mynster, one of the church's better leaders and role models, who had also been his father's pastor.

Because of their small readership, these books stirred up little reaction. Initially Kierkegaard did not mind, but after a time he felt the need to take a more public stance. Though he would have preferred to remain in the background, he experienced an inner compulsion that would not go away. He knew that to speak out would break not only his own heart but also those of various people dear to him, including the bishop. He knew that ultimately he had no choice and had to call institutional religion what it was: a Sunday religion that was neither rooted deeply enough in the soul nor applied radically enough to daily life. Even after Bishop Mynster died, in deference to his theological teacher's desire to become the bishop's successor, he waited almost twelve months before he spoke out. In 1854 he wrote twenty articles in a journal, *The Fatherland*, and continued the attack in nine editions of his own periodical, *The Instant* (now gathered together under the title *Attack upon Christendom*). Many of these critiques focused on the compromised position of the clergy as salaried functionaries of the state. For him, the idea of a Christian nation, indeed, of Christendom itself, was a betrayal of the gospel.

Kierkegaard found himself at the center of an acrimonious public controversy. Though the clergy bitterly opposed him, this time the common people responded to his message. All of a sudden he was popular again, and even some of his earlier books began to sell. He was uncomfortable with his newfound celebrity status. It was something he had neither anticipated nor desired. As John Gates says, Kierkegaard regarded himself "not as a reformer, but as a detective ferreting out the evidence." He was simply trying to tell the truth, not become the center of a public controversy surrounded by admirers or detractors.[8] He did not feel equipped to handle the pressure this created, the misunderstanding it involved, and the abuse it generated. Some people find themselves at home in the glare of publicity. They even warm to the prospect of battle. Instead of feeling overwhelmed by criticism and ridicule, they are motivated by them into even greater efforts. For Kierkegaard, however, the more combative the discussion became, the more he wanted to stay in the background. Though he worked hard at relating to others socially and could be a congenial and stimulating companion, he was essentially a private, introspective, and sensitive person. If God wanted him to operate in the limelight, why had he not been given the temperament to do so? By nature he was retiring and nonconfrontational. Why had God placed him in this position? Why not someone who was better suited to the task?

But the more Kierkegaard pondered his situation, the more he began to see a divine logic to it. While, from one angle, it made sense to place in the public spotlight someone who was constitutionally equipped to deal with it, from another, doing so involved a greater risk. Such a person would be more vulnerable to the temptations of public life. He would be more likely to allow his public position, or the public attention he received, to go to his head. A more private person is largely protected from these temptations, preferring to withdraw from the limelight, not get lost in it, and more likely to fall into self-doubt than into vanity. What appeared at first sight to be a mismatch of personality and position, therefore, made sense as long as the person in question possessed other abilities—sharpness of mind, a passion for truth, and a capacity to communicate—to undertake the task.

Kierkegaard died as he was preparing the final *Instant* for publication. He was only forty-two years old. While his work had limited influence during his lifetime, almost a century later his writings became available to a wider audience and began to receive their full due. Since then he has had a major impact on a continuing line of novelists, intellectuals, philosophers, and theologians, not to mention a wide range of thoughtful people who have read his works.

Implications

In these days of pervasive personality tests, we need to be especially careful not to tie a particular personality too closely to a specific task, occupation, or position. Such tests do reveal factors that should be taken into consideration, but these factors should not be determinative. There is always the danger of introducing inadequate cultural assumptions into an assessment of what a person can or should do.

Theological considerations must also be taken into account. On the one hand, assessments can inform us of the potentialities God has built into us and of the qualities he has given to us as he has nurtured and guided us. But on the other hand, they are not always good predictors of the positions into which God wishes to place us. This is partly because there are other factors at stake than simply matching personality to position. Other factors may include the unavailability of someone more appropriate for the job. Ideally, we may not be the best person for a particular position, but we are, from God's or others' point of view, the best person for the moment. Or, by casting us against type, God may wish to widen our own or other people's perceptions of what a position does or does not demand. Perhaps our efforts will galvanize someone to step up and do a more thorough job. Or it could be that God wants to display in and through us his divine versatility and power by enabling us to accomplish what under normal circumstances would be beyond our reach.

In addition, a person whose personality may not be seen as an ideal match for a position may bring a unique experience, perspective, and style to the task. At the very least, such a person may avoid falling too quickly into a business-as-usual approach. At the most, this person may need to rely on creative and experimental ways of tackling problems and may, by facing challenges, become an effective leader.

An analogy from cinema might be helpful here. In casting a film, a director usually chooses an actor whose persona and track record fit a particular role. In some cases, actors go through their entire careers playing similar kinds of roles. Such roles, it is assumed, are what they do best. In the language of the trade, they are cast according to type. Occasionally, however, this rule of thumb is broken. The history of cinema contains some wonderful examples of actors who have managed to play a part at odds with their established persona. The results can be powerful. One thinks of such matinee idols as Cary Grant playing a Cockney crook in *None but the Lonely Heart*, Tyrone Power playing a man who is seduced into the depths of depravity in *Nightmare Alley*, Robert Mitchum playing a timid schoolteacher in *Ryan's Daughter*, Robin Williams playing a psychologically disturbed murderer in *Insomnia*, and Charlize Theron playing a serial killer in *Monster*. The struggle to play a role that differs from their usual persona often gives the performance an extra edge and strength.

Is Leadership Only about Fulfilling One's Potential or Relinquishing It to Fulfill Others'?

These days there is much talk about the importance of people fulfilling their potential. This involves actualizing and maximizing inherent gifts and learned capabilities and using them in the kinds of work for which one is best suited. There is, of course, something to all of this. People should be aware of their gifts and abilities, for they come from the Creator's hand or are the result of God's providence in their lives. Not acknowledging these things would be an act of ingratitude. The trouble with the language of fulfillment and potential is that it is too self-regarding and can too easily lead to self-centeredness. The focus is too resolutely on oneself and only secondarily on what one can do for others. If the words "fulfillment" and "potential" are used when discussing leadership, talk should focus on fulfilling others' potential. Paradoxically, as people seek to do that, genuine leadership takes place.

Power plays a role in the fulfillment of potential. Whether some people recognize it or not, making leadership a goal often springs from a latent desire to exercise power, to be in charge, to take control. As Max De Pree often said in workshops, even the most enlightened forms of leadership involve "a serious meddling in the lives of others."[9] This is even more the case with less enlightened forms. Unless leaders exercise great care, they will have a tendency to coerce or manipulate those under their authority. This diminishes rather than fulfills their workers' potential, and it also hinders and distorts their own. The real task is to empower others, to play whatever part one can in enhancing their innate gifts and learned capacities so that they are able to contribute as fully and as creatively as possible to their organizations and to others.

Sometimes people realize that fulfilling their potential or even seeking to empower others springs too much from an unconscious or limited desire to focus on self rather than on others. This realization often takes place at the halfway stage in life, when people reevaluate whether they have made the best use of their time.[10] Sometimes it occurs when they hit a personal or occupational wall. In such cases, people who are already in leadership positions may undergo a radical reevaluation of their lives, leave behind much of what they have been doing, and take up a new form of work or way of working that is more other-focused. The story of one such person—who helped to redefine power in more other-centered ways and contributed the idea of "hitting the wall" to workplace literature on spirituality—follows.

Janet Hagberg: A For-Profit to a Not-for-Profit Leader

Janet Hagberg was born in Minnesota to parents who seriously sought to live out evangelical Lutheran convictions. From a young age she attended church and several times underwent the experience of being born again. Through early efforts at playing the piano and singing in the choir, she became actively involved in the congregation. She also enjoyed and excelled at a private Christian high school that reinforced her church's strict, conservative pattern of belief and morality. Both her church and school emphasized sin and atonement at the expense of grace. The dominant mood was one of guilt and shame, the dominant attitude one of unquestioning obedience. In this environment, she said, "I learned early to be a leader by getting involved and doing things . . . but at the same time, always wondering about all my myriads of questions."[11] In her late teens, she became a member of a crusade team that went to various parts of her state, providing opportunities for singing and speaking that both she and others regarded as a benchmark of genuine faith.

After completing high school, Hagberg attended the University of Minnesota. It was the 1960s, and the air was full of slogans such as "God is dead" and of protests against the Vietnam War. During this time, partly because of the more open atmosphere and partly because of a more academic approach to faith, she began to question the rigid, performance-oriented, literalist faith in which she had been raised. This resulted in a decade-long questioning of religious faith and practice, including a period of agnosticism. She became, by her own account, both intellectually factious and self-sufficient. Marriage after college to a pastor's son who was also rebelling against the church only exacerbated her questioning. She became an infrequent attender of a Unitarian church. The lack of a truly supportive community made it difficult for her to handle the additional spiritual issues that arose as a result of her mother's early death.

After completing her first degree, Hagberg began a master's program in psychology and social work, which became fields of alternative spiritual exploration. As she wrote later, "That led me into an adventure into humanistic psychology, creativity, psychic experiences, Eastern thought, meditation, other levels of consciousness, and New Age awareness. It was a whirlwind period of discovering new ways to be and think."[12] She gained a faculty position at the University of Minnesota, and everything she touched seemed to work out perfectly. Everything appeared to be going according to plan. She was unaware that her ability to realize her ambitions and her assumption that she had control over her life had heightened her vulnerability to the unexpected.

Riding this wave of achievement, she left the academic world to start her own business. She formed the Hagberg Company, a firm that specialized in training and management for business, higher education, and government. This too became highly successful. In time she found herself called in to advise a range of Fortune 500 companies, among them Alcoa, Honeywell, and General Mills. Meanwhile, her involvement in adult education and government gave her the opportunity to try her hand at creating specialized programs. During the mid-1970s, in collaboration with a consultant involved in career development, she devised a program focusing on self- and occupational renewal for the 3M Company. Its purpose was to help people explore new options and possibilities, both personally and vocationally, including life and career changes. In 1978 this was released in book form and has since gone through several editions.[13]

The book reveals a concern for being as well as doing, personal identity as well as career path, and leadership as well as vocational achievement. It stresses the need for both an inward and an outward journey, which is essential to a satisfactory and satisfying direction in life.

Ironically, it was around the time this program was published that her own life began to unravel. Her marriage fell apart, leading to divorce and a deep sense of personal failure. She began a period of self-examination, during which she wrote in a journal, thought seriously about God, and began visiting churches— eventually finding one in Edina, Minnesota, that attracted other seekers and sought to help people keep head and heart, belief and life together. Through its loving and caring support, this community was instrumental in helping her to regain her self-esteem and a renewed desire to achieve. She began to find a productive place in the church, using the skills she had employed so successfully in the business world, and it was not long before she began to take the lead in various projects both inside the church and in the wider community.

At the same time, her consulting work gained increasing attention, and she found herself reflecting more deeply on the nature, exercise, and abuse of power by individuals and institutions. Her book *Real Power*, she said, "was written for individuals who aspire to power, who long to understand what power really is; for leaders, to provoke their thinking about what true leadership is; for organizations, as a practical tool for developing people and vision for the future."[14]

In this book, as noted earlier, Hagberg set out six stages or levels of power. In order they are powerlessness, power by association, power by symbols, power by reflection, and power by purpose. A final level, attained by very few, power by gestalt (or embodiment), is manifested chiefly as wisdom. This book, which developed out of not only Hagberg's substantial thinking about the issue but also her personal development and growth, was well received and is still considered by some to make the most sense of the various types of power at work in organizations. Its reception opened new doors for Hagberg's work as a consultant and led to further opportunities as a public speaker.

In all of this, Hagberg was responding to abilities she had and to opportunities that came her way but was also beginning to glimpse something deeper and more challenging. While she still had the desire to be a success and to conquer fresh fields, at a certain point she became aware that despite her growing influence and recognition, something was still not quite right. She felt the need for a greater consistency between her work and her Christian faith. This led her to give up much of the consulting and training work she was doing to focus on understanding and becoming involved in spiritual direction. Increasingly, this became the focus of the time she spent with others in the workplace. Only by letting go of the reputation and status she had achieved was she able to enter into this.

Hagberg went on to cofound a nonprofit organization to eradicate the violence inflicted against women in spousal abuse. The organization is called Silent Witness, and their goal is zero cases of domestic violence homicides by 2020. Although Hagberg is the highest-profile person in this organization, she deliberately takes a low-profile stance, encouraging, facilitating, and empowering others to undertake the work. As the organization grows in a grassroots way, she finds herself responding to its spontaneous growth rather than serving as a catalyst for it.

Implications

Enjoying the power and prestige that come with success is seductive because the more we receive, the more we want. Leaders who seek only to fulfill their own personal potential eventually fall prey to this seduction. But success for the sake of success is much like shaky scaffolding; eventually, it becomes too weak to sustain the weight of power and prestige and falls to the ground.

Henri Nouwen offers an important insight into this question of self-fulfillment. Nouwen asks: "What makes the temptation to power so seemingly irresistible? Maybe it is that power offers an easy substitute for the hard task of love. It seems easier to be God than to love God, easier to own life than to love life. . . . The temptation of power is greatest when intimacy is a threat."[15]

There are times when the desire to fulfill one's potential leads to emptiness, which is a lack of intimacy, and the yearning for something more. The longing to give one's life to work that goes beyond the immediacy of personal fulfillment—to contribute to something long-lasting—often occurs at the point in life when one is open to letting go of self-fulfillment in favor of service to others. At this juncture of letting go, a leader comes face-to-face with a critical and existential question: Am I doing the work to which I was called? Paul speaks of this in Philippians 3, where he makes a plea to continue pressing toward the goal and to "take hold of that for which Christ Jesus took hold of me" (Phil. 3:12). Paul rightly understood the importance of reaching for and firmly grasping one's calling. The challenge is to move from leadership built on power to leadership in which we critically discern where God is calling us to serve. For our work to be a calling, we must first know who we are and what we stand for. Sometimes it takes coming to grips with the emptiness of fulfilling one's own potential to discover these things.

Leadership is rooted in helping others fulfill their potential and letting go of one's need for self-fulfillment. As Robert Greenleaf so aptly put it, "The servant leader is servant first. It begins with the conscious feeling that one wants to serve first—and that conscious choice brings one to aspire to lead."[16] Hagberg realizes that her greatest contribution is to serve those who suffer spousal abuse and to take action to eradicate this form of violence. From this calling to serve came her aspiration to lead—to let go of self-fulfillment in favor of helping victims of abuse recover their potential.

Are Leaders Primarily Exercising Power or Empowering Others?

For most people, climbing the ladder of leadership is about attaining a position of power over resources, systems, and others. It is precisely this understanding of power, however, that has come under criticism in most of the recent literature on leadership. Max De Pree is fond of saying that, contrary to usual expectations, the more one climbs the corporate ladder, the more one becomes an amateur rather than an expert. The more responsibility a person has, the more that person has to know about everything. The more encompassing one's work, the more one realizes the multiple levels of complexity in an organization and the magnitude of decisions concerning it. Consequently, De Pree says, leaders need to know their limitations, become learners, and "abandon themselves to the strengths of others."[17] Instead of regarding themselves as in control of an organization, good leaders know that control is in a range of hands, indeed, all the way down the line. They seek to recognize, affirm, and enhance the power of all involved. They view power as pervasive within or distributed throughout an organization. A leader's special responsibility is to discern where wisdom and expertise lie and then make the best use of both and help them to develop further.

It is in empowering others that power is most effectively exercised and multiplied. Instead of this resulting in the diminution of a leader's power, it reveals its true nature and operation. As with self, according to Jesus in the Gospels, so with power: "Whoever loses their life . . . will save it" (Mark 8:35). For the most part, however, leaders find it in a different form. The more transformative forms of power will be most in evidence and are the most effective.

This discussion reveals yet another instance of a reversal of values that paradoxically results in things turning out for the best.

Gordon Cosby: A Mission Church Leader

Gordon Cosby was not ranked among the high priests of church renewal in North America such as Bill Hybels, Joel Osteen, and Rick Warren, or among the public figures engaged in creative mission such as Jim Wallis and Ray Bakke. Yet he helped to fashion one of the most innovative and influential congregations of the past half-century, whose members radically give their lives away to others in their immediate community as well as to people in the wider marketplace. Unlike most of his well-known peers, Cosby hardly put anything into print, did not run a radio or a television ministry, and did not hold seminars focusing on his church. He simply—and quietly—performed the job to which he felt called. He had no interest in creating disciples in his or his church's likeness. The church's name, Church of the Savior, is better known than his, and that is the way Cosby preferred it. He simply saw himself as facilitating the vision and mission of his church in the most committed, discerning, and empowering way.

Cosby passed away in 2013. He was raised in a supportive and ecumenical family in Lynchburg, Virginia. He attended a Presbyterian church in the morning with one parent and a Baptist church in the evening with the other parent. In his mid-teens he started to work among youth in the Baptist church and soon became close friends with the minister's daughter, Mary, whom he later married. In his early twenties, he attended simultaneously a college and a seminary. After he was ordained in 1942, he became a chaplain in the army and took part in the Normandy invasion. He was twice decorated for bravery under fire.

In the army he concluded that the only way he could reach all the men in his regiment was to decentralize the work of the chapel by forming twelve fellowship and mission bands headed by the most spiritually mature men in each company. Each of these leaders had around him a committed core group. As a result of this experience, he began to dream of founding a church that would revolve around the quality of its members' commitment rather than the size of its membership and that would also cut across denominational boundaries. This grew from his conviction that "no one had all the truth. Each of us had a part . . . and the best way to retain this truth . . . was to share it with others to keep it by giving it away."[18] This was also true, he realized, of the way leadership operates: No one person, not even the designated leader of an organization, possesses the whole truth. It lies in the group and can be discovered only through everyone having a voice, listening carefully to others, and searching in the Spirit for a common mind.

After demobilization, Gordon and his wife began to frame a more concrete vision for such a community as well as to look for a few others who might become founding members. After several months, a small group began to meet for corporate worship on Sunday afternoons in a borrowed church building, after which they would adjourn to a local restaurant for dinner. Conversation centered on how people's faith should impact their busy, weekday activities. Those who were interested attended weekly studies of the meaning of discipleship. Within two years, the church was able to purchase a four-story house in a run-down part of the city. It was refitted to include offices, a library, classrooms, a reception hall, a dining room, and a chapel. When the renovations were complete, a core group of nine people pledged to become a mission community that—to use Elton Trueblood's provocative words—took "unlimited liability" for one another over the long term.[19] As the church's first brochure warned, doing this is "dangerous, for if one becomes committed in this way, all life will be different and every sphere of one's existence involved in the change."

In 1950 the church moved to a larger house and later a coffee shop before diversifying into nine smaller communities meeting in their own premises. Even today the church has no identifiable church building. Its membership has grown but, by the standards of "successful" congregations, remains relatively small because of the high level of commitment it requires. The church does not rely on one person; rather, each member learns how to pastor the others.

Rather than being centralized in one place, the church has several congregations, each of which is also a mission. They meet at a coffeehouse, a housing project, an arts center, a renewal farm, and a suburban home. All are organized and led by their members. This way of being the church and doing mission runs counter to traditional Christian culture.

From the outset, all major decisions were made by the entire community. While, in the initial stages, Cosby often exhibited more discernment than others as to the way forward, this was not always the case. He and his wife expected and encouraged others to be involved in strategic planning, and frequently a specific vision or plan of action emerged from someone else in the group or as a result of group reflection. In such cases, Cosby energetically supported whatever decisions were made and whoever was chosen to implement them. As the church grew, other congregations were formed. The size of these groups allowed the members to maintain the quality of relationships and accountability experienced by the original group and also distributed the pastoral care of members throughout the entire congregation. Another empowering structure was a class in which each member received help from the others to discern his or her calling. From the earliest days, there was never a sense that their service was primarily an extension of their pastor's work.

As for Cosby himself, he was bound by the same covenant, shared equally in the life of the community, and like everyone else was accountable to its members. He did not operate from a privileged position in the congregation but as one among them. Though he could and often did speak prophetically, his views had power primarily because of the credibility he had gained through his daily and down to earth participation in the community. Like everyone else, he was also involved in serving and rebuilding the local neighborhood. Rather than diminishing Cosby's influence in the church, however, his actions and equal status supported the church's ethos and way of operating.

The most important development in the church's life and, in some respects, the most vital test and demonstration of Cosby's approach to leadership took place in the 1970s. Membership in the church had grown to over one hundred members. Cosby declared that he could no longer fulfill his general pastoral responsibility in the community. He could not give sufficient support even to those who were most active in the congregation and in mission. He suggested that they could either add more church staff or decentralize the operation by dividing the church into smaller units and giving more authority to others. He asked:

> Is it possible that we can divide into different combinations cohering around different worship centers and, in the process of creating the new, not losing what we value? There are many, many people in the life of this community with rare gifts

of leadership that are not being used. . . . It can be exciting, if we do not decide to hang on . . . [but] trust that the same Spirit which brought us to this point will still be around. We as an organization have been blessed, and my guess is that leadership might be developed at an even deeper level than we have known it.[20]

This challenge was the beginning of a wholesale restructuring of the church into a cluster of mission congregations, each with its own leadership and decision-making processes. Although Cosby remained part of the core group to which each center was accountable, he was in no sense the key figure and influence in the various centers.

Although, from one point of view, Cosby increasingly divested himself of leadership in the congregation, from another he demonstrated how profound his practice of it was. He refused to be the one to whom others always looked for guidance and instead released them to take the lead and then assisted in any way he could. What was at the heart of Cosby's capacity to do this? According to Elizabeth O'Connor, a key member of the community and the chief chronicler of its activities, it was his "willingness to question" and his readiness "to give up the old and embrace the new."[21] This sprung, she says, from a wonderful "flexibility of spirit." Cosby also displayed an acute capacity to listen to God, not only in moments of withdrawal but also in the most ordinary situations. For example, the idea for a coffeehouse that would be a hospitable place not only for church members but also for people in the neighborhood looking for a place to hang out did not come during a time of secluded prayer, but as Cosby reflected on the liveliness and interaction in a tavern compared to a dull church service he had just visited. "I realized that there was more warmth and fellowship in that tavern than there was in the church. If Jesus of Nazareth had his choice He would probably have come to the tavern rather than to the church we visited."[22]

Cosby also had a commitment to affirm others. Because he gave "to those he touche[d] a sense of worth and destiny," it is not surprising that others gravitated toward him and felt empowered by him. His belief that everyone can be a special person of God means that ordinary members of the church were "entrusted in ways it has not seen before."[23] Because he was committed to helping people become who God wanted them to be and doing what God wanted them to do, he could give freedom to each of the mission communities to find and implement its own vision.

Implications

Some years ago, a theological student attended a cluster of informal churches meeting in homes to learn more about a nontraditional way of being and doing church. The first meeting he attended began midmorning and ran over lunch until early afternoon. There were roughly twenty-five people present. Every so often during the gathering, he wrote down something that struck or puzzled him. When the meeting ended, he went over to a small group of people and thanked them for their hospitality in allowing him to observe. "There is, however, one aspect of your time together that particularly puzzles me," he said.

"And what's that?" asked one of the others.

"Well, although I kept a careful watch of what took place, I was not able to determine who your leader is!" So many people had participated in such a variety of ways that no one person had stood out from the rest. As it happened, one couple had played a major role in providing a framework for the service, but they had not been visible during the service. This is often the case when a commitment to empowering others rather than exercising power over others is at work. Much empowering takes place out of the spotlight. While it may seem easier for this to happen at the kind of meeting just described, it can also occur at larger, more public occasions. For example, a three-day national consultation was discreetly facilitated by Leighton Ford. Anyone present would have found it extremely difficult to identify him as the key instigator and leader of the event. Likewise, anyone walking into the coffee shop known as the Potter's House in downtown Washington would have found it difficult to pinpoint the key person in the network of congregations and missions of which it is a part. In the broad cross section of people, one would have been hard-pressed to pick the elderly man engaged in a relaxed conversation at one of the tables.

conclusion: the
future of leadership

Not long ago, Max De Pree asked a paradoxical question: "Does leadership have a future?"[1] Intertwined in this provocative question is concern about the rising ineffectiveness and selfishness among leaders. If leadership is to have a future, some important principles need to be preserved. These principles can be illuminated by asking the right questions. While good leaders do not have all the answers, they should possess the wisdom and the insight to raise important questions that search for deeper meaning. Such questions are critical because they help leaders and organizations to find and determine their direction. The leaders just profiled asked some powerful questions of themselves and those around them. Some of their questions correspond with those De Pree sees as important. If leadership is to have a future, these questions must be addressed.

Who do I intend to be? This is not the same as asking, "What do I intend to do?" which is always a consequence of who one intends to be. A person can address this central question by asking, "What do I believe? What is my purpose in life? To what am I, as a leader, devoted?" These questions bring to the foreground the centrality of purpose, virtue, and truth, all of which lead to hope. Without purpose, virtue, and truth, it is difficult to experience hope. An absence of virtues and the presence of deceit do not create the conditions necessary for hope to survive. For leadership to endure, it must be intertwined with hope—hope in the sense of looking forward to the future with expectation. If leadership has a future, leaders must be able to articulate, find, and live out their own sense of hope. Hope grows dim as people deviate from their core values but grows stronger and becomes contagious in the context of shared hope within a community.

What is the source of our humanity? As Christians, we believe that the source of our humanity is found in being created in God's image. This has profound

157

implications for how to treat people in organizations. Seeing each person as created in God's image compels leaders to offer respect, create opportunities for contribution, and affirm the gifts of others.

In the company cafeteria, how good should the bagels be? This is a question of quality. Society seems to care more about numbers than quality, particularly in an increasingly competitive marketplace. What is the quality of our relationships, and what do things such as opportunity, access, and reconciliation have to do with quality?

What will I die for? In other words, what is most essential, what matters most? This is a question of purpose and integrity. When leaders have a clear sense of calling, they serve as models and mentors for others to find and live out their callings.

What may a leader not delegate? For leadership to thrive, leaders need to be clear about what they alone can and therefore must do. Leaders build and maintain trust as well as share responsibilities. They hold both themselves and the organizations they serve accountable. One thing they do not delegate is the obligation to be prepared to lead.[2]

Last, De Pree points to four critical questions that leaders must ponder consistently over the course of their leading:

1. What is my purpose in life?
2. What do I owe?
3. What will I promise?
4. What may I keep?

De Pree insightfully notes that as a society we need to care more about faithfulness than success, more about the potential of communities than individual accomplishment, and more about inclusiveness than winning. The values of society are not always the best guide and indeed often fail to reflect the true essence of leadership. If leadership is to survive, there must be an environment of high moral standards among leaders and followers, and this has the best chance of coming to expression as faith-based leaders live out their core convictions and Christian faith in everyday life and work.

Also critical for the future of leadership is the finding or creating of conducive contexts in which leadership can most effectively develop. Leadership does not come merely from gaining knowledge about it through a set of seminars or a course, though these may certainly be helpful. Some of what is entailed in faithful leadership can come through observing those who embody and practice it. But more is needed.

First, leaders must place people in self-directed teams with intrinsic as well as extrinsic rewards for their performance. People can learn from those working with them how to identify, handle, and evaluate issues related to faithfulness. Group wisdom has much to offer, even when people tackle issues in different ways. Where possible, tackling situations in pairs rather than alone can increase learning curves and improve responses. When there is no agreement on the best course of action, observing the ways others deal with issues allows people to see the strengths and weaknesses of different approaches.

Second, people should be encouraged to become involved in a voluntary organization. In such a setting, acceptance and influence are earned differently—for example, by showing a commitment to the purpose of the organization and by exhibiting a capacity to work well with others. Leighton Ford has said that anyone seeking to become a leader in the church should first gain some experience in the voluntary sector. This is the best context in which to learn whether one has the qualities and attributes required for leadership in a changing world and among the coming generation. Only earned, not expected, authority will now do. In the same way, direct participation in nonprofit organizations creates opportunities for leaders to use and improve their skills. For example, it can help them to move from a reward mentality to a service mind-set, or from a rugged individualism to a commitment to the general good.

Third, people should be shown the benefit of being part of an informal group of people at a similar level. When trust is present in such a group, people feel free to discuss questions related to faithfulness and to ask for help with individual struggles in this area.

In addition, there is always a place for ongoing connections with people who already exhibit faithful leading at work. Much can be gained from a mentoring experience. Anyone who invites a mentoree into such a relationship or finds a mentor with whom he or she can meet several times a year is bound to enhance the prospects for the future of leadership.

Max De Pree, the acclaimed author and former chairman of the board and CEO of Herman Miller Inc.—and to whom this book is dedicated—knows a great deal about creating a legacy. During his stint as CEO from 1980 to 1987, profits at the office furniture manufacturer soared, and people in the company excelled. His values-based leadership earned him a spot in *Fortune* magazine's National Business Hall of Fame, and the Business Enterprise Trust awarded him the lifetime achievement award for his innovative approach to business.

Max's father, D. J. De Pree, founded Herman Miller in the 1920s, grew it, and handed it over to his oldest son, Hugh, in 1962. When Hugh retired in 1980, he passed the torch to Max, who was a vice president in the company at the time. Max understood well the legacy he had inherited from his father and his brother, and he continued to build on the spirit and the practices established by his predecessors. In the following excerpt from his third book,

Leading without Power: Finding Hope in Serving Community, he reflects on the idea of legacy:

> It's important to distinguish between strategic planning and leaving a legacy. A strategic plan is a long-term commitment to something we intend to do. A legacy results from the facts of our behavior that remain in the minds of others, the cumulative, informal record of how close we came to the person we intended to be. It is important to remember that what we do will always be a consequence of who we become. What you plan to do differs enormously from what you leave behind. Becoming an effective leader requires us to think purposefully about legacy. Everyone leaves a legacy, a legacy may consist of words, a building, a single deed. One powerful moment may be our legacy, and we may not even realize it at the time. We must think consciously about what kind of legacy we want to leave our organizations, our communities, and our families.[3]

According to DePree, building a legacy is intentional and takes place over time through actions. It involves the following dimensions:

- *Establishing and maintaining good relationships:* This is at the center of organizational life. Effective leaders cannot be successful without mastering relationships. Relational competence derives from selflessness and real concern for people and is based on understanding and acting on the truth that people are created in the image of God. Competence in relationships results in civility, love, and devotion to a common good. Nothing guarantees it; no leader succeeds without it.
- *Formulating a direction that is clearly observable:* A legacy always reflects a vision. A clear sense of direction is the necessary foundation for a life of service.
- *Defending the truth:* Truth has to be the first level of quality. Without truth, people react in a temporary way to daily pressure. A legacy helps others to preserve and illuminate the truth. Truth can become part of a legacy only when it is lived.
- *Becoming personally accountable:* Many circumstances in life cannot be controlled, but a person can make a choice to accept responsibility for him- or herself and not to deprive others of this important aspect of life.
- *Setting standards that endure:* Such standards are not just of performance but also of dignity and servanthood, good manners, good taste, and decorum. Society cries out for the civility that results from high standards.
- *Lifting the spirit of others:* A spirit-lifting presence is an important part of a legacy. Leaders who have the gift to lift the spirits of those with whom they work inspire others to do the same.

- *Developing constructive constraints and simplicity in work:* Constraints for creative people are not a problem but an opportunity and a guide. Ability does not mandate use. The most powerful people wield their power carefully.
- *Serving to integrate life and faith:* This involves bringing work up to the standards of belief and acting on those beliefs.
- *Enabling others to live up to their full potential:* A legacy extends beyond a person and enables others to achieve. Mentoring, which can happen unintentionally, is a way to pass on wisdom, knowledge, and experience.
- *Saying thank you to the organization and the people with whom one works:* Work can become an expression of gratitude for the chance to contribute. What a person leaves behind, more than anything that person does or says, tells the world what he or she thought of the organization and its work.[4]

A leadership legacy is something that is built over time during each day of one's life. Are we ready for the moment when our convictions will be tested? Have we taken the long view and considered what our actions today will mean years from now? When we think in terms of legacy, work and life take on a new meaning and purpose, and we see things from a new perspective. It is then that our leadership is fully realized, and, if God grants it, it will continue to exercise its influence long after we have passed from the scene.

notes

Introduction

1. Miller, *God at Work*.
2. Banks, *Faith Goes to Work*.
3. Delbecq, "Christian Spirituality and Contemporary Business Leadership."
4. Faber, "Arjay Miller Thinks Business Schools Should Stress Ethics."
5. Ignon, "More MBA Programs Introduce Ethics Courses."
6. Burns, *Leadership*.
7. Fiedler, *Theory of Leadership Effectiveness*.
8. Rost, *Leadership for the Twenty-First Century*.
9. Northouse, *Leadership*.
10. Goethals and Sorenson, *Quest for a General Theory of Leadership*.
11. Kellerman, "Leadership Warts and All."
12. Banks and Ledbetter, *Reviewing Leadership*.
13. Podolny, Khurana, and Besharov, *Revisiting the Meaning of Leadership*, 5.
14. Weber, *From Max Weber*, 6.
15. Hegel, *Philosophy of Right*.
16. Rousseau, *Social Contract and Discourses*.
17. Durkheim, *Division of Labor in Society*.
18. Epstein, "Religion and Business"; Tombaugh and Tombaugh, "Can Spiritual Leadership Lead Us Not into Temptation?"
19. Cullen and Victor, "Ethical Climate Questionnaire."
20. Cullen, Praveen, and Victor, "Effects of Ethical Climates on Organizational Commitment."
21. Fry, Vitucci, and Cedillo, "Spiritual Leadership and Army Transformation."
22. Fry, "Toward a Theory of Spiritual Leadership"; Fry and Slocum, "Maximizing the Triple Bottom Line."
23. Delbecq, "Christian Spirituality and Contemporary Business Leadership."
24. Delbecq, "Spiritual Challenge of Power."
25. Giacalone, "What Are Expansive Values Adherents?"
26. Patel, *Pluralism, Prejudice, and the Promise of America*.
27. Mitroff and Denton, "A Study of Spirituality in the Workplace," 83.
28. Wheatley, "Leadership in Turbulent Times Is Spiritual," 20.
29. Benefiel, "Mapping the Terrain of Spirituality in Organizations Research"; Benefiel, *Soul at Work*.
30. Neal, Lichtenstein, and Banner, "Spiritual Perspectives on Individual, Organizational, and Societal Transformation"; Neal, "Spirituality in the Workplace."

31. Lips-Wiersma, Dean, and Fornaciari, "Theorizing the Dark Side of the Workplace Spirituality Movement."

Chapter 1 Leadership: An Emerging Academic Discipline

1. Kellerman, "Leadership Warts and All."
2. See www.smartbrief.com/industry/business/leadership.
3. Ciulla, *Nature of Leadership*, 509.
4. Rost, *Leadership for the Twenty-First Century*, 104.
5. Ciulla, *Nature of Leadership*, 512.
6. B. V. Moore, "May Conference on Leadership," 124.
7. Parks, *Leadership Can Be Taught*, 35.
8. Stodgill, "Personal Factors Associated with Leadership," 64.
9. Jackson and Parry, *Very Short, Fairly Interesting and Reasonably Cheap Book*.
10. Day and Antonakis, *Nature of Leadership*.
11. Burns, *Leadership*.
12. Bennis, *On Becoming a Leader*.
13. Kouzes and Posner, *Leadership Challenge* (2007).
14. Mintzberg, "Manager's Job," 24.
15. Ibid.
16. House et al., *Culture, Leadership, and Organizations*.
17. Pearce and Conger, "All Those Years Ago."
18. Stodgill, *Handbook of Leadership*.
19. Ibid.
20. Fiedler, "Contingency Model of Leadership Effectiveness."
21. Hersey and Blanchard, "Life-Cycle Theory of Leadership."
22. House, "Path-Goal Theory of Leader Effectiveness."
23. Dansereau, Graen, and Haga, "Vertical Dyad Linkage Approach."
24. Jackson and Parry, *Very Short, Fairly Interesting and Reasonably Cheap Book*.
25. Fiedler, "Contingency Model of Leadership Effectiveness."
26. Hersey and Blanchard, "Life-Cycle Theory of Leadership."
27. House, "Path-Goal Theory of Leader Effectiveness."
28. Dansereau, Graen, and Haga, "Vertical Dyad Linkage Approach."
29. Greenleaf, *Servant Leadership*.
30. Ibid., 27.
31. Schein, *Organizational Culture and Leadership*.
32. Hofstede, *Culture's Consequences*.
33. House et al. *Culture, Leadership, and Organizations*.
34. Dorfman, "International Cross-Cultural Leadership Research."
35. Bernard, *Research Methods in Anthropology*, 23.
36. Carroll, Levy, and Richmond, "Leadership as Practice."
37. Bekker, "Towards a Theoretical Model of Christian Leadership."
38. Benefiel, *Soul at Work*, 9.

Chapter 2 Biblical, Historical, and Denominational Perspectives on Leadership

1. See further Stevens, *Leadership Roles of the Old Testament*. On Moses, note Wildavsky, *Moses as a Political Leader*; on Solomon, Manz et al., *Wisdom of Solomon*.
2. For some examples, see Goldingay, *Men Behaving Badly*: "The Man Born to Be Tough," "The Man Who Didn't Want to Be Responsible," "The Man Who Made Little Mistakes," "The Man Who Lost His Grip," etc.

3. See Ellul, *Politics of God and the Politics of Man*, especially his "Meditation on Utility" (190–99), evaluating the life and work of seven early Israelite leaders.

4. Strom, *Lead with Wisdom*, 249.

5. Anscough and Cotton, *Passionate Visionary*.

6. Strom, *Lead with Wisdom*, 243–55.

7. See Banks, *Paul's Idea of Community*; Banks, "Pauline Church Order and Governance"; Doohan, *Leadership in Paul*; Sanders, *Paul the Leader*; and Rinehart, *Upside Down*, 94–98, 106–7.

8. See Banks, "Pauline Church Order and Governance."

9. Whittington et al., "Legacy Leadership," 753.

10. Ibid.

11. Anscough and Cotton, *Passionate Visionary*.

12. See Lewis, *Models and Meanings in the History of Jewish Leadership*, which analyzes leadership paradigms through the biblical, rabbinic, medieval, and contemporary periods.

13. See O'Keefe, "The Benedictine Abbot."

14. Benedict, *The Rule of Saint Benedict*.

15. Lull, "Underachievers? Or Reformers?"

16. See Bavinck, *Our Reasonable Faith*, 32.

17. Mouw, "Leadership and the Threefold Office of Christ."

18. Keiser and Keiser, "Quaker Principles in the Crucible of Practice."

19. Smith, *Quaker Book of Wisdom*, 182.

20. Wood, "Christ Has Come to Teach His People Himself."

21. Weems, *Leadership in the Wesleyan Spirit*.

22. Ibid., 48.

23. Robeck, "Pentecostal Perspective on Leadership."

24. See, e.g., Gooch, *English Democratic Ideas in the Seventeenth Century*.

25. Shekerjian, *Uncommon Genius*, 101–2.

Chapter 3 Spiritual and Religious Dimensions of Leadership: The Ethical Foundation

1. Oman, "Defining Religion and Spirituality."

2. Hill et al., "Conceptualizing Religion and Spirituality," 66.

3. Fry, "Toward a Theory of Spiritual Leadership," 694–95.

4. Jackson and Parry, *A Very Short, Fairly Interesting and Reasonably Cheap Book*.

5. Wong and Vinsky, "Speaking from the Margins."

6. Klenke, "Internal Theater of the Authentic Leader."

7. Hackett et al., "The Global Religious Landscape."

8. Epstein, "Religion and Business"; Tombaugh and Tombaugh, "Can Spiritual Leadership Lead Us Not into Temptation?"

9. Josephson, "Teaching Ethical Decision-Making and Principled Reasoning," 88.

10. Hanh, *Peace Is Every Step*.

11. S. J. Reynolds, "Moral Attentiveness."

12. Pruzan, "Question of Organizational Consciousness."

13. Ruedy and Schweitzer, "In the Moment."

14. Pruzan, "Spirituality as the Context for Leadership."

15. Karakas and Sarigollu, "Role of Leadership in Creating Virtuous and Compassionate Organizations."

16. Sutton and Rao, *Scaling Up Excellence*, 33–65.

17. Schulte, *Overwhelmed*, 27, 10.

18. Covey, *Seven Habits of Highly Effective People*.

19. Covey, *Principle-Centered Leadership*.

20. Covey, Merrill, and Merrill, *First Things First*.

21. Wolfe, "White Magic."

22. Covey, *Principle-Centered Leadership*, 40–47.

23. Ibid., 33–39.

24. Wolfe, "White Magic," 32.

25. As in Conger, *Spirit at Work*.

26. Cf. Hillman, *Soul's Code*; Hawley, *Reawakening the Spirit in Work*; and Briskin, *Stirring of Soul in the Workplace*.

27. Cf. W. C. Miller, "How Do We Put Our Spiritual Values to Work?"; Fox, *Reinvention of Work*; Hendricks and Ludeman, *Corporate Mystic*; Orsborn, *Inner Excellence*; and the interviews with Matthew Fox, Keshavan Nair, and Barry Schieber in Garfield, *Soul of Business*, 73–98, 123–46, 169–92.

28. Bolman and Deal, *Leading with Soul*.

29. Moxley, *Leadership and Spirit*.

30. Ibid., xiv.

31. Ibid., 24.

32. Vaill, *Spirited Leading and Learning*.

33. Hartshorne, *Reality as Social Process*.

34. Vaill, *Spirited Leading and Learning*, 5.

35. Ibid., 179.

36. Ibid., 180.

37. Ibid., 208.

38. Ibid., 219.

39. Ibid., 208.

40. D. W. Miller, *God at Work*.

41. Ibid.

42. Sire, *Václav Havel*.

43. Haughey, "Leader's Conscience," 43.

44. Havel, *Disturbing the Peace*, 199.

45. Ibid., 120, 123.

46. Havel, *Letters to Olga*, 331–33.

47. Sire, *Václav Havel*, 98.

48. Havel, *Disturbing the Peace*, 102.

49. Vladilav, *Václav Havel*, 12.

50. Havel, *Disturbing the Peace*, 8.

51. Ibid., 11.

52. Havel, "Revolution Has Just Begun," 15.

53. Havel, *Disturbing the Peace*, 203.

54. Ibid., 204–5.

55. Cf. Haughey, *Converting 9 to 5*; Palmer, *Active Life*; Diehl, *Monday Connection*; Jacobsen, *Hearts to God, Hands to Work*; and most recently, Pierce, *Spirituality at Work*.

56. Brown, *Learning to Lead from Your Spiritual Center*.

57. Ibid., 11.

58. Ibid.

59. De Pree, *Leading without Power*.

Chapter 4 Faith-Based Approaches to Leadership

1. Nair, *Higher Standard of Leadership*; Edelman and Crain, *Tao of Negotiation*; Autry and Mitchell, *Real Power*; Renesch, *Leadership in a New Era*; Bolman and Deal, *Leading with Soul*; some of the essays in Renesch, *New Traditions in Business*. Others have drawn on the New Science, often drawing out its spiritual implications. Such works include Jaworski, *Synchronicity*; Wheatley, *Leadership and the New Science*.

2. Autry, *Confessions of an Accidental Businessman*; Beckett, *Loving Monday*; Blanchard, Hybels, and Hodges, *Leadership by the Book*; Chappell, *Soul of a Business*; Melrose, *Making the Grass Greener on Your Side*; Novak, *Business as a Calling*; Pollard, *Soul of the Firm*; some material in Conger, *Spirit at Work*; Spears, *Insights on Leadership*, 197–267; and Baron and Padwa, *Moses on Management*. Two substantial empirically-based studies of the way religiously-inclined leaders function are Nash, *Believers in Business*; and Pascarella, *Christ-Centered Leadership*.

3. Baron and Padwa, *Moses on Management*, 278–84.

4. Jones, *Jesus CEO*, 317. Other books along similar lines are Briner, *Leadership Lessons of Jesus*; and Briner and Pritchard, *More Leadership Lessons of Jesus*.

5. Jones, *Jesus CEO*, preface.

6. Ibid., 295–302.

7. Ibid., 296–99.

8. Ibid., 16.

9. Ibid., 17.

10. Ibid., 295.

11. Manz, *Leadership Wisdom of Jesus*.

12. De Pree, *Leadership Is an Art*; De Pree, *Leadership Jazz*; De Pree, *Leading without Power*.

13. Cruikshank and Malcolm, *Herman Miller, Inc.*

14. De Pree, *Leading without Power*, 127–29.

15. Ibid.

16. Le Peau, *Paths of Leadership*.

17. See Banks, *Reenvisioning Theological Education*.

18. Cadbury, *Peril of Modernizing Jesus*, 4.

19. Ibid., 9.

20. Barton, *Man Nobody Knows*, 11.

21. Cadbury, *Peril of Modernizing Jesus*, 123–24.

22. Ibid., 141–42.

23. Ibid., 77.

24. Ibid., 99–100.

25. Ibid., 101–2.

26. See Hauerwas, *Peaceable Kingdom*, 72–95.

27. Ibid., 96–115.

28. Goldingay, *Men Behaving Badly*.

29. Wright, *Relational Leadership*.

30. Clinton, *Making of a Leader*.

31. Ibid., 181.

32. Clinton, "Emerging Leader," 28.

33. Banks, *Faith Goes to Work*, 18–30.

34. Diehl, *In Search of Faithfulness*.

35. Peters and Waterman, *In Search of Excellence*.

36. Schumacher, *To Live and Work*; Schumacher, *God in Work*.

37. Sayers, *Mind of the Maker*.

38. Preece, *Trinitarian Perspective on Work*.

39. Moltmann, *Trinity and the Kingdom of God*; Volf, *Work in the Spirit*.

40. LaCugna, *God for Us*.

41. Senge, *Fifth Discipline*.

42. Moxley, *Leadership and Spirit*.

43. De Pree, "What Is Leadership?," 131.

44. Block and Koestenbaum, *Freedom and Accountability at Work*, 30.

45. Rinehart, *Upside Down*.

46. Ibid., 88–90, 104–6. For a critique of the Orthodox view of the Trinity as too hierarchical and containing no democratic element, see Volf, *Trinity and Community*, where the writings of John D. Zizioulas, especially his *Being as Communion*, are particularly in view.

47. Williams and McKibben, *Oriented Leadership*.

48. Ibid., 22–23.

49. Ibid., 24, 29.

50. Ibid., 139.

51. Naisbitt and Aburdene, *Megatrends 2000*, 36.

52. OECD, "Gender and Sustainable Development."

53. Warner, "Fact Sheet: The Women's Leadership Gap"; OECD, "Gender and Sustainable Development"; Catalyst, "The Ripple Effect."

54. Catalyst, "The Case for Gender Diversity in Japan."

55. Elborgh-Woytek et al., "Women, Work and the Economy."

56. Daimon, "New Group of Female Executives Hopes to Boost Ranks in Japan Inc."

57. Brasor, "Attitude Change Needed to Shake Up the Workforce."

58. Prime and Salib, "Inclusive Leadership."

59. Tyree-Hyche, "In Keeping with the Spirit."

60. Ulrich, "Talent Trifecta."

61. *Fortune* Editors, "The International Power 50."

62. James, *Thinking in the Future Tense*, 214.

63. Ibid., 226.

64. Hagberg, *Real Power*, xxi.

65. Ibid.

Chapter 5 Practicing Leadership through Faithfulness, Integrity, and Service

1. Clutterbuck, *Doing It Different*.

2. See ibid. See also Vaill, *Managing as a Performing Art*; and Pitcher, *Drama of Leadership*.

3. Lakoff and Johnson, *Metaphors We Live By*.

4. Morgan, *Images of Organization*.

5. Goleman, *Emotional Intelligence*; Goleman, *Working with Emotional Intelligence*; and Goleman, Boyatzis, and McKee, *Primal Leadership*.

6. Raimundo, *Relational Capital*.

7. Mant, *Intelligent Leadership*.

8. See Dalla Costa, *Working Wisdom*.

9. Strom, *Lead with Wisdom*, esp. 244–51.

10. La Barre, "Do You Have the Will to Lead?"

11. Ibid.

12. Kouzes and Posner, "Seven Lessons for Leading the Voyage to the Future," 102–3.

13. Alford and Naughton, *Managing as If Faith Mattered*, 70–96. See further MacIntyre, *After Virtue*; and Hauerwas, *Vision and Virtue*.

14. Jinkins and Jinkins, *Character of Leadership*, 101–6.

15. Bellah, *Habits of the Heart*; and Covey, *Seven Habits of Highly Effective People*.

16. De Pree, *Leading without Power*, 127, 129.

17. Kouzes and Posner, *Credibility*.

18. Reichheld with Teal, *Loyalty Effect*, 303–4.

19. Thomas, "Ethical Integrity and Organizational Mortal Culture."

20. Emler and Cook, "Moral Integrity in Leadership."

21. Pearson, *Integrity in Organizations*.

22. Graham, "Servant-Leadership and Enterprise Strategy," esp. 151–55.

23. Carter, *Integrity*, 5–6.

24. Solomon, *Ethics and Excellence*, 168.

25. Higginson, *Transforming Leadership*, 58.

26. Kraybill and Good, *Perils of Professionalism*.

27. See further Higginson, *Transforming Leadership*, 54–55.

28. See Autry, *Love and Profit*.

29. Amann and Stachowicz-Stanusch, *Integrity in Organizations*.

30. Bonhoeffer, *Ethics*, 67, 125–43.

31. Higginson, *Transforming Leadership*, 78.

32. Greenleaf, "Life's Choices and Markers." This appears in Greenleaf's seminal essay, *The Servant as Leader*, partly reprinted in Spears, *Insights on Leadership*, 15–20; and more fully in Greenleaf, *Servant Leadership*.

33. Nielsen, "Quaker Foundations for Greenleaf's Servant Leadership."

34. Greenleaf, *Seeker and Servant*, 201.

35. Fraker, "Robert K. Greenleaf and Business Ethics," 37. See Greenleaf, *Servant Leadership*, 28–29.

36. DiStefano, "Tracing the Vision and Impact of Robert K. Greenleaf," 63.

37. See Greenleaf, *Servant Leadership*, 28–29.

38. Ibid., 186.

39. Ibid., 29–30, 81.

40. Spears, *Reflections on Leadership*, 4–7; and Batten, "Servant-Leadership."

41. Wright, *Relational Leadership*, 13–17.

42. Block, *Empowered Manager*.

43. Block, *Stewardship: Choosing Service over Self-Interest*.

44. Ibid., xx.

45. Block, "Stewardship: From Leadership to Citizenship," 88.

46. Trompenaars and Voerman, *Servant-Leadership across Cultures*.

47. Blanchard, "Servant-Leadership Revisited," 27.

48. Greenleaf, *Old Age*, 2.

49. See Greenleaf, *Spirituality and Leadership*.

50. Roels, *Moving beyond Servant Leadership*.

51. Dunfee, *Beyond Servanthood*. Cf. Isasi-Díaz, "Un Poquito de Justicia."

52. Zaragoza, *No Longer Servants but Friends*, 38–39.

53. Tan, *Full Service*, 43.

54. See now also Tan, *Full Service*, 55.

55. E. Peterson, "Follow the Leader."

Chapter 6 Leader Development: Leaving a Legacy

1. McCall, "Recasting Leadership Development."

2. Kegan, *Evolving Self*.

3. Colvin, "Personal Bests."

4. Mumford et al., "Leadership Skills for a Changing World."

5. King, "I Have a Dream." www.american.rhetoric.com/speeches/mlkihaveadream.htm.

6. Gilligan and Attanucci, "Two Moral Orientations."

7. Smetana, Killen, and Turiel, "Children's Reasoning about Interpersonal and Moral Conflicts."

8. Connor and Becker, "Personal Value Systems and Decision-Making Styles of Public Managers."

9. Piaget, *Moral Judgment of the Child*.

10. Braithwaite and Scott, "Values," 745.

11. Rokeach, *Understanding Human Values*; S. H. Schwartz, "Universals in the Content and Structure of Values."

12. Rokeach, *Understanding Human Values*.

13. Piaget, *Moral Judgment of the Child*.

14. Kohlberg, "Moral Stages and the Idea of Justice."

15. Ledbetter, "Values Approach to Advancing Women in Leadership."
16. Blake and Mouton, *Managerial Grid III*.
17. Burns, *Leadership*.
18. Ledbetter, "Values Approach to Advancing Women in Leadership."
19. Ibid.
20. Damon, *Moral Child*.
21. Crittenden, *Learning to Be Moral*.
22. Fairholm, *Perspectives on Leadership*.
23. Trevino, Hartman, and Brown, "Moral Person and Moral Manager."
24. S. J. Reynolds, "Moral Attentiveness."
25. Reynolds, Owens, and Rubenstein, "Moral Stress," 493.
26. Badaracco, *Defining Moments*, 5.
27. Reynolds, Owens, and Rubenstein, "Moral Stress," 497.
28. Almedom and Glandon, "Resilience Is Not the Absence of PTSD"; Zautra, "Resilience."
29. Almedom and Glandon, "Resilience Is Not the Absence of PTSD"; Coutu, "How Resilience Works."
30. Zautra, "Resilience," 1936.
31. Reynolds, Owens, and Rubenstein, "Moral Stress."
32. Coutu, "How Resilience Works."
33. Almedom and Glandon, "Resilience Is Not the Absence of PTSD," 131.
34. "Hijrah: Resilience and Resolve," para. 5.
35. Reave, "Spiritual Values and Practices Related to Leadership Effectiveness."
36. Patterson, "Resilience in the Face of Adversity."
37. Pavlovich, "Educating for Consciousness."
38. Chopra, *Soul of Leadership*.
39. Weick and Putnam, "Organizing for Mindfulness"; Brown, Ryan, and Creswell, "Mindfulness."
40. Palmer, *Active Life*.
41. Ibid., 25.
42. Palmer, "To Whom Do You Report?," 20.
43. Palmer, *Active Life*, 31.
44. Tyree-Hyche, "In Keeping with the Spirit."
45. Fowler, *Stages of Faith*.
46. Quackenbush and Barnett, "Recollection and Evaluation of Critical Experience in Moral Development," 56.
47. Loder, *Logic of the Spirit*.
48. Ibid., 293.
49. Whittington et al., "Legacy Leadership."
50. Wildavsky, *Nursing Father*.
51. Whittington et al., "Legacy Leadership."
52. Ibid.
53. Stanley, *Visioneering Sisters*.

Chapter 7 Governance: Practicing Faith-Based Leadership

1. Forbes and Milliken, "Cognition and Corporate Governance," 492.
2. Bayrasli, "Building Successful Non-Profit Boards." *Forbes*. http://www.forbes.com/sites/elmirabayrasli/2011/06/06/building-successful-non-profit-boards.
3. Groysberg and Bell, "Joining Boards."
4. Tonello, "Corporate Director Selection and Recruitment."
5. Casal and Caspar, "Building a Forward-Looking Board," para. 10.
6. De Pree, *Leadership Is an Art*.
7. Burton, Obel, and DeSanctis, *Organizational Design*.

8. Ludwig and Longnecker, "Bathsheba Syndrome."

9. Goldsmith, "Success Delusion."

10. De Pree, *Leadership Jazz*.

11. Fairholm, *Perspectives on Leadership*.

12. Burns, *Leadership*, 20.

13. Fairholm, *Perspectives on Leadership*.

14. Carver, "Revisiting Values in Policy Governance."

15. Brown, Ferris, and Kolodinsky, "Political Skill, Servant Leadership, and Workplace Spirituality," 133.

16. Mintzberg, *Power in and around Organizations*.

17. Ibid.

18. Ferris et al., "Political Skill in Organizations."

19. Kovacs, "Theoretical Foundation of Buddhist Management Practices."

20. Thera, *Threefold Division of the Noble Eightfold Path*.

21. Hanh, *Walking the Noble Path*.

22. Zsolnai, "Buddhist Economic Strategy."

23. Sacks, "Patagonia CEO Rose Marcario Fights the Fights Worth Fighting."

24. Marcario, "Repair is a Radical Act."

25. Patagonia, "Company History."

26. Beekun, "Character Centered Leadership," 1003.

27. Ibid., 1006.

28. Bass and Steidlmeier, "Ethics, Character and Authentic Transformational Leadership Behavior."

29. Beekun, "Character Centered Leadership," 1008.

30. Said, *The World, the Text, and the Critic*.

31. Beekun, "Character Centered Leadership," 1010.

32. Ibid., 1012.

33. IFYC, "About Eboo."

34. Ibid.

35. Pearce and Conger, "All Those Years Ago," 1.

36. Vandewaerde et al., "Board Team Leadership Revisited."

37. Bligh, Pearce, and Kohles, "Importance of Self- and Shared Leadership in Team Based Knowledge Work."

38. Vandewaerde et al., "Board Team Leadership Revisited," 408.

39. Strom, "'To Know as We Are Known,'" 87.

40. Ibid.

41. Orpheus Chamber Orchestra. http://orpheusnyc.org/about-orpheus/mission-process/.

42. Lubans, "Invisible Leader."

43. Pearce and Conger, "All Those Years Ago," 1.

44. Hosking, "Organizing, Leadership, and Skillful Process"; Uhl-Bien, "Relational Leadership Theory."

Chapter 8 Christian Leadership in Action: Some Exemplary Case Studies

1. Lean, *On the Tail of a Comet*, 43.

2. Quoted in ibid., 2.

3. Van Dusen, "Apostle to the Twentieth Century," 1–2.

4. Cf. Lean, *On the Tail of a Comet*, 461.

5. Howard, *Frank Buchman's Secret*, 13.

6. Lean, *On the Tail of a Comet*, 175.

7. Frank Buchman, New Year's address, 1943.

8. Gates, *Life and Thought of Kierkegaard for Everyman*, 141.

9. De Pree, *Leadership Jazz*, 219.

10. Buford, *Halftime*.

11. Hagberg and Guelich, *Critical Journey*, 21.

12. Ibid., 23.

13. Hagberg and Leider, *Inventurers*.

14. Hagberg, *Real Power*, viii.

15. Nouwen, *In the Name of Jesus*, 59–60.

16. Greenleaf, *Servant Leadership*, 13.

17. De Pree, *Leadership Is an Art*, xxi.

18. O'Connor, *Call to Commitment*, 13.

19. Trueblood, *Incendiary Fellowship*, 86.

20. O'Connor, *New Community*, 91–92.

21. O'Connor, *Call to Commitment*, 5.

22. Ibid., 109.

23. Ibid., 42, 86.

Conclusion: The Future of Leadership

1. De Pree, *Does Leadership Have a Future?*

2. Ibid., 14–15.

3. De Pree, "Leaving a Legacy."

4. De Pree, *Leading without Power*, 166–75.

bibliography

Alford, Helen J., and Michael J. Naughton. *Managing as If Faith Mattered: Christian Social Principles in the Modern Organization*. Notre Dame, IN: University of Notre Dame Press, 2001.

Almedom, A. M., and D. Glandon. "Resilience Is Not the Absence of PTSD Any More Than Health Is the Absence of Disease." *Journal of Loss and Trauma* 12 (2007): 127–43.

Amann, W., and A. Stachowicz-Stanusch. *Integrity in Organizations*. New York: Palgrave Macmillan, 2013.

Anscough, Richard S., and Sandy Cotton. *Passionate Visionary: Leadership Lessons from the Apostle Paul*. Ottawa: Novalis, 2005.

Aubrey, Robert, and Paul M. Cohen. *Working Wisdom*. San Francisco: Jossey-Bass, 1995.

Autry, James A. *Confessions of an Accidental Businessman*. San Francisco: Berrett-Koehler, 1996.

———. *Life and Work: A Manager's Search for Meaning*. New York: Morrow, 1994.

———. *Love and Profit: The Art of Caring Leadership*. New York: Morrow, 1991.

Autry, James A., and Stephen Mitchell. *Real Power: Business Lessons from the Tao Te Ching*. New York: Riverhead Books, 1998.

Avolio, Bruce. *Full Range Leadership Development*. Thousand Oaks, CA: Sage, 2011.

Badaracco, Joseph L., Jr. *Defining Moments: When Managers Must Choose between Right and Right*. Boston: Harvard Business School Press, 1997.

———. *Leadership and the Quest of Integrity*. Boston: Harvard Business School Press, 1989.

Banks, Robert, ed. *Faith Goes to Work: Reflections from the Marketplace*. Washington, DC: Alban Institute, 1993.

———. "Pauline Church Order and Governance." In *Dictionary of Paul and His Letters*, edited by Gerald F. Hawthorne and Ralph P. Martin, 131–37. Downers Grove, IL: InterVarsity, 1993.

———. *Paul's Idea of Community: The Early House Churches in Their Historical Setting.* Peabody, MA: Hendrickson, 1994.

———. *Reenvisioning Theological Education: Exploring a Missional Alternative to Current Models.* Grand Rapids: Eerdmans, 1999.

Banks, Robert J., and Bernice M. Ledbetter. *Reviewing Leadership: A Christian Evaluation of Current Approaches.* Grand Rapids: Baker Academic, 2004.

Baron, David, and Lynette Padwa. *Moses on Management: Fifty Leadership Lessons from the Greatest Manager of All Time.* New York: Pocket Books, 1999.

Barton, Bruce. *The Man Nobody Knows.* Indianapolis: Bobbs-Merrill, 1925.

Bass, Bernard M. *Leadership and Performance beyond Expectations.* New York: Free Press, 1985.

———. *Transformational Leadership: Industrial, Military, and Educational Impact.* Mahwah, NJ: Lawrence Earlbaum, 1998.

Bass, Bernard M., and P. Steidlmeier. "Ethics, Character and Authentic Transformational Leadership Behavior." *Leadership Quarterly* 10, no. 2 (1999): 181–217.

Batten, Joe D. "Servant-Leadership: A Passion to Serve." In *Insights on Leadership*, edited by Larry C. Spears, 47–60. New York: Wiley, 1998.

———. *Tough-Minded Leadership.* New York: Amacom, 1989.

Bavinck, Herman. *Our Reasonable Faith: A Survey of Christian Doctrine.* Grand Rapids: Eerdmans, 1956.

Bayrasli, E. "Building Successful Non-Profit Boards." *Forbes*, June 6, 2011. http://www.forbes.com/sites/elmirabayrasli/2011/06/06/building-successful-non-profit-boards.

Beckett, John. *Loving Monday.* Downers Grove, IL: InterVarsity, 1998.

Beckhard, Richard. *Changing the Essence.* San Francisco: Jossey-Bass, 1992.

Beekun, R. I. "Character Centered Leadership: Muhammad as an Ethical Role Model for CEOs." *Journal of Management Development* 31, no. 10 (2012): 1003–20.

Bekker, Corné. "Towards a Theoretical Model of Christian Leadership." *Journal of Biblical Perspectives in Leadership* 2, no. 2 (2009): 142–52.

Belasco, James A. *Teaching the Elephant to Dance.* New York: Plume, 1990.

Bellah, Robert N. *Habits of the Heart: Individualism and Commitment in American Life.* New York: Harper & Row, 1985.

Below, Patrick J., George L. Morrisey, and Betty L. Acomb. *The Executive Guide to Strategic Planning.* San Francisco: Jossey-Bass, 1987.

Benedict (Saint Abbot of Monte Cassino). *The Rule of Saint Benedict.* Translated by A. C. Meisel and M. L. Maestro. Garden City, NY: Image Books, 1975.

Benefiel, Margaret. "Mapping the Terrain of Spirituality in Organizations Research." *Journal of Organizational Change Management* 16, no. 4 (2003): 367–77.

———. *Soul at Work: Spiritual Leadership in Organizations.* New York: Seabury Books, 2005.

Benfari, Robert. *Understanding and Changing Your Management Style*. San Francisco: Jossey-Bass, 1999.

Bennis, Warren. *On Becoming a Leader*. Reading, MA: Addison-Wesley, 1989.

———. *Why Leaders Can't Lead: The Unconscious Conspiracy Continues*. San Francisco: Jossey-Bass, 1989.

Bennis, Warren, and Joan Goldsmith. *Learning to Lead*. Reading, MA: Addison-Wesley, 1994.

Bennis, Warren, and Burt Nanus. *Leaders: Strategies for Taking Charge*. Rev. ed. New York: Harper & Row, 1997.

Bennis, Warren, Jagdish Parikh, and Ronnie Lessem. *Beyond Leadership: Balancing Economics, Ethics, and Ecology*. Oxford: Blackwell, 1994.

Benton, Debra A. *Secrets of a CEO Coach: Your Personal Training Guide to Thinking Like a Leader and Acting Like a CEO*. New York: McGraw-Hill, 1999.

Bernard, H. Russell. *Research Methods in Anthropology: Qualitative and Quantitative Approaches*, 4th ed. Oxford: AltaMira, 2006.

Blake, Robert R., and Jane S. Mouton. *The Managerial Grid III: A New Look at the Classic That Has Boosted Productivity and Profits for Thousands of Corporations Worldwide*. Houston: Gulf, 1985.

Blanchard, Kenneth. "Servant-Leadership Revisited." In *Insights on Leadership*, edited by Larry C. Spears, 21–28. New York: Wiley, 1998.

Blanchard, Kenneth, Bill Hybels, and Phil Hodges. *Leadership by the Book: Tools to Transform Your Workplace*. New York: Morrow, 1999.

Blanchard, Kenneth, and Terry Waghorn. *Mission Possible: Becoming a World-Class Organization While There's Still Time*. New York: McGraw-Hill, 1997.

Bligh, M. C., C. L. Pearce, and J. C. Kohles. "The Importance of Self- and Shared Leadership in Team Based Knowledge Work: A Meso-Level Model of Leadership Dynamics." *Journal of Managerial Psychology* 21, no. 4 (2006): 296–318.

Block, Peter. *The Empowered Manager*. San Francisco: Jossey-Bass, 1987.

———. *Stewardship: Choosing Service over Self-Interest*. San Francisco: Berrett-Koehler, 1993.

———. "Stewardship: From Leadership to Citizenship." In *Insights on Leadership*, edited by Larry C. Spears, 87–95. New York: Wiley, 1998.

Block, Peter, and Peter Koestenbaum. *Freedom and Accountability at Work: Applying Philosophical Insight to the Real World*. San Francisco: Jossey-Bass, 2001.

Bolles, Richard Nelson. *What Color Is Your Parachute?* San Francisco: Berrett-Koehler, 1993.

Bolman, Lee G., and Terrence E. Deal. *Leading with Soul: An Uncommon Journey of Spirit*. San Francisco: Jossey-Bass, 1995.

———. *Reframing Organizations*. San Francisco: Jossey-Bass, 1991.

Bonhoeffer, Dietrich. *Ethics*. London: SCM, 1986.

Bouque, E. Grady. *The Enemies of Leadership: Lessons for Leaders in Education*. Bloomington, IN: Phi Delta Kappa Educational Foundation, 1985.

———. *Leadership by Design: Strengthening Integrity in Higher Education*. San Francisco: Jossey-Bass, 1994.

Bracey, Hyler, Jack Rosenblum, Aubrey Sanford, and Roy Trueblood. *Managing from the Heart*. New York: Delacorte Press, 1990.

Braithwaite, Valerie A., and William A. Scott. "Values." In *Measures of Personality and Social Psychological Attitudes*, edited by J. P. Robinson, P. R. Shaver, and L. S. Wrightsman, 661–753. San Diego: Academic Press, 1991.

Brasor, Philip. "Attitude Change Needed to Shake Up the Workforce." *Japan Times*, November 25, 2012. http://www.japantimes.co.jp/news/2012/11/25/national/attitude -change-needed-to-shake-up-the-workforce/#.VAAA-vldWSp.

Brim, Gilbert. *Ambition: How We Manage Success and Failure throughout Our Lives*. New York: Basic Books, 1992.

Briner, Bob. *The Leadership Lessons of Jesus: A Timeless Model for Today's Leaders*. Nashville: Broadman & Holman, 1997.

Briner, Bob, and Ray Pritchard. *More Leadership Lessons of Jesus: A Timeless Model for Today's Leaders*. Nashville: Broadman & Holman, 1998.

Briskin, Alan. *The Stirring of Soul in the Workplace*. San Francisco: Jossey-Bass, 1996.

Brown, K. W., R. M. Ryan, and J. D. Creswell. "Mindfulness: Theoretical Foundations and Evidence for Its Salutary Effects." *Psychological Inquiry* 18 (2007): 1–27.

Brown, Michael G., Gerald R. Ferris, and Robert W. Kolodinsky. "Political Skill, Servant Leadership, and Workplace Spirituality in the Creation of Effective Work Environments." In *Handbook of Workplace Spirituality and Organizational Performance*, 2nd ed., edited by Robert A. Giacalone and Carole L. Jurkiewicz, 126–42. Armonk, NY: M. E. Sharpe, 2010.

Brown, Patricia D. *Learning to Lead from Your Spiritual Center*. Nashville: Abingdon, 1996.

Brueggemann, Walter, Sharon Parks, and Thomas H. Groome. *To Act Justly, Love Tenderly, Walk Humbly: An Agenda for Ministers*. New York: Paulist Press, 1986.

Bryman, Alan. *Charisma and Leadership in Organizations*. London: Sage, 1992.

Bryson, John M., and Barbara C. Crosby. *Leadership for the Common Good: Tackling Public Problems in a Shared-Power World*. San Francisco: Jossey-Bass, 1992.

Buford, Bob. *Halftime: Changing Your Game Plan from Success to Significance*. Grand Rapids: Zondervan, 1994.

Burns, James MacGregor. *Leadership*. New York: Harper & Row, 1978.

Burton, R. M., B. Obel, and G. DeSanctis. *Organizational Design: A Step-by-Step Approach*. 2nd ed. New York: Cambridge University Press, 2011.

Cadbury, Henry. *The Peril of Modernizing Jesus*. London: SPCK, 1962.

Cairnes, Margot. *Approaching the Corporate Heart: Breaking through to New Horizons of Personal and Professional Success*. New York: Simon & Schuster, 1998.

Callahan, Kennon L. *Effective Church Leadership: Building on the Twelve Keys*. San Francisco: Harper & Row, 1990.

Carroll, Brigid, Lester Levy, and David Richmond. "Leadership as Practice: Challenging the Competency Paradigm." Paper presented at the International Conference for Studying Leadership, University of Warwick, December 14–15, 2007.

Carter, Stephen L. *Integrity*. New York: Basic Books, 1996.

Carver, J. "Revisiting Values in Policy Governance." *Board Leadership* (July–August 2007): 7–8.

Casal, C., and C. Caspar. "Building a Forward-Looking Board." *McKinsey Quarterly* 2 (2014): 119–26. http://www.mckinsey.com/insights/strategy/building_a_forward -looking_board.

Catalyst. "The Case for Gender Diversity in Japan." May 21, 2014. http://www.catalyst .org/knowledge/gender-diversity-japan.

———. "The Ripple Effect: What's Good for Women Is Good for the World." March 3, 2014. http://www.catalyst.org/knowledge/ripple-effect-women-world.

Chait, Richard P., Thomas P. Holland, and Barbara E. Taylor. *The Effective Board of Trustees*. Phoenix: Oryx Press, 1993.

Champy, James. *Reengineering Management: The Mandate for New Leadership*. New York: HarperBusiness, 1995.

Champy, James, and Nitin Nohria. *The Arc of Ambition: Defining the Leadership Journey*. Cambridge, MA: Perseus Books, 2000.

Chappell, Tom. *The Soul of a Business: Managing for Profit and the Common Good*. New York: Bantam Books, 1993.

Childress, John R., and Larry E. Senn. *In the Eye of the Storm: Reengineering Corporate Culture*. Los Angeles: Leadership Press, 1995.

Chopra, Deepak. *The Soul of Leadership*. New York: Harmony Books, 2010.

Ciulla, Joanne B. "Ethics and Effectiveness: The Nature of Good Leadership." In *The Nature of Leadership*, 2nd ed., edited by David V. Day and John Antonakis, 508–40. Los Angeles: Sage, 2012.

———. *Ethics: The Heart of Leadership*. 2nd ed. Westport, CT: Praeger, 2004.

———. *The Nature of Leadership*. Thousand Oaks, CA: Sage, 2004.

Clark, Kenneth E., and Miriam B. Clark, eds. *Measures of Leadership*. West Orange, NJ: Leadership Library of America, 1990.

Clawson, James G. *Level Three Leadership: Getting Below the Surface*. 2nd ed. Upper Saddle River, NJ: Prentice-Hall, 1999.

Clinton, J. Robert. "The Emerging Leader." *Theology, News, and Notes* (June 1987): 28.

———. *The Making of a Leader: Recognizing the Lessons and Stages of Leadership Development*. Colorado Springs: NavPress, 1988.

———. *A Short History of Leadership*. Altadena, CA: Barnabas, 1992.

Clutterbuck, David. *Doing It Different: Lessons for the Imaginative Manager*. London: Orion Business Books, 1999.

Cohen, Allan R., and David L. Bradford. *Influence without Authority*. New York: Wiley, 1990.

Coles, Robert. *The Call of Service: A Witness to Idealism*. Boston: Houghton-Mifflin, 1993.

Collins, James C., and Jerry I. Porras. *Built to Last: Successful Habits of Visionary Companies*. New York: HarperBusiness, 1994.

Colvin, Geoff. "Personal Bests." *Fortune* 171, no. 4 (March 15, 2015): 106–10.

Conger, Jay A. *The Charismatic Leader: Behind the Mystique of Exceptional Leadership*. San Francisco: Jossey-Bass, 1989.

———. *Learning to Lead: The Art of Transforming Managers into Leaders*. San Francisco: Jossey-Bass, 1992.

———, ed. *Spirit at Work: Discovering the Spirituality in Leadership*. San Francisco: Jossey-Bass, 1994.

Conger, Jay A., and Beth Benjamin. *Building Leaders: How Successful Companies Develop the Next Generation*. San Francisco: Jossey-Bass, 1999.

Conger, Jay A., Gretchen M. Spreitzer, and Edward E. Lawler III, eds. *The Leader's Change Handbook: An Essential Guide to Setting Direction and Taking Action*. San Francisco: Jossey-Bass, 1999.

Connor, P. E., and B. Becker. "Personal Value Systems and Decision-Making Styles of Public Managers." *Public Personnel Management* 32, no. 1 (1991): 155–80.

Coutu, Diane L. "How Resilience Works." *Harvard Business Review* 80, no. 5 (2002): 46–51.

Covey, Stephen R. *Principle-Centered Leadership*. New York: Summit Books, 1991.

———. *The Seven Habits of Highly Effective People: Restoring the Character Ethic*. New York: Simon & Schuster, 1989.

Covey, Stephen R., A. Roger Merrill, and Rebecca R. Merrill. *First Things First: To Live, to Love, to Learn, to Leave a Legacy*. New York: Simon & Schuster, 1994.

Cox, Danny, with John Hoover. *Leadership When the Heat's On*. New York: McGraw-Hill, 1992.

Cramer, Kathryn D. *Staying on Top When Your World Turns Upside Down: How to Triumph over Trauma and Adversity*. New York: Viking, 1990.

Crittenden, P. *Learning to Be Moral: Philosophical Thoughts about Moral Development*. Atlantic Highlands, NJ: Humanities Press International, 1990.

Crocker, H. W., III. *Robert E. Lee on Leadership: Executive Lessons in Character, Courage, and Vision*. Rocklin, CA: Forum, 1999.

Cruikshank, Jeffrey L., and Clark Malcolm. *Herman Miller, Inc.: Buildings and Beliefs*. Washington, DC: American Institute of Architects Press, 1994.

Cullen, J. B., P. K. Praveen, and B. Victor. "The Effects of Ethical Climates on Organizational Commitment: A Two-Study Analysis." *Journal of Business Ethics* 46, no. 2 (2003): 127–41.

Cullen, J. B., and B. Victor. "The Ethical Climate Questionnaire: An Assessment of Its Development and Validity." *Psychological Reports* 73, no. 2 (1993): 667–74.

Daimon, Sayuri. "New Group of Female Executives Hopes to Boost Ranks in Japan Inc." *Japan Times*, May 9, 2013. http://japantimes.co.jp/news/2013/05/09/national/new -group-of-female-executives-hopes-to-boost-ranks-in-japan-inc/#.VAAFfPldWSo.

Dale, Robert D. *Good News from Great Leaders*. Washington, DC: Alban Institute, 1992.

Dalla Costa, John. *Working Wisdom: The Ultimate Value in the New Economy*. Toronto: Stoddart, 1995.

Damon, W. *The Moral Child: Nurturing Children's Natural Moral Growth*. New York: Free Press, 1988.

Dansereau, F., G. G. Graen, and W. Haga. "A Vertical Dyad Linkage Approach to Leadership in Formal Organizations." *Organizational Behavior and Human Performance* 13 (1975): 46–78.

Dattner, Fabian, Jim Luscombe, and Kenneth Grant. *Three Spirits of Leadership: The United Voice of the Entrepreneur, the Corporation, and the Community*. Crows Nest, Australia: Allen & Unwin, 1999.

Day, David D., and John Antonakis. *The Nature of Leadership*. Thousand Oaks, CA: Sage, 2012.

Delbecq, Andre L. "Christian Spirituality and Contemporary Business Leadership." *Journal of Organizational Change* 12, no. 4 (1999): 345–49.

———. "The Spiritual Challenge of Power: Humility and Love as Offsets to Leadership Hubris." *Journal of Management, Spirituality and Religion* 3, no. 1 (2006): 141–54.

———. "Spirituality and Business: One Scholar's Perspective." *Journal of Management, Spirituality and Religion* 6, no. 1 (2009): 3–13.

De Pree, Max. *Does Leadership Have a Future? Questions and Stories for Leaders*. Pasadena, CA: De Pree Leadership Center, 2000.

———. *Leadership Is an Art*. New York: Doubleday, 1989.

———. *Leadership Jazz*. New York: Currency Doubleday, 1992.

———. *Leading without Power: Finding Hope in Serving Community*. San Francisco: Jossey-Bass, 1997.

———. "Leaving a Legacy." Speech given at the De Pree Leadership Center, Pasadena, CA, March 3, 1997.

———. "What Is Leadership?" In *Leading Organizations: Perspectives for a New Era*, edited by Gill Robinson Hickman, 130–32. Thousand Oaks, CA: Sage, 1998.

Diehl, William E. *In Search of Faithfulness: Lessons from the Christian Community*. Philadelphia: Fortress, 1987.

———. *The Monday Connection: A Spirituality of Competence, Affirmation, and Support in the Workplace*. San Francisco: HarperSanFrancisco, 1991.

DiStefano, Joseph J. "Tracing the Vision and Impact of Robert K. Greenleaf." In *Reflections on Leadership*, edited by Larry C. Spears, 61–78. New York: Wiley, 1995.

Doohan, Helen. *Leadership in Paul*. Wilmington, DE: Michael Glazier, 1984.

Dorfman, P. W. "International and Cross-Cultural Leadership Research." In *Handbook for International Management Research*, edited by B. J. Punnett and O. Shenkar, 265–355. Ann Arbor: University of Michigan Press, 2003.

Drath, Wilfred H., and Charles J. Palus. *Making Common Sense: Leadership as Meaning-Making in a Community of Practice*. Greensboro, NC: Center for Creative Leadership, 1994.

Drucker, Peter F. *The Effective Executive*. New York: Harper & Row, 1967.

———. *Innovation and Entrepreneurship: Practice and Principles*. New York: Harper & Row, 1985.

———. *Management Challenges for the Twenty-First Century*. New York: HarperBusiness, 1999.

———. *Managing in Turbulent Times*. New York: Harper & Row, 1980.

Dunfee, Susan N. *Beyond Servanthood: Christianity and the Liberation of Women*. Lanham, MD: University Press of America, 1989.

Dunphy, Dexter, and Andrew Griffiths. *The Sustainable Corporation: Organisational Renewal in Australia*. Sydney: Allen & Unwin, 1999.

Durkheim, Émile. *The Division of Labor in Society*. Translated by G. Simpson. Glencoe, IL: The Free Press, 1947.

Edelman, Joel, and Mary Beth Crain. *The Tao of Negotiation: How You Can Prevent, Resolve, and Transcend Conflict in Work and Everyday Life*. New York: HarperBusiness, 1993.

Egan, Gerard. *Adding Value: A Systematic Guide to Business-Driven Management and Leadership*. San Francisco: Jossey-Bass, 1993.

Elborgh-Woytek, Katrin, et al. "Women, Work and the Economy: Macroeconomic Gains from Gender Equity." International Monetary Fund. September 2013. http://www.imf.org/external/pubs/ft/sdn/2013/sdn1310.pdf.

Ellul, J. *The Politics of God and the Politics of Man*. Grand Rapids: Eerdmans, 1972.

Emler, N. C., and T. Cook. "Moral Integrity in Leadership: Why It Matters and Why It May Be Difficult to Achieve." *Personality Psychology in the Workplace. Decade of Behavior* 15, no. 337 (2001): 277–98.

Engstrom, Ted W., and Edward R. Dayton. *The Art of Management for Christian Leaders*. Grand Rapids: Pyranee Books, 1989.

Epstein, E. "Religion and Business: The Critical Role of Religious Traditions in Management Education." *Journal of Business Ethics* 38, no. 1/2 (2001): 91–96.

Evans, John S. *The Management of Human Capacity: An Approach to the Ideas of Elliott Jacques*. Bradford, UK: MCB Human Resources, 1979.

Faber, Nancy. "Arjay Miller Thinks Business Schools Should Stress Ethics, But the Bottom Line Isn't Bad: His Grads Start at $27,500." *People Magazine*, June 25, 1979. http://www.people.com/people/archive/article/0,,20073975,00.html.

Fairholm, G. W. *Perspectives on Leadership: From the Science of Management to Its Spiritual Heart*. Westport, CT: Praeger, 2000.

Farson, Richard. *Management of the Absurd: Paradoxes in Leadership*. New York: Simon & Schuster, 1996.

Feldman, H. D., and R. C. Thompson. "Teaching Business Ethics: A Challenge for Business Educators in the 1990s." *Journal of Marketing Education* 12, no. 2 (1990): 10–23.

Ferris, P. L., G. R. Treadway, D. C. Perrewe, R. L. Brouer, and S. Lux. "Political Skill in Organizations." *Journal of Management* 33, no. 3 (2007): 290–320.

Fiedler, Frederick E. "A Contingency Model of Leadership Effectiveness." In *Advances in Experimental Social Psychology*, edited by L. Berkowitz, 1:149–90. New York: Academic Press, 1964.

———. *A Theory of Leadership Effectiveness*. New York: McGraw-Hill, 1967.

Finzel, Hans. *The Top Ten Mistakes Leaders Make*. Wheaton: Victor Books, 1994.

Fisher, Roger, and William Ury. *Getting to Yes: Negotiating Agreement without Giving In*. New York: Penguin Books, 1993.

Fitzgerald, Catherine, and Linda K. Kirby, eds. *Developing Leaders: Research and Applications in Psychological Type and Leadership Development*. Palo Alto, CA: Davies-Black, 1997.

Flood, Robert Louis. *Rethinking the Fifth Discipline: Learning within the Unknowable*. New York: Routledge, 1999.

Forbes, D. P., and F. J. Milliken. "Cognition and Corporate Governance: Understanding Boards of Directors as Strategic Decision-Making Groups." *The Academy of Management Review* 24, no. 3 (1999): 489–505.

Ford, Leighton. *Jesus: The Transforming Leader*. London: Hodder & Stoughton, 1991.

———. *Transforming Leadership: Jesus' Way of Creating Vision, Shaping Values, and Empowering Change*. Downers Grove, IL: InterVarsity, 1991.

Fortune Editors. "The International Power 50: Fortune's Most Powerful Women." *Fortune*, October 10, 2013. http://fortune.com/2013/10/10/most-powerful-women-the-international-power-50/?iid=MPW13_sp_lead2.

Fowler, James. *Stages of Faith: The Psychology of Human Development and the Quest for Meaning*. New York: Harper & Row, 1981.

Fox, Matthew. *The Reinvention of Work: A New Vision of Livelihood for Our Time*. San Francisco: HarperSanFrancisco, 1994.

Fraker, Anne. "Robert K. Greenleaf and Business Ethics." In *Reflections on Leadership*, edited by Larry C. Spears, 37–48. New York: Wiley, 1995.

Fraker, Anne T., and Larry C. Spears, eds. *Seeker and Servant: Reflections on Religious Leadership*. San Francisco: Jossey-Bass, 1996.

Fromm, Bill, and Len Schlesinger. *The Real Heroes of Business and Not a CEO among Them*. New York: Doubleday, 1993.

Fry, L. W. "Toward a Theory of Spiritual Leadership." *Leadership Quarterly* 14, no. 6 (2003): 693–727.

Fry, L. W., and J. W. Slocum Jr. "Maximizing the Triple Bottom Line through Spiritual Leadership." *Organizational Dynamics* 37, no. 1 (2008): 86–96.

Fry, L. W., S. Vitucci, and M. Cedillo. "Spiritual Leadership and Army Transformation: Theory, Measurement, and Establishing a Baseline." *Leadership Quarterly* 16, no. 5 (2005): 835–62.

Fukuyama, Francis. *Trust: The Social Virtues and the Creation of Prosperity*. New York: Free Press, 1995.

Fullan, Michael. *Educational Leadership*. San Francisco: Jossey-Bass, 2000.

Fuller, Timothy, ed. *Leading and Leadership*. Notre Dame, IN: University of Notre Dame Press, 2000.

Galpin, Timothy J. *The Human Side of Change: A Practical Guide to Organization Redesign*. San Francisco: Jossey-Bass, 1996.

Gardner, Howard. *Leading Minds: An Anatomy of Leadership*. New York: Basic Books, 1995.

Gardner, John W. *Building Community*. New York: Independent Sector, 1991.

———. *On Leadership*. New York: Free Press, 1990.

Gardner, W. L., B. J. Avolio, and F. O. Walumbwa, eds. *Authentic Leadership Theory and Practice: Origins, Effects and Development*. Bingley, UK: Emerald Group, 2008.

Garfield, Charles, with Michael Toms. *The Soul of Business: New Dimensions*. Carlsbad, CA: Hay House, 1997.

Gates, John A. *The Life and Thought of Kierkegaard for Everyman*. London: Hodder & Stoughton, 1960.

Giacalone, Robert. "What Are Expansive Values Adherents?" *Science & Religion Today*, September 2, 2011, http://www.scienceandreligiontoday.com/2011/09/02/what-are -expansive-values-adherents/.

Giacalone, Robert A., and Carole L. Jurkiewicz. *Handbook of Workplace Spirituality and Organizational Performance*. 2nd ed. Armonk, NY: M. E. Sharpe, 2010.

Gilligan, C., and J. Attanucci. "Two Moral Orientations: Gender Differences and Similarities." *Merrill-Palmer Quarterly* 34, no. 3 (1988): 223–37.

Goethals, George, and Georgia L. J. Sorenson. *The Quest for a General Theory of Leadership*. Northampton, MA: Edward Elgar, 2006.

Goldingay, John. *Men Behaving Badly*. Exeter, UK: Paternoster, 2000.

Goldsmith, M. "The Success Delusion: Why It Can Be So Hard for Successful Leaders to Change." *Journal of Applied Christian Leadership* 3, no. 2 (2009): 84–92.

Goleman, Daniel. *Emotional Intelligence*. New York: Bantam Books, 1995.

———. *Working with Emotional Intelligence*. New York: Bantam Books, 1998.

Goleman, Daniel, Richard Boyatzis, and Annie McKee. *Primal Leadership: Realizing the Power of Emotional Intelligence*. Boston: Harvard Business School Press, 2002.

Gooch, G. P. *English Democratic Ideas in the Seventeenth Century*. New York: Harper, 1959.

Gouillart, Francis J., and James N. Kelly. *Transforming the Organization*. New York: McGraw-Hill, 1995.

Gozdz, Kazimierz. *Community Building: Renewing Spirit and Learning*. Pleasanton, CA: New Leaders Press, 1995.

Graham, Jill W. "Servant-Leadership and Enterprise Strategy." In *Insights on Leadership*, edited by Larry C. Spears, 145–56. New York: Wiley, 1998.

Greenleaf, Robert K. "Life's Choices and Markers." In *Reflections on Leadership: How Robert K. Greenleaf's Theory of Servant-Leadership Influenced Today's Top Management Thinkers*, edited by Larry C. Spears, 17–20. New York: Wiley, 1995.

———. *Old Age: The Ultimate Test of Spirit*. Indianapolis: Robert K. Greenleaf Center, 1987.

———. *Seeker and Servant: Reflections on Religious Leadership*. San Francisco: Jossey-Bass, 1996.

———. *The Servant as Leader*. Indianapolis: Robert K. Greenleaf Center, 1970.

———. *Servant Leadership: A Journey into the Nature of Legitimate Power and Greatness*. New York: Paulist Press, 1977.

———. *Spirituality and Leadership*. Indianapolis: Robert K. Greenleaf Center, 1988.

Greenleaf, Robert K., Don M. Frick, and Larry C. Spears, eds. *On Becoming a Servant-Leader*. San Francisco: Jossey-Bass, 1996.

Greenslade, Philip. *Leadership*. London: Marshall Pickering, 1984.

Gregg, Samuel, and Gordon Preece. *Christianity and Entrepreneurship: Protestant and Catholic Thoughts*. Sydney: Centre for Independent Studies, 1999.

Griffin, Emilie. *The Reflective Executive: A Spirituality of Business and Enterprise*. New York: Crossroad, 1993.

Grint, Keith. *Leadership: A Very Short Introduction*. Oxford: Oxford University Press, 2010.

Groysberg, Borris, and Deborah Bell. "Joining Boards: It's Not Just Who You Know That Matters." *Harvard Business Review*, July 16, 2013. https://hbr.org/2013/07/joining-a -board-who-you-know-m.

Gunderson, Denny. *The Leadership Paradox: A Challenge to Servant Leadership in a Power Hungry World*. Seattle: YWAM, 1997.

Hackett, Conrad, et al. "The Global Religious Landscape." Pew Research Center, December 18, 2012. www.pewforum.org/2012/12/18/global-religious-landscape-exec/.

Hagberg, Janet O. *Real Power: The Stages of Personal Power in Organizations*. Minneapolis: Winston, 1984.

Hagberg, Janet O., and Robert A. Guelich. *The Critical Journey: Stages in the Life of Faith*. Dallas: Word, 1990.

Hagberg, Janet O., and Richard J. Leider. *The Inventurers: Excursions in Life and Career Renewal*. 3rd ed. Reading, MA: Addison-Wesley, 1988.

Haggai, John. *Lead On! Leadership That Endures in a Changing World*. Waco: Word, 1986.

Hamilton, Nigel. *Monty: The Making of a General, 1887–1942*. New York: McGraw-Hill, 1981.

Handy, Charles. *The Age of Unreason*. Boston: Harvard Business School Press, 1989.

———. *Beyond Certainty: The Changing Worlds of Organizations*. Boston: Harvard Business School Press, 1996.

———. *Gods of Management: The Changing Work of Organizations*. New York: Oxford University Press, 1995.

———. *The Hungry Spirit: Beyond Capitalism: A Quest for Purpose in the Modern World*. New York: Broadway Books, 1998.

———. *The New Alchemists: How Visionary People Make Something out of Nothing*. London: Hutchinson, 1999.

———. *Understanding Organizations*. New York: Oxford University Press, 1993.

———. *Waiting for the Mountain to Move: Reflections on Work and Life*. San Francisco: Jossey-Bass, 1999.

Hanh, Thich Nhat. *Peace Is Every Step: The Path of Mindfulness in Everyday Life*. New York: Bantam, 1992.

———. *Walking the Noble Path: The Five Mindfulness Trainings*. Berkeley: Parallax Press, 2012.

Hartshorne, Charles. *Reality as Social Process: Studies in Metaphysics and Religion*. Glencoe, IL: Free Press, 1953.

Hass, Howard, with Bob Tamarkin. *The Leader Within: An Empowering Path of Self-Discovery*. New York: HarperBusiness, 1992.

Hauerwas, Stanley. *The Peaceable Kingdom: A Primer in Christian Ethics*. Philadelphia: SCM, 1983.

———. *Vision and Virtue: Essays in Christian Ethical Reflection*. Notre Dame, IN: University of Notre Dame Press, 1974.

Haughey, John C. *Converting 9 to 5: A Spirituality of Daily Work*. New York: Crossroad, 1989.

———. "A Leader's Conscience: The Integrity and Spirituality of Václav Havel." In *Spirit at Work: Discovering the Spirituality in Leadership*, edited by Jay A. Conger, 41–62. San Francisco: Jossey-Bass, 1994.

Havel, Václav. *Disturbing the Peace: A Conversation with Karel Hvízdala*. Translated by Paul Wilson. New York: Knopf, 1990.

———. *Letters to Olga: June 1979–September 1982*. Translated by Paul Wilson. New York: Holt, 1989.

———. "The Revolution Has Just Begun." *Time*, March 5, 1990, 14–15.

Hawley, Jack. *Reawakening the Spirit in Work: The Power of Dharmic Management*. San Francisco: Berrett-Koehler, 1993.

Hegel, G. W. F. *The Philosophy of Right*. Translated by T. M. Know. New York: Oxford University Press, 1952.

Heifetz, Ronald A. *Leadership without Easy Answers*. Cambridge: Belknap Press of Harvard University Press, 1994.

Helgesen, Sally. *The Female Advantage: Women's Ways of Leadership*. New York: Doubleday Currency, 1990.

———. *The Web of Inclusion: A New Architecture for Building Great Organizations*. New York: Doubleday Currency, 1995.

Hendricks, Gay, and Kate Ludeman. *The Corporate Mystic: A Guidebook for Visionaries with Their Feet on the Ground*. New York: Bantam Books, 1996.

Hersey, Paul, and Kenneth H. Blanchard. "Life-Cycle Theory of Leadership." *Training and Development Journal* 23 (1969): 26–34.

Hersey, Paul, Kenneth H. Blanchard, and Dewey E. Johnson. *Management of Organizational Behavior: Utilizing Human Resources*. Upper Saddle River, NJ: Prentice-Hall, 1996.

Hess, J. Daniel. *Integrity: Let Your Yea Be Yea*. Scottdale, PA: Herald Press, 1978.

Hesselbein, Frances, Marshall Goldsmith, and Richard Beckhard, eds. *The Leader of the Future: New Visions, Strategies, and Practices for the Next Era*. San Francisco: Jossey-Bass, 1996.

———. *The Organization of the Future*. San Francisco: Jossey-Bass, 1997.

Hesselbein, Frances, Marshall Goldsmith, Richard Beckhard, and Richard Schubert, eds. *The Community of the Future*. San Francisco: Jossey-Bass, 1998.

Hickman, Craig R. *Mind of a Manager, Soul of a Leader*. New York: Wiley, 1990.

Higginson, Richard. *Transforming Leadership: A Christian Approach to Management*. London: SPCK, 1996.

"Hijrah: Resilience and Resolve." http://www.islamweb.net/emainpage/printarticle.php?id=155742&lang=E.

Hill, P. C., et al. "Conceptualizing Religion and Spirituality: Points of Commonality, Points of Departure." *Journal for the Theory of Social Behavior* 30 (2000): 51–77.

Hillman, James. *The Soul's Code: In Search of Character and Calling*. New York: Random House, 1996.

Hodgkinson, Christopher. *The Philosophy of Leadership*. New York: St. Martin's Press, 1983.

Hofstede, G. *Culture's Consequences: International Differences in Work-Related Values*. Beverly Hills, CA: Sage, 1980.

Holmes, Arthur F. *Shaping Character: Moral Education in the Christian College*. Grand Rapids: Eerdmans, 1991.

Hosking, D. M. "Organizing, Leadership, and Skillful Process." *Journal of Management Studies* 25, no. 2 (1988): 147–66.

House, Robert J. "A 1976 Theory of Charismatic Leadership." In *Leadership: The Cutting Edge*, edited by J. G. Hunt and L. L. Larson, 189–207. Carbondale: Southern Illinois University Press, 1977.

———. "A Path-Goal Theory of Leader Effectiveness." *Administrative Science Quarterly* 16 (1971): 321–28.

House, Robert J., Paul J. Hanges, Mansour Javidan, Peter W. Dorfman, and Vipin Gupta. *Culture, Leadership, and Organizations: The Globe Study of 62 Societies*. Thousand Oaks, CA: Sage, 2004.

Howard, Peter. *Frank Buchman's Secret*. London: Heinemann, 1961.

Hughes, Richard L., Robert C. Ginnett, and Gordon J. Curphy. *Leadership: Enhancing the Lessons of Experience*. 2nd ed. Chicago: Irwin, 1996.

Huszczo, Gregory E. *Tools for Team Excellence: Getting Your Team into High Gear and Keeping It There*. Palo Alto, CA: Davies-Black, 1996.

Hybels, Bill. "Finding Your Leadership Style: Ten Different Ways to Lead God's People." *Leadership* (Winter 1998): 84–89.

Hyland, Bruce N., and Merle J. Yost. *Reflections for Managers*. New York: McGraw-Hill, 1994.

IFYC. "About Eboo." Interfaith Youth Corp. http://www.ifyc.org/about-us/eboo-patel.

Ignon, L. "More MBA Programs Introduce Ethics Courses. Economics: The Scandals of the 1980s Have Prompted Some Professors to Rethink the Way that Business Is Taught." *Los Angeles Times*, May 20, 1990. http://articles.latimes.com/1990-05-12/business/fi-1130_1_business-professor.

Isasi-Díaz, A. M. "Un Poquito de Justicia—A Little Bit of Justice: A Mujerta Account of Justice." In *Hispanic/Latino Theology: Challenge and Promise*, edited by A. M. Isasi-Díaz and F. F. Segovia, 325–29. Minneapolis: Fortress, 1996.

Jackson, Brad, and Ken Parry. *A Very Short, Fairly Interesting and Reasonably Cheap Book about Studying Leadership*. Thousand Oaks, CA: Sage, 2011.

Jacobsen, Steve. *Hearts to God, Hands to Work: Connecting Spirituality and Work*. Washington, DC: Alban Institute, 1997.

James, Jennifer. *Thinking in the Future Tense: Leadership Skills for a New Age*. New York: Simon & Schuster, 1996.

Janov, Jill. *The Inventive Organization: Hope and Daring at Work*. San Francisco: Jossey-Bass, 1994.

Jaworski, Joseph. *Synchronicity: The Inner Path of Leadership*. San Francisco: Berrett-Koehler, 1996.

Jinkins, Michael, and Deborah Bradshaw Jinkins. *The Character of Leadership: Political Realism and Public Virtue in Nonprofit Organizations*. San Francisco: Jossey-Bass, 1998.

Johnson, Barry. *Polarity Management: Identifying and Managing Unsolvable Problems*. Amherst, MA: HRD Press, 1992.

Jones, Laura Beth. *Jesus CEO: Using Ancient Wisdom for Visionary Leadership*. New York: Hyperion, 1995.

————. *The Path*. New York: Hyperion, 1996.

Josephson, Michael. "Teaching Ethical Decision-Making and Principled Reasoning." In *Business Ethics: Readings and Cases in Corporate Morality*, 4th ed., edited by W. M. Hoffman, R. E. Frederick, and M. S. Schwartz, 87–94. New York: McGraw-Hill, 2001.

Kanter, Rosabeth Moss. *Rosabeth Moss Kanter on the Frontiers of Management*. Boston: Harvard Business School Press, 1997.

Kanter, Rosabeth Moss, Barry A. Stein, and Todd D. Jick. *The Challenge of Organizational Change: How Companies Experience It and Leaders Guide It*. New York: Free Press, 1992.

Karakas, F., and E. Sarigollu. "The Role of Leadership in Creating Virtuous and Compassionate Organizations: Narratives of Benevolent Leadership in an Anatolian Tiger." *Journal of Business Ethics* 113, no. 4 (2013): 663–78.

Keating, Charles J. *The Leadership Book*. Rev. ed. New York: Paulist Press, 1982.

Kegan, Robert. *The Evolving Self: Problem and Process in Human Development*. Cambridge, MA: Harvard University Press, 1982.

Keiser, Elizabeth B., and R. Melvin Keiser. "Quaker Principles in the Crucible of Practice." *Cross Currents* 43, no. 4 (Winter 1993): 476–84.

Kellerman, Barbara. *The End of Leadership*. New York: HarperCollins, 2012.

————. "Leadership Warts and All." *Harvard Business Review* 82, no. 1 (2004): 40–45.

Kerr, Alan. *Guided Journey*. Gundaroo, Australia: Brolga Press, 1998.

Kets de Vries, Manfred F. R. *Life and Death in the Executive Fast Lane: Essays on Irrational Organizations and Their Leaders*. San Francisco: Jossey-Bass, 1995.

————. *Prisoners of Leadership*. New York: Wiley, 1989.

Klenke, Karin. "The Internal Theater of the Authentic Leader: Integrating Cognitive, Affective, Conative, and Spiritual Facets of Authentic Leadership." In *Authentic Leadership Theory and Practice: Origins, Effects and Development*, edited by W. L. Gardner, B. J. Avolio, and F. O. Walumbwa, 155–82. Bingley, UK: Emerald Group, 2008.

Koestenbaum, Peter. *Leadership: The Inner Side of Greatness*. San Francisco: Jossey-Bass, 1991.

Kohlberg, Lawrence. "Moral Stages and the Idea of Justice." In *Essays on Moral Development*, vol. 1, *The Philosophy of Moral Development*, edited by Lawrence Kohlberg, 311–72. San Francisco: Harper & Row, 1981.

Kotter, John P. *A Force for Change: How Leadership Differs from Management*. New York: Free Press, 1990.

————. *Leading Change*. Boston: Harvard Business Review Press, 2012.

————. *The New Rules: How to Succeed in Today's Post-Corporate World*. New York: Free Press, 1995.

Kouzes, James M., and Barry Z. Posner. *Credibility: How Leaders Gain and Lose It, Why People Demand It*. San Francisco: Jossey-Bass, 1993.

————. *The Leadership Challenge*. 4th ed. San Francisco: Jossey-Bass, 2007.

———. *The Leadership Challenge: How to Make Extraordinary Things Happen in Organizations*. San Francisco: Wiley, 2012.

———. "Seven Lessons for Leading the Voyage to the Future." In *The Leader of the Future: New Visions, Strategies, and Practices for the Next Era*, edited by Frances Hesselbein, Marshall Goldsmith, and Richard Beckhard, 99–110. San Francisco: Jossey-Bass, 1996.

Kovacs, G. "The Theoretical Foundation of Buddhist Management Practices." *Journal of Management Development* 33, no. 8/9 (2014): 751–62.

Kraybill, Donald B., and Phyllis Pellman Good, eds. *Perils of Professionalism: Essays on Christian Faith and Professionalism*. Scottdale, PA: Herald Press, 1982.

Kundtz, David. *Stopping*. New York: MJF Books, 1998.

La Barre, Patricia. "Do You Have the Will to Lead?" *Fast Company* 32 (March 2000): 222.

LaCugna, Catherine Mowry. *God for Us: The Trinity and Christian Life*. San Francisco: HarperCollins, 1993.

Lakoff, G., and M. Johnson. *Metaphors We Live By*. Chicago: University of Chicago Press, 1980.

Lean, Garth. *On the Tail of a Comet: The Life of Frank Buchman*. Colorado Springs: Helmers & Howard, 1988.

Ledbetter, Bernice. "A Values Approach to Advancing Women in Leadership: Using Talent Management to Change the Equation." *Graziadio Business Review* 17, no. 3 (2014), available at http://gbr.pepperdine.edu/2014/12/a-values-approach-to-advancing-women-in-leadership.

Leider, Richard J. *The Power of Purpose: Creating Meaning in Your Life and Work*. San Francisco: Berrett-Koehler, 1997.

Lencioni, Patrick. *The Five Temptations of a CEO: A Leadership Fable*. San Francisco: Jossey-Bass, 1998.

Le Peau, Andrew T. *Paths of Leadership: Guiding Others toward Growth in Christ through Serving, Following, Teaching, Modeling, Envisioning*. Downers Grove, IL: InterVarsity, 1983.

Lewis, H. M. *Models and Meanings in the History of Jewish Leadership*. New York: Edwin Mellen, 2004.

Lipman-Blumen, Jean. *The Connective Edge: Leading in an Independent World*. San Francisco: Jossey-Bass, 1996.

Lips-Wiersma, M., K. L. Dean, and C. J. Fornaciari. "Theorizing the Dark Side of the Workplace Spirituality Movement." *Journal of Management Inquiry* 18, no. 4 (2009): 288–300.

Loder, James E. *The Logic of the Spirit: Human Development in Theological Perspective*. San Francisco: Jossey-Bass, 2001.

Lubans, J., Jr. "The Invisible Leader: Lessons for Leaders from The Orpheus Chamber Orchestra." *OD Practitioner* 38, no. 2 (2006): 5–9.

Ludwig, D., and C. Longnecker. "The Bathsheba Syndrome: The Ethical Failure of Successful Leaders." In *The Ethics of Leadership*, edited by Joanne B. Ciulla, 70–80. Belmont, CA: Wadsworth/Thomson Learning, 2003.

Lull, Timothy F. "Underachievers? Or Reformers? Lutherans Exercising Daily Life Leadership." Paper presented at the meeting Traditions in Leadership, De Pree Leadership Center, Pasadena, CA, June 1999.

Lynch, Richard. *Lead! How Public and Nonprofit Managers Can Bring Out the Best in Themselves and Their Organizations.* San Francisco: Jossey-Bass, 1993.

MacIntyre, Alasdair. *After Virtue: A Study in Moral Theory.* 2nd ed. Notre Dame, IN: University of Notre Dame Press, 1984.

Mallison, John. *Mentoring to Develop Disciples and Leaders.* Sydney: Scripture Union/ Open Book, 1998.

Mant, Alistair. *Intelligent Leadership.* Crows Nest, Australia: Allen & Unwin, 1997.

Manz, C. C., K. P. Manz, R. D. Marx, and C. P. Neck. *The Wisdom of Solomon: Ancient Virtues for Living and Leading.* New York: Berrett-Koehler, 2001.

Manz, Charles C. *The Leadership Wisdom of Jesus: Practical Lessons for Today.* San Francisco: Berrett-Koehler, 1998.

Manz, Charles C., and Henry P. Simms. *Superleadership: Leading Others to Lead Themselves.* Don Mills, ON: Pearson Education Canada, 1989.

Marcario, Rose. "Repair is a Radical Act." Patagonia. http://www.patagonia.com/us /worn-wear/. First appeared on Quartz, November 25, 2015. http://qz.com/581854 /the-case-for-quitting-your-job-without-a-backup-plan.

Marcic, Dorothy. *Managing with Wisdom of Love: Uncovering Virtue in People and Organizations.* San Francisco: Jossey-Bass, 1997.

Maxwell, John C. *Developing the Leader within You.* Nashville: Thomas Nelson, 1993.

———. *The Twenty-One Irrefutable Laws of Leadership: Follow Them and People Will Follow You.* Nashville: Thomas Nelson, 1998.

McCall, M. "Recasting Leadership Development." *Industrial Organizational Psychology* 3 (2010): 3–19.

McCauley, Cynthia D., Russ S. Moxley, and Ellen Van Velsor, eds. *The Center for Creative Leadership Handbook of Leadership Development.* San Francisco: Jossey-Bass, 1998.

Melrose, Ken. *Making the Grass Greener on Your Side: A CEO's Journey to Leading by Serving.* San Francisco: Berrett-Koehler, 1995.

Miller, David W. *God at Work: The History and Promise of the Faith at Work Movement.* New York: Oxford University Press, 2007.

Miller, William C. "How Do We Put Our Spiritual Values to Work?" In *New Traditions in Business: Spirit and Leadership in the Twenty-First Century*, edited by John Renesch, 69–77. San Francisco: Berrett-Koehler, 1992.

Milton-Smith, J. "Business Ethics in Australia and New Zealand," *Journal of Business Ethics* 16, no. 14 (1997): 1485–97.

Mintzberg, Henry. "The Manager's Job: Folklore and Fact." In *Harvard Business Review on Leadership*, 1–36. Cambridge, MA: Harvard Business School Press, 1998.

———. *Power in and around Organizations*. Englewood Cliffs, NJ: Prentice-Hall, 1983.

———. *Simply Managing: What Managers Do—and Can Do Better*. San Francisco: Berrett-Koehler, 2013.

Mitchell, John J. "Why Ethics in the Business School Curriculum?" *AllBusiness.com*, March 1, 1991, http://www.allbusiness.com/human-resources/employee-develop ment-employee-ethics/251403-1.html#ixzz1Z2ZLU4kG.

Mitroff, Ian I., and Elizabeth A. Denton. "A Study of Spirituality in the Workplace." *Sloan Management Review* 40 (1999): 83–84.

Mohrman, Allan M., Jr., Susan Albers Mohrman, and Gerald E. Ledford. *Large-Scale Organizational Change*. San Francisco: Jossey-Bass, 1989.

Moltmann, Jürgen. *The Trinity and the Kingdom of God*. Philadelphia: Fortress, 1993.

Moore, B. V. "The May Conference on Leadership." *Personnel Journal* 6 (1927): 124–28.

Moore, George Foot. *Judaism in the First Centuries of the Christian Era: The Age of the Tannaim*, 2nd ed. Cambridge, MA: Harvard University Press, 1927.

Morgan, Gareth. *Images of Organization*. London: Sage, 1986.

Mouw, Richard J. "Leadership and the Threefold Office of Christ." Paper presented at the meeting Traditions in Leadership, De Pree Leadership Center, Pasadena, CA, June 1999.

Moxley, Russ S. *Leadership and Spirit: Breathing New Vitality and Energy into Individuals and Organizations*. San Francisco: Jossey-Bass, 2000.

Mumford, M. D., S. J. Zaccaro, F. D. Harding, T. O. Jacobs, and E. A. Fleishman. "Leadership Skills for a Changing World: Solving Complex Social Problems." *Leadership Quarterly* 11, no. 1 (2000): 12–35.

Nader, Jonar C. *How to Lose Friends and Infuriate People*. Cherrybrook, Australia: Plutonium, 1999.

Nair, Keshavan. *A Higher Standard of Leadership: Lessons from the Life of Gandhi*. San Francisco: Berrett-Koehler, 1994.

Naisbitt, John, and Patricia Aburdene. *Megatrends 2000: Ten New Directions for the 1990s*. New York: Morrow, 1990.

Nanus, Burt. *The Leader's Edge: The Seven Keys to Leadership in a Turbulent World*. Chicago: Contemporary Books, 1989.

———. *Visionary Leadership*. San Francisco: Jossey-Bass, 1992.

Nash, Laura L. *Believers in Business*. Nashville: Thomas Nelson, 1994.

Nash, Laura L., and Scotty McLennan. *Church on Sunday, Work on Monday: The Challenge of Fusing Christian Values with Business Life*. San Francisco: Jossey-Bass, 2001.

Neal, J., B. Lichtenstein, and D. Banner. "Spiritual Perspectives on Individual, Organizational, and Societal Transformation." *Journal of Organizational Change Management* 12, no. 3 (1999): 175–85.

Neal, Judith. "Spirituality in the Workplace: An Emerging Phenomenon." *Studies in Spirituality* 15, no. 1 (2005): 267–82.

Nielsen, Richard P. "Quaker Foundations for Greenleaf's Servant Leadership and 'Friendly Disentangling' Method." In *Insights on Leadership*, edited by Larry C. Spears, 126–44. New York: Wiley, 1998.

Nix, William H. *Character Works*. Nashville: Broadman & Holman, 1999.

Northouse, Peter G. *Leadership: Theory and Practice*. 7th ed. Thousand Oaks, CA: Sage, 2015.

Nouwen, Henri J. M. *In the Name of Jesus: Reflections on Christian Leadership*. New York: Crossroad, 1995.

Novak, Michael. *Business as a Calling: Work and the Examined Life*. New York: Free Press, 1996.

Oakley, Ed, and Doug Krug. *Enlightened Leadership: Getting to the Heart of Change*. New York: Simon & Schuster, 1994.

O'Connor, Elizabeth. *Call to Commitment: The Story of the Church of the Savior, Washington, D.C.* New York: Harper & Row, 1963.

———. *The New Community*. New York: Harper & Row, 1976.

OECD. "Gender and Sustainable Development: Maximising the Economic, Social and Environmental Role of Women." 2008. http://www.oecd.org/social/40881538.pdf.

O'Keefe, Mark, OSB. "The Benedictine Abbot: Creative Tensions in Leadership." Unpublished paper for the De Pree Leadership Center, 1999.

Oman, D. "Defining Religion and Spirituality." In *Handbook of the Psychology of Religion and Spirituality*, 2nd ed., edited by R. F. Paloutzian and C. L. Park, 23–47. New York: Guilford, 2013.

Orsborn, Carol. *Inner Excellence: Spiritual Principles of Life-Driven Business*. San Rafael, CA: New World Library, 1992.

O'Toole, James. *Leading Change: Overcoming the Ideology of Comfort and the Tyranny of Custom*. San Francisco: Jossey-Bass, 1995.

Palmer, Parker J. *The Active Life: A Spirituality of Work, Creativity, and Caring*. San Francisco: Harper & Row, 1990.

———. *Leading from Within: Reflections on Spirituality and Leadership*. Washington, DC: Servant Leadership School, 1990.

———. *The Promise of Paradox: A Celebration of Contradictions in the Christian Life*. Washington, DC: Servant Leadership School, 1993.

———. "To Whom Do You Report?" *Journal for Quality & Participation* 24, no. 3 (2001): 19–20.

Paloutzian, R. F., and C. L. Park, eds. *Handbook of the Psychology of Religion and Spirituality*. New York: Guilford Press, 2013.

Parker, Glenn M. *Team Players and Teamwork: The New Competitive Business Strategy*. San Francisco: Jossey-Bass, 1990.

Parks, Sharon Daloz. *Leadership Can Be Taught: A Bold Approach for a Complex World.* Boston: Harvard Business School Publishing, 2005.

Pascale, Richard Tanner. *Managing on the Edge: How the Smartest Companies Use Conflict to Stay Ahead.* New York: Simon & Schuster, 1990.

Pascarella, Perry. *Christ-Centered Leadership: Thriving in Business by Putting God in Charge.* Rocklin, CA: Prima, 1999.

Patagonia. "Company History." http://www.patagonia.com/us/patagonia.go?assetid=3351.

Patel, Eboo. *Pluralism, Prejudice, and the Promise of America.* Boston: Beacon, 2012.

Patterson, J. "Resilience in the Face of Adversity." *School Administrator* 58, no. 6 (2001): 18–24.

Pattison, Stephen. *The Faith of the Managers: When Management Becomes Religion.* London: Cassell, 1997.

———. "Recognizing Leaders' Hidden Beliefs." In *Faith and Leadership: How Leaders Live Out Their Faith in Their Work and Why It Matters,* edited by Robert Banks and Kim Powell, 169–81. San Francisco: Jossey-Bass, 2000.

Pavlovich, K. "Educating for Consciousness." *Journal of Management, Spirituality and Religion* 7, no. 3 (2010): 193–208.

Pearce, C. L., and J. A. Conger. "All Those Years Ago: The Historical Underpinnings of Shared Leadership." In *Shared Leadership: Reframing the Hows and Whys of Leadership,* edited by C. L. Pearce and J. A. Conger, 1–18. Thousand Oaks, CA: Sage, 2003.

Pearce, Terry. *Leading Out Loud: The Authentic Speaker, the Credible Leader.* San Francisco: Jossey-Bass, 1995.

Pearman, Roger R. *Hard Wired Leadership: Unleashing the Power of Personality to Become a New Millennium Leader.* Palo Alto, CA: Davies-Black, 1998.

Pearson, Gordon. *Integrity in Organizations: An Alternative Business Ethic.* New York: McGraw-Hill, 1995.

Perkins, Dennis N. T. *Leading at the Edge: Leadership Lessons from the Extraordinary Saga of Shackleton's Antarctic Expedition.* New York: Amacom, 2000.

Peters, Thomas. *Liberation Management: Necessary Disorganization for the Nanosecond Nineties.* New York: Knopf, 1992.

———. "Rule #3: Leadership Is as Confusing as Hell." *Fast Company* 44 (March 2001): 124–40.

———. *Thriving on Chaos: Handbook for a Management Revolution.* New York: Knopf, 1987.

Peters, Thomas, and Robert H. Waterman Jr. *In Search of Excellence: Lessons from America's Best-Run Companies.* New York: Harper & Row, 1982.

Peterson, Eugene. "Follow the Leader." *Fuller Focus* (Fall 2001): 31.

Peterson, Linda. *Starting Out, Starting Over: Finding the Work That's Waiting for You.* Palo Alto, CA: Davies-Black, 1995.

Phillips, Donald T. *Lincoln on Leadership: Executive Strategies for Tough Times.* New York: Warner Books, 1992.

Piaget, Jean. *The Moral Judgment of the Child*. New York: Harcourt, Brace, 1932.

Pierce, Gregory F. A. *Spirituality at Work: Ten Ways to Balance Your Life on the Job*. Chicago: Loyola, 2001.

Pinchot, Gifford. *Creating Organizations with Many Leaders*. San Francisco: Jossey-Bass, 1996.

Pinchot, Gifford, and Elizabeth Pinchot. *The End of Bureaucracy and the Rise of the Intelligent Organization*. San Francisco: Berrett-Koehler, 1993.

Pitcher, Patricia. *The Drama of Leadership*. New York: Wiley, 1997.

Podolny, J. M., R. Khurana, and M. L. Besharov. *Revisiting the Meaning of Leadership*. Boston: Harvard Business Press, 2010.

Pollard, C. William. *The Soul of the Firm*. New York: HarperBusiness, 1996.

Powell, James Lawrence. *Pathways to Leadership: How to Achieve and Sustain Success*. San Francisco: Jossey-Bass, 1995.

Preece, Gordon. *A Trinitarian Perspective on Work*. New York: Edward Mellen, 1998.

Prime, Jeanine, and Elizabeth R. Salib. "Inclusive Leadership: A View from Six Countries." Catalyst 2014. http://www.catalyst.org/system/files/inclusive_leadership_the_view _from_six_countries_O.pdf.

Pruzan, Peter. "The Question of Organizational Consciousness: Can Organizations Have Values, Virtues, and Visions?" *Journal of Business Ethics* 29 (2001): 271–84.

———. "Spirituality as the Context for Leadership." In *Spirituality and Ethics in Management*, edited by L. Zsolnai, 15–31. Dordrecht: Kluwer Academic Publishers, 2004.

Quackenbush, S. W., and M. A. Barnett. "Recollection and Evaluation of Critical Experience in Moral Development: A Cross-Sectional Examination." *Basic and Applied Social Psychology* 23, no. 1 (2001): 55–64.

Quinn, Robert E. *Beyond Rational Management: Mastering the Paradoxes and Competing Demands of High Performance*. San Francisco: Jossey-Bass, 1988.

———. *Deep Change: Discovering the Leader Within*. San Francisco: Jossey-Bass, 1996.

Raimundo, Carlos. *Relational Capital: True Success through Coaching and Managing Relationships in Business and Life*. Sydney: Prentice-Hall, 2002.

Reave, Laura. "Spiritual Values and Practices Related to Leadership Effectiveness." *Leadership Quarterly* 16, no. 5 (2005): 655–87.

Reichheld, Frederick F., with Thomas Teal. *The Loyalty Effect: The Hidden Force behind Growth, Profits, and Lasting Value*. Boston: Harvard Business School Press, 2001.

Renesch, John. *Leadership in a New Era: Visionary Perspectives on the Big Issues of Our Time*. San Francisco: New Leaders Press, 1994.

———, ed. *New Traditions in Business: Spirit and Leadership in the Twenty-First Century*. San Francisco: Berrett-Koehler, 1992.

Reynolds, Joe. *Out Front Leadership: Discovering, Developing, and Delivering Your Potential*. Austin: Mott & Carlisle, 1993.

Reynolds, S. J. "Moral Attentiveness: Who Pays Attention to the Moral Aspects of Life?" *Journal of Applied Psychology* 93 (2008): 1027–41.

Reynolds, S. J., B. P. Owens, and A. L. Rubenstein. "Moral Stress: Considering the Nature and Effects of Managerial Moral Uncertainty." *Journal of Business Ethics* 106 (2012): 491–502.

Rinehart, Stacy T. *Upside Down: The Paradox of Servant Leadership*. Colorado Springs: NavPress, 1998.

Rion, Michael. *The Responsible Manager: Practical Strategies for Ethical Decision Making*. San Francisco: Harper & Row, 1990.

Robeck, Cecil M. "A Pentecostal Perspective on Leadership." Paper presented at the meeting Traditions in Leadership, De Pree Leadership Center, Pasadena, CA, June 1999.

Roels, Shirley. *Moving beyond Servant Leadership*. Pasadena, CA: De Pree Leadership Center, 1999.

Rokeach, M. *Understanding Human Values: Individual and Societal*. New York: Free Press, 1979.

Rost, Joseph. *Leadership for the Twenty-First Century*. Newport: Praeger, 1991.

Rousseau, Jean-Jacques. *The Social Contract and Discourses*. Translated by G. D. H. Cole. London: Everyman, 1993.

Ruedy, N. E., and M. E. Schweitzer. "In the Moment: The Effect of Mindfulness on Ethical Decision Making." *Journal of Business Ethics* 95 (2002): 73–87.

Sacks, Danielle. "Patagonia CEO Rose Marcario Fights the Fights Worth Fighting." *Fast Company*, February 2015. http://www.fastcompany.com/3039739/creative-conversations/patagonia-ceo-rose-marcario-fights-the-fights-worth-fighting.

Said, Edward W. *The World, the Text, and the Critic*. Cambridge, MA: Harvard University Press, 1983.

Sakenfeld, Katharine Doob. *Faithfulness in Action: Loyalty in Biblical Perspective*. Philadelphia: Fortress, 1985.

Salkin, Jeffrey K. *Being God's Partner: How to Find the Hidden Link between Spirituality and Your Work*. Woodstock, VT: Jewish Lights Publishing, 1994.

Sanders, J. Oswald. *Paul the Leader: A Vision for Christian Leadership Today*. Eastbourne, UK: Kingsway, 1983.

———. *Spiritual Leadership*. Rev. ed. Chicago: Moody, 1980.

Sarros, John C., and Oleh Butchatsky. *Leadership: Australia's Top CEOs: Finding Out What Makes Them the Best*. New York: HarperBusiness, 1996.

Sayers, Dorothy L. *The Mind of the Maker*. London: Methuen, 1941.

Schaef, Anne Wilson, and Diane Fassel. *The Addictive Organization*. San Francisco: Harper & Row, 1988.

Schein, Edgar H. *The Corporate Culture Survival Guide: Sense and Nonsense about Culture Change*. San Francisco: Jossey-Bass, 1999.

———. *Organizational Culture and Leadership*. 3rd ed. San Francisco: Jossey-Bass, 2004.

Schulte, Brigid. *Overwhelmed: How to Work, Love, and Play When No One Has the Time.* New York: Picador, 2015.

Schumacher, Christian. *God in Work: Discovering the Divine Pattern for Work in the New Millennium.* Oxford, UK: Lion, 1998.

———. *To Live and Work: A Theological Interpretation.* Bromley, UK: Marc, 1987.

Schwartz, Peter. *The Art of the Long View: Planning for the Future in an Uncertain World.* New York: Currency Doubleday, 1995.

Schwartz, S. H. "Universals in the Content and Structure of Values: Theoretical Advances and Empirical Tests in 20 Countries." *Advances in Experimental Social Psychology* 25 (1992): 1–65.

Senge, Peter M. *The Fifth Discipline: The Art and Practice of the Learning Organization.* New York: Currency Doubleday, 1990.

Sennett, Richard. *The Corrosion of Character: The Personal Consequences of Work in the New Capitalism.* New York: Norton, 1998.

Shamir, Boas. *Follower-Centered Perspectives on Leadership: A Tribute to the Memory of James R. Meindl.* Charlotte: Information Age Publishing, 2007.

Shekerjian, Denise. *Uncommon Genius: How Great Ideas Are Born.* New York: Penguin, 1990.

Simon, Sidney B., Leland W. Howe, and Howard Kirschenbaum. *Values Clarification.* Rev. ed. New York: Warner Books, 1995.

Sinclair, Amanda. *Doing Leadership Differently: Gender, Power, and Sexuality in a Changing Business Culture.* Victoria, Australia: Melbourne University Press, 1998.

Sinetar, Marsha. *Do What You Love, the Money Will Follow: Discovering Your Right Livelihood.* New York: Dell, 1989.

Sire, James W. *Václav Havel: The Intellectual Conscience of International Politics: An Introduction, Appreciation, and Critique.* Downers Grove, IL: InterVarsity, 2001.

Smedes, Lewis. *Choices: Making Right Decisions in a Complex World.* San Francisco: HarperSanFrancisco, 1991.

Smetana, J. G., M. Killen, and E. Turiel. "Children's Reasoning about Interpersonal and Moral Conflicts." *Child Development* 62 (1991): 629–44.

Smith, Robert Lawrence. *A Quaker Book of Wisdom: Life Lessons in Simplicity, Service, and Common Sense.* New York: Eagle Brook, 1998.

Sofield, Loughlan, and Donald H. Kuhn. *The Collaborative Leader: Listening to the Wisdom of God's People.* Notre Dame, IN: Ave Maria Press, 1995.

Solomon, Robert C. *Ethics and Excellence: Cooperation and Integrity in Business.* New York: Oxford University Press, 1992.

Spears, Larry C., ed. *Insights on Leadership: Service, Stewardship, Spirit, and Servant-Leadership.* New York: Wiley, 1998.

———. *Reflections on Leadership: How Robert K. Greenleaf's Theory of Servant-Leadership Influenced Today's Top Management Thinkers.* New York: Wiley, 1995.

Spink, Kathryn. *Mother Teresa: A Complete Authorized Biography*. San Francisco: Harper SanFrancisco, 1997.

Stanley, A. *Visioneering Sisters*. Portland, OR: Multnomah, 1999.

Stevens, M. E. *Leadership Roles of the Old Testament: King, Prophet, Priest, Sage*. Eugene, OR: Cascade Books, 2012.

Stevens, R. Paul, and Phil Collins. *The Equipping Pastor: A Systems Approach to Congregational Leadership*. Washington, DC: Alban Institute, 1993.

Stodgill, Ralph M. *Handbook of Leadership: A Survey of Theory and Research*. New York: Free Press, 1974.

———. "Personal Factors Associated with Leadership: A Survey of the Literature." *Journal of Psychology* 25 (1948): 35–71.

Strom, Mark. *Lead with Wisdom: How Wisdom Transforms Good Leaders into Great Leaders*. Melbourne: John Wiley, 2014.

———. "'To Know as We Are Known': Locating an Ancient Alternative to Virtues." In *Wise Management in Organizational Complexity*, edited by M. J. Thompson and D. Bevan, 85–105. New York: Palgrave Macmillan, 2013.

Sullivan, William M. *Work and Integrity: The Crisis and Promise of Professionalism in America*. New York: HarperBusiness, 1995.

Sutton, Robert, and Hayagreeva Rao. *Scaling Up Excellence: Getting to More without Settling for Less*. New York: Crown, 2014.

Swain, Bernard F. *Liberating Leadership: Practical Styles for Pastoral Ministry*. San Francisco: Harper & Row, 1986.

Swiss, Deborah. *Women Breaking Through: Overcoming the Final Ten Obstacles at Work*. Princeton: Peterson's/Pacesetter Books, 1996.

Tan, S-Y. *Full Service: Moving from Self-Serve Christianity to Total Servanthood*. Grand Rapids: Baker Books, 2006.

Terry, Robert W. *Authentic Leadership: Courage in Action*. San Francisco: Jossey-Bass, 1993.

Theobald, Robert. *Reworking Success: New Communities at the Millennium*. Gabriola Island, BC: New Society Publishers, 1997.

Thera, Piyadassi. *The Threefold Division of the Noble Eightfold Path*. Kandy, Sri Lanka: Buddhist Publication Society, 2010. Available at http://www.bps.lk/olib/bl/bl032.pdf.

Thomas, J. C. "Ethical Integrity and Organizational Mortal Culture." *Leadership* 4, no. 4, (2008): 418–42.

Thrall, Bill, Bruce McElrath, and Jim McNichol. *The Ascent of the Leader: How Ordinary Relationships Develop Extraordinary Character and Influence*. Hoboken, NJ: Wiley, 1999.

Tomasko, Robert M. *Downsizing: Reshaping the Corporation for the Future*. New York: Amacom, 1990.

Tombaugh, J. R., and E. F. Tombaugh. "Can Spiritual Leadership Lead Us Not into Temptation?" *Business & Professional Ethics Journal* 28, nos. 1–4 (2009): 95–119.

Tonello, Matteo. "Corporate Director Selection and Recruitment: A Matrix." Harvard Law School Forum on Corporate Governance and Financial Regulation, June 2, 2013. http://corpgov.law.harvard.edu/2013/06/02/corporate-director-selection-and -recruitment-a-matrix.

Trevino, L. K., L. P. Hartman, and M. Brown. "Moral Person and Moral Manager: How Executives Develop a Reputation for Ethical Leadership." *California Management Review* 42, no. 4 (2000): 128–42.

Trompenaars, F., and E. Voerman. *Servant-Leadership across Cultures: Harnessing the Strengths of the World's Most Powerful Management Philosophy*. New York: McGraw-Hill, 2009.

Trueblood, E. *The Incendiary Fellowship*. New York: Harper & Row, 1967.

Tyree-Hyche, I. "In Keeping with the Spirit: Workplace Spirituality Draws on Ethics, Values, Motivation, Work/Life Balance and Leadership." *Women Lawyers Journal* 99, no. 1/2 (2014): 26–30.

Uhl-Bien, M. "Relational Leadership Theory: Exploring the Social Processes of Leadership and Organizing." *Leadership Quarterly* 17, no. 6 (2006): 654–76.

Ulrich, D. "The Talent Trifecta." *Workforce Management* 17, no. 10 (2007): 32–33.

Ury, William. *Getting Past No: Negotiating Your Way from Confrontation to Cooperation*. Rev. ed. New York: Bantam Books, 1993.

Vaill, Peter B. *Managing as a Performing Art: New Ideas for a World of Chaotic Change*. San Francisco: Jossey-Bass, 1989.

———. *Spirited Leading and Learning: Process Wisdom for a New Age*. San Francisco: Jossey-Bass, 1998.

Vandewaerde, Maaeten, Wim Voordeckers, Frank Lambrechts, and Yannick Bammens. "Board Team Leadership Revisited: A Conceptual Model of Shared Leadership in the Boardroom." *Journal of Business Ethics* 104, no. 3 (2011): 403–20.

van Dusen, Henry. "Apostle to the Twentieth Century." *Atlantic Monthly*, July 1934, 1–16.

Vladilav, J., ed. *Václav Havel, or Living in Truth*. London: Faber & Faber, 1990.

Volf, Miroslav. *Trinity and Community: An Ecumenical Ecclesiology*. Grand Rapids: Eerdmans, 1997.

———. *Work in the Spirit: Toward a Theology of Work*. New York: Oxford University Press, 1991.

Warner, Judith. "Fact Sheet: The Women's Leadership Gap: Women's Leadership by the Numbers." Center for American Progress, March 7, 2014. http://www.american progress.org/issues/women/report/2014/03/07/85457/fact-sheet-the-womens-leader ship-gap.

Waterman, Robert H., Jr. *Adhocracy: The Power to Change*. New York: Norton, 1990.

Weber, Max. *From Max Weber: Essays on Sociology*. Edited by H. H. Gerth and C. W. Mills. New York: Oxford University Press, 1946.

Weems, L. H., Jr. *Leadership in the Wesleyan Spirit*. Nashville: Abingdon, 1999.

Weick, K., and T. Putnam. "Organizing for Mindfulness: Eastern Wisdom and Western Knowledge." *Journal of Management Inquiry* 15, no. 3 (2006): 275–87.

Wheatley, Margaret J. *Leadership and the New Science: Learning about Organization from an Orderly Universe*. San Francisco: Berrett-Koehler, 1992.

———. "Leadership in Turbulent Times Is Spiritual." *Frontiers of Health Services Management* 18, no. 4 (2003): 19–26.

White, John. *Excellence in Leadership: Reaching Goals with Prayer, Courage, and Determination*. Downers Grove, IL: InterVarsity, 1986.

Whittington, J. L., T. M. Pitts, W. V. Kageler, and V. L. Goodwin. "Legacy Leadership: The Leadership Wisdom of the Apostle Paul." *Leadership Quarterly* 16, no. 5 (2005): 749–70.

Whyte, David. *The Heart Aroused: Poetry and the Preservation of the Soul in Corporate America*. New York: Currency Doubleday, 1994.

Wildavsky, A. *Moses as a Political Leader*. Jerusalem: Shalom Press, 2005.

———. *The Nursing Father: Moses as a Political Leader*. Tuscaloosa: University of Alabama Press, 1984.

Wilkins, Alan L. *Developing Corporate Character: How to Successfully Change an Organization without Destroying It*. San Francisco: Jossey-Bass, 1989.

Williams, Benjamin D., and Michael T. McKibben. *Oriented Leadership: Why All Christians Need It*. Wayne, NJ: Orthodox Christian Publications Center, 1994.

Williams, Oliver F., and John W. Houck, eds. *A Virtuous Life in Business: Stories of Courage and Integrity in the Corporate World*. Lanham, MD: Rowman & Littlefield, 1992.

Wills, Garry. *Certain Trumpets: The Call of Leaders*. New York: Simon & Schuster, 1994.

Wolfe, Alan. "White Magic: Capitalism, Mormonism, and the Doctrines of Stephen Covey." *The New Republic*, February 23, 1998, 26–34.

Wong, Y. R., and J. Vinsky. "Speaking from the Margins: A Critical Reflection on the 'Spiritual-but-Not-Religious' Discourse in Social Work." *British Journal of Social Work* 39 (2009): 1343–59.

Wood, Richard J. "Christ Has Come to Teach His People Himself: Quaker Ambiguities about Leadership." Paper presented at the meeting Traditions in Leadership, De Pree Leadership Center, Pasadena, CA, June 1999.

Wren, J. Thomas. *The Leader's Companion: Insights on Leadership through the Ages*. New York: Free Press, 1995.

Wright, Walter C. *Relational Leadership: A Biblical Model for Leadership Service*. Exeter, UK: Paternoster, 2000.

Yukl, Gary A. *Leadership in Organizations*. 3rd ed. Englewood Cliffs, NJ: Prentice-Hall, 1989.

Zaragoza, Edward. *No Longer Servants but Friends*. Abingdon: Nashville, 1999.

Zautra, A. "Resilience: One Part Recovery, Two Parts Sustainability." *Journal of Personality* 77, no. 6 (2009): 1936–43.

Zizioulas, John D. *Being as Communion: Studies in Personhood and the Church*. Crestwood, NY: St. Vladimir's Seminary Press, 1985.

Zohar, Danah. *Rewiring the Corporate Brain: Using the New Science to Rethink How We Structure and Lead Organizations*. San Francisco: Berrett-Koehler, 1997.

Zsolnai, Laszlo. "Buddhist Economic Strategy." In *Frugality: Rebalancing Material and Spiritual Values in Economic Life*, edited by L. Bouckaert, H. Opdebeeck, and L. Zsolnai, Frontiers of Business Ethics, 279–304. Bern, Switzerland: Peter Lang, 2008.

———, ed. *Spirituality and Ethics in Management*. Dordrecht: Kluwer Academic Publishers, 2004.

index